Judy Krumm
216 Welch Hall

Public Authorities, Special Districts and Local Government

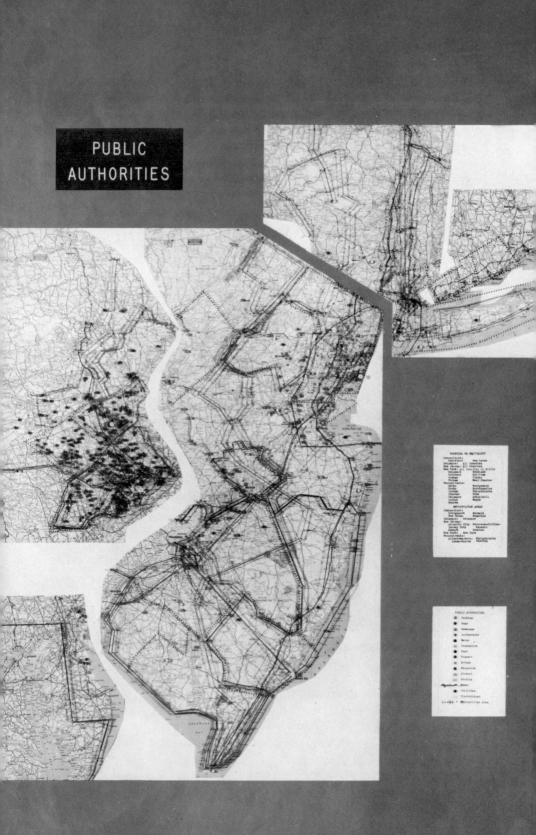

PUBLIC
AUTHORITIES

Public Authorities, Special Districts

and

Local Government

ROBERT G. SMITH

Professor of Political Science

Drew University

NATIONAL ASSOCIATION OF COUNTIES

Research Foundation

1001 Connecticut Avenue, N.W.

Washington, D. C. 20036

The frontispiece shows public authorities, and
their lines of jurisdiction, in the five-State
area chosen for the studies reported in this
book. Counties, or their equivalent, included
are: in Connecticut: Fairfield, New Haven;
all the counties in Delaware and New Jersey;
in New York: Bronx, Delaware, Dutchess,
Kings, New York, Orange, Putnam, Queens,
Richmond, Rockland, Sullivan, Ulster, West
Chester; Pennsylvania: Berks, Bucks, Carbon,
Chester, Delaware, Lehigh, Monroe, Montgomery,
Northhampton, Philadelphia, Pike, Schuylkill,
and Wayne. Categories of authorities included
are: parking, highways, sewerage, water,
recreation, port, transit, bridge, education,
airport, housing, power, and discontinued
authorities.

To

Lois, Bob, Don

Foreword

ONE NEW UNIT of local government has been created somewhere in the United States each and every day for the past five years. They are called authorities (or sometimes special districts). There are now more authorities (18,323) than cities (17,997), and six times as many authorities as there are counties (3,043).

County and city officials are deeply concerned. Is this spectacular growth in authorities "good" or "bad"? What does this fragmentation of governmental functions in single-purpose authorities mean to the future of city, county and state government, and to our representative democracy?

The plain fact is that nobody really knows much about authorities. They are relatively new on the American scene and have by their very nature escaped the careful scrutiny that scholars have given other levels of government. They are quasi-public and, therefore, take on some aspects of both government and business and thus, in many respects, are exempt from many of the public controls exercised over both business and government.

We in the National Association of Counties Research Foundation are proud to publish this painstaking analysis

by Dr. Robert G. Smith of one type of these authorities —
namely, those that in general are single purpose in function
and financed by revenue bonds and special user charges.
The author has carefully examined five so-called "advantages" of authorities and has discovered that some of
these supposed advantages are, in part at least, myths.

This book will be highly controversial. It attempts to
"bring to bear on the problem, for the local government
official, arguments for and against the formation of public
authorities, or special districts, from the viewpoint of their
effect on county and local governments, and to present
results of case studies relevant to this issue." We hope
that those who have strong pro-authority or anti-authority
feelings will come forward and make their case. Dr. Smith
has clearly identified the issues and amassed an impres-
sive array of facts which should keep the debate on course.

As the first step in bringing authorities under closer
public scrutiny, we would urge all city and county officials
and community leaders everywhere to study carefully this
book as an important new addition to our national understanding of authorities.

> Bernard F. Hillenbrand
> Executive Director
> National Association of Counties
> Research Foundation

Preface

IN A PROLONGED DEBATE by the Middlesex, New Jersey, County Board of Chosen Freeholders in 1963 over a proposal to create a County public authority to purchase, develop, and resell land vacated by the federal government at Raritan Arsenal, one of the Freeholders was reported to have told a newspaper correspondent: "Individuals have changed their minds from one time to another based on new bits of information. I have mixed feelings. At one point, I was somewhat opposed, then for it. Now I don't know what I am."(1)

Most local officials find themselves in a similarly ambivalent position in regard to continual suggestions for the establishment of public authorities, or special districts, for countless local functions ranging from recreation to public utilities. Literature on these special agencies of government is not lacking altogether; it is sparse, but what there is is quite good. It has not been directed, however, to the specific problem which confronts the local official: namely, what effect will the formation of such a unit of government, outside the normal structure of governments, have on the existing governments? He would be hard-put to find in any one source an indication of what the result would be on the Middlesex County government, and the Borough government of Metuchen, in which Raritan Arsenal is situated, of the establishment of a quasi-public, quasi-private public authority to deal with the phasing out of the federal arsenal. Information of help to him is, indeed, to be found in "bits" and the already too busy official would have to piece together the pros and cons from a wide variety of periodical and journal articles. Most of this information, moreover, is in the form of generalizations unsupported by actual case studies. It is little wonder that he comes out of a debate on this issue with "mixed feelings."

Decisions as to the creation of public authorities, or special districts, are being made, however, and in great numbers on the local levels. This category constitutes the most rapidly proliferating unit of government in the United States, and, indeed, throughout the world. Between the 1957 census of governments and the more recent count in 1962, special districts increased by more than 2,200, or about 15 percent. Three States, Illinois, California, and Pennsylvania, have more than 1,000 of these special agencies; seven other States have more than 700, including New York, Kansas, Washington, Nebraska, Missouri, Texas, and Oregon; and four States have more than 300: Colorado, Georgia, Idaho, and Indiana. Every State authorizes their creation, and there is no State today without them. The newest States, Alaska and Hawaii list 6 and 16 special districts respectively, but under the State Constitution of Alaska no new districts may be established.

The imposition of these 18,323 special districts on existing governments cannot help but have a marked effect on governments on all levels. In far too many instances, however, they are being established to meet exigencies of the moment with no consideration of what effect they will have on the very governments that give them birth. Those of greatest concern to local governments are not forced on local officials by State action, but rather are the very creation of the local governments themselves under permissive State enabling acts. Reliance is placed on the notion that, having performed their special function, such as the building of a turnpike, a sewer system, a park, or some other capital construction, and having paid off their indebtedness on the revenue bonds floated for that purpose, they will cease to exist and the functions will revert to the more conventional local governments. This concept of self-liquidation of special districts, or authorities, is but one of a whole series of generalizations about them which needs to be subjected to the test of actual experience.

Experience there has been, as special districts as such date back in the United States to the Eighteenth Century, and may well be traced historically to the medieval guilds. There is need now to correlate for the local government official the best thinking on this subject of special districts and authorities that relates directly to the problem of their effect on county and municipal governments, and to suggest certain conclusions which may be reached by an application of these generalizations to case studies of the interrelationships of these agencies and the standard local governments in given areas.

This book attempts to fulfill this function: namely to bring to bear on the problem, for the local government official, arguments for and against the formation of public authorities, or special districts, from the viewpoint of their effect on county and local governments, and to present results of case studies relevant to this issue.

This is not to suggest, of course, that there is any ready answer which can be prefabricated for the official, especially in view of the fact that one of the assets of the public authority device is its flexibility which enables it to be tailored to local situations. Cautions, however, growing from trial and error elsewhere may serve as guideposts of concern when considering the application of the principles of the semi-independent agency device to local circumstances.

The need for such an approach was recognized as early as 1940 when the Committee on Public Administration issued a report entitled, "Research in the Use of the Government Corporation." Its recommendation was that the public corporation "be tested at every point to see when it is merely accidental, when its qualities make it a convenient means of surmounting obstacles, and when, if ever, the form itself is of basic importance." The report posed lists of questions which the Committee on Public Administration thought should be examined in regard not only to the government corporations on the federal level, but to the interstate, state, and local public corporations, as well, including "toll bridges, toll highways, hydro-electric projects, state universities, and 'development corporations' " together with the "commissions or authorities set up to handle irrigation, water supply, housing, public markets, sanitation, and other matters."(2)

A number of the questions concerned the relationships between the public corporation, on the one hand, and existing governments, on the other:

"Does the corporate form offer a convenient way of avoiding legal, financial, and operating requirements customarily imposed on the traditional government agency?"

"Is there evidence to show that the device has been used to popularize activities that seem to encroach on private fields of activity because it carries the connotation of efficient, 'business-like' action?"

"Could these functions be handled as adequately by another form of organization?"

"Are there constitutional obstacles to the granting of the same powers and immunities to ordinary agencies of government as to corporations?"

"What has been the experience of state and local corporations or authorities in bond flotation?"

"What is the significance and what are the implications of the growing use of 'revenue bond' financing?"

"What effect does corporation debt have on the total debt of the government?"

"What mechanisms are there to insure that a government corporation will be amenable to substantial shifts in public sentiment concerning the operations of that corporation?"

"To what extent have corporations been freed from restraints in providing 'publicity' service that are imposed upon other government agencies?"

"(I)s there a special problem of control or approval of the plans of corporations by a chief executive or other agency to insure agreement with more general public planning?"

"Are governments more willing to engage in cooperative activities where the concept of incorporation is used?"

It is of interest to note that even then the Research Council singled out for special recommendation two approaches, the case study and the comparative, and spotlighted a pioneer work in each: John McDiarmid's Government Corporations and Federal Funds (1938), and Ruth G. Weintraub's Government Corporations and State Law (1939), respectively.

Many of the other questions asked have been discussed in more recent publications. These questions of intergovernmental relationships on the local level have, for the most part, been subordinated to considerations of the administrative aspects of the public authorities and concern for the large interstate or regional authority. The great proliferation has come on the county and municipal levels with almost an inverse ratio of discussion of their meaning for local governments as against the effect of the bi-state and state agencies.

The promise of the few books that have been published on the subject of special districts and authorities in general should have encouraged others.

John C. Bollens' comprehensive analysis of the Special District Governments in the United States is, to be sure, as recent as 1957, but the fact that it was reprinted in 1961 attests to the impact it has had and is certain to continue to have. Bollens emphasized the spread of the special district into local areas, and prompted all sorts of queries into their meaning there. "Governments exist and function in an intergovernmental environment," he

concludes. "There is a need, often long-standing, in practically every state for comprehensive state governmental
study and appropriate action regarding the modern-day
sufficiency of all classes of local governments . . . . Although at present regarded as detrimental, the growth of
special districts may sooner or later serve as the impetus
necessary to bring about needed and long overdue changes
across the whole fabric of local government."(3)

The study of public authorities which had preceded
Bollen's work by four years, made by the Council of State
Governments, consciously had excluded from its scope
those "authorities which are created locally, although
usually under state enabling legislation, and largely serving only a single community."(4)

The intensive investigation of public authorities by
the Temporary Commission on Coordination of State Activities in New York State, a report which merits even
more attention than it has been accorded, also was published prior to Bollen's book. This report concerned itself
with authorities on all levels of government, but addressed
itself primarily to the administrative implications: "If a
public authority is responsible for the management of a
public enterprise, then the entrepreneurial decisions
necessary to the economical and efficient operation of a
public enterprise may more likely be kept out of the
political arena."(5)

Nathaniel S. Preston's doctoral dissertation at Princeton University in 1960, "The Use and Control of Public
Authorities in American State and Local Governments,"
accumulates valuable data and suggests an interesting
taxonomy of authorities, but again stresses the need to
consider the authority "as an adaptable administrative
device."

The symposium on "Public Authorities" published by
the Law School of Duke University in 1961 "to describe
both generally and through a detailed analysis of significant
examples, experience with public authorities in the United
States and abroad," focuses its concern most effectively
on international, supranational, and interstate public

authorities, on port authorities and highway authorities, and on the problem in underdeveloped countries, in France, and in a socialist state, but draws relatively few of its illustrations from the county and municipal levels in this country.

The body of literature on the subject, illustrated by the books and dissertation mentioned, and a few others referred to in the bibliography, supplemented by a selected list of articles numbering about 400, constitutes a source of knowledge of immense value for the local official. Hopefully, this present book may add something to the slowly evolving reservoir of studies by testing some of the generalizations on the actual functioning of public authorities in a given geographic area, and by pulling together in one short book arguments for and against the use of such authorities from the standpoint of their effects on existing local governments.

One reason for the fact that there are relatively few books on the subject of authorities curiously is the sheer problem of defining these agencies. Having grown up outside the regular framework of governments, they have acquired various designations not only inconsistent from one part of the country to another, but not even uniform within any one part of the nation. With the extensive proliferation of these special agencies, however, the problem must be confronted and somehow resolved.

At the core of the difficulty of definition is the necessity to differentiate between two large categories of these agencies, one known as special districts, and the other as public authorities. Inasmuch as even these two terms are used interchangeably throughout the country students of the subject have tended to despair of distinguishing between them and have lumped them together. For any kind of critical appraisal, however, this grouping simply will not suffice. Distinctions between the two large classifications must be drawn, or studies of them will serve merely to compound the confusion.

The author of this book attempts to face the semantic issue squarely. At the risk of oversimplification, he has tried to single out one feature that can be used as a meaningful distinction between special districts and public authorities. Drawing on the traditional concept of the significance of the control of the purse strings in government, he takes their method of finance as the principal difference between the two categories. For this study, therefore, special districts are considered those agencies operating outside the regular structure of government which rely primarily upon special taxes within the district; public authorities, on the other hand, are differentiated as those agencies functioning outside the regular structure of government which rely primarily upon revenue-bond issues to be amortized by the collection of user charges.

The author recognizes full well the validity of the arguments for taking into account other distinctions bearing on the degree of independence of these agencies from their parent governments or other governmental levels. Certainly significant in this regard are such controls as auditing and reporting, dependence on the parent government for policy-making decisions, and the like. The complex number of variables thereby created for the student of these special agencies, however, serves to deter recognition of the overall impact of these thousands of agencies on the total framework of American government and to bog him down in questions of semantics.

Despite the undoubted importance of machinery for regulating their operations, such as requirements for annual audits and reports, the need now is to go beyond such formal organization in our studies and to attempt to analyze these agencies in the whole political realm of government. These are policy-making units, not mere administrative automata, and, accordingly, they never will be understood except through a realization of the informal as well as the formal methods through which they function.

The system of financing their operations serves the student of them well in this more comprehensive view of their role. An entirely different frame of reference is conceived for those agencies which depend for their income on special taxes levied on the people within the district in which the agency functions as against those agencies which finance themselves through the issuance of revenue bonds to be paid off by charges for the use of the facilities constructed by them. In the first instance, those benefitting from the functions of the agency live within the agency district and are taxed for the functions. In the other, however, the buyers of the bonds may live anywhere in the country, or in the world for that matter, and may exercise a kind of absentee regulation over the functions being performed by the agency.

When these agencies are viewed as not mere administrative units, but policy-making in their own right, the differences in constituencies and accountability alone are much more sharply etched by a recognition of the method of finance as the most important distinction between special districts and public authorities.

The book accepts this distinction and attempts throughout to illustrate its significance. Its concern is with those agencies operating outside the regular governments which finance their function or functions by the issuance of revenue bonds and which pay for these bonds by the collection of user charges. These the author refers to as public authorities, as distinct from the other such category of agencies which depend primarily upon special taxation within a district.

It so happens that the definition fits rather well such agencies within the geographic area covered in the studies for this book. In focusing on governmental interrelationships on the local level the author required for his studies a given geographic region of considerable extent. The area chosen involved the five contiguous States of New York, New Jersey, Connecticut, Pennsylvania, and Delaware. Within these States, the term, public authority, generally refers to the revenue-bond type unit, and the term, special district, more often indicates the agency relying on special taxes. Inconsistencies even within these States, however, can be pointed to. In other parts of the country the terminology becomes even more confused. The meaning of the two methods of financing can be drawn anywhere regardless of the name applied to the unit, and that distinction in the long run is of greater importance than the nomenclature itself.

Two of the five States selected for this study, Pennsylvania and New York, have the third and fourth largest numbers of special districts in the country, and Pennsylvania has the largest number of such agencies which use the term, "authority." Two others, Connecticut and Delaware, have among the fewest number of public authorities in the United States. Connecticut resisted the tendency of this part of the country to make its thruway a public authority, contrary to the practices of other States in the given area. Within the five States are public authorities of every level of government, including international, interstate, state, regional, county, and municipal, in addition to inter-county and inter-municipal. Two of the three interstate port authorities in the United States are situated therein, one at the Philadelphia port and the other at the New York port, and one river authority of great size, the St. Lawrence Seaway Authority, are in operation here.

The use of the five States makes possible a comparison of enabling acts and laws of the States relating to authorities.

The five States contain extensive urban, suburban, and rural areas, and authorities are found in all three. New Jersey is the most suburban of all States, and the five States together contain 15% of all the Standard Metropolitan Statistical Areas. Sections of all five are subsumed under the name, "Megalopolis," or spread city.

This region encompasses, also, the greatest concentration of governments in the nation -- Robert Wood's 1400 governments -- and includes, therefore, ample illustrations of the effects of public authorities on counties and municipalities, and on the local areas of Connecticut where counties have been abolished.

Studies for the book cover an eighteen-year period from World War II to the present, the years of great proliferation of public authorities particularly in the suburban sections. The author observed authorities in the region at first-hand during this period, meeting with authority personnel and studying public reaction to these agencies. Helpful in the assessment of public opinion was the regular reading of newspapers selected to represent geographic parts of the area, such as the Poughkeepsie Journal; The Evening Bulletin of Philadelphia; Evening Journal of Wilmington, Delaware; Newark Evening News of Newark, New Jersey; Morris County's Daily Record, of Morris County, New Jersey; The Madison Eagle of Madison, New Jersey; and The New York Times, New York Herald-Tribune, The Wall Street Journal, and the New York Post, of New York City.

Part of the research resulted from a grant-in-aid from the Eagleton Institute.

Students who helped with research include: David E. Allen, who investigated the activities of the Jersey Jetport Site Association, the Great Swamp Committee, and other organizations opposing the proposed location of a jetport by the Port of New York Authority in Green Village, New Jersey; Irwin Bloch, the Morristown, New Jersey, Parking Authority; Mrs. Dorothy Brady, the role of commercial banks in authority financing; Robert Catlin, a survey of the extent of teaching of public authorities in colleges in and near New York City; William Dickinson, the dissolution of the Dover, New Jersey, Parking Authority; Ellen Earp, public relations of the New York City Transit Authority; Jane Fink, the strike of employees of the New Jersey Turnpike Authority; John Foreman, the delay in the appointment of an Executive Director for the Delaware River Port Authority; Gordon Friedman, three newspapers' coverage of the Port Authority jetport controversy; Jeffrey Gillman, Robert Moses and public authorities; Herman Hansen, the Jersey City Sewerage Authority; Robert Harrall, Jersey City Incinerator Authority; Russell Hawke, authorities in Pennsylvania; William Hayes, the St. Lawrence Seaway Authority; Barbara Jahreis, the Port of New York Authority; Marilyn Holt, Florham Park Sewer Authority; Adam Kaufman, suit against Robert Moses, Chairman of the Triborough Bridge and Tunnel Authority, by the New York Post; Lillian Kozuma, the Morris County Municipal Utilities Authority; George Kullgren, the Port of New York Authority's proposal on the jetport; Grace Leoser, the surplus of the New Jersey Turnpike Authority; Herman Mertins, authorities in New Jersey; Philip Moore, the court decision in favor of Moonachie against tax exemption of an industrial facility at the Teterboro Airport of the Port of New York Authority; Alan Petty, Camden Township's attempt to attract the 'Phillies' Baseball Team from Philadelphia by the creation of the Camden County Improvement Authority; D. Logan Potts, hearings of the subcommittee of the Committee on the Judiciary of the House of Representatives on the Port of New York Authority; Shannon Rafferty, the construction of the garage under Military Park by the Newark, New Jersey, Parking Authority; Richard Ricciardi, the establishment of the Bridgewater, New Jersey, Sewerage Authority to attempt to gain a right of way through Somerville; and Donald Scott, the beginnings of the New Jersey Expressway Authority.

June 1964
Washington, D. C.

ROBERT G. SMITH

REFERENCES

1. Newark Evening News, January 7, 1963.

2. (New York, 1940) pp. 4-5.

3. (Berkeley and Los Angeles, University of California Press, 1961) pp. 262, 263.

4. Public Authorities in the States, A Report to the Governors' Conference (Chicago, 1953), introductory statement to Appendix B.

5. State of New York, Temporary State Commission on Coordination of State Activities, Staff Report on Public Authorities under New York State, Legislative Document No. 46 (1956) (Albany, March 21, 1956), p. 55.

Table of Contents

Index of Illustrations

Chapter One

"Authoritycin"

IN AN AGE in which their constituents have become addicted to 'miracle' medicines, it may not be so surprising to find county and municipal officials reflecting a similar desire for 'cure-all' remedies for the problems of government. One of the more striking manifestations of this reflection is the increasing prescription by local officials of large doses of what the London Economist has referred to as "the wonder-drug authoritycin," – the public-authority device.(1)

Communities have seized upon the authority technique as a panacea for needed sewerage, roads, playgrounds, airports, seaports, school buildings, parking lots, housing projects, industrial parks, and numerous other functions, with the same sort of unquestioning faith with which long-suffering patients grasp at news of a medical 'breakthrough.' "To quell grumblings of an irritated populace and concerned industry," reported Pennsylvania's local-government journal, "something had to be done to create for Chester a source where clean water could be obtained and plenty of it. It would be a colossal feat requiring millions of dollars. The only answer was the creation of an Authority."(2)

The immediate remedy is, to be sure, painless. In Pennsylvania, in which Chester is located, the Pennsylvania Municipal Authorities Association provides even a simple eight-page booklet, entitled, "Organizing a Municipal Authority in Pennsylvania — A practical 'How to do it' manual."

Pennsylvania by 1960 could list 1,364 municipal authorities to cover a myriad of functions, and with 48 such authorities identified merely as "No Known Purpose Municipal Authorities."(3) And, as was noted in the Preface to this book, Pennsylvania stood only third in the country, topped by Illinois and California, in total numbers of special districts, of which public authorities are a part.

Moreover, not only is the proliferation widespread in this country, but the public-authority unit is extending throughout a large part of the world. Their titles indicate their geographic spread: Port of London Authority, Ghana Housing Corporation, Volta River Authority, Israel Port Authority, Amun-Israel Housing Corporation, Greek Port Authority, Suez Canal Authority, West Pakistan Water and Power Development Authority, Domodar Valley Corporation, Snowy Mountain Hydro-Electric Authority, Teito Rapid Transit Authority, Hong Kong Housing Authority, Puerto Rico Water Resources Authority, the "autonomous institutes" of Venezuela, and literally hundreds of others. In its report on Cooperation for Progress in Latin America in 1961, the Committee for Economic Development advised in general against government involvement in private enterprises, but added: "Where government does carry on business activity, experience has shown that this is more efficiently done through government corporations or authorities than through regular government departments."(4)

As in the case of the antibiotics, the potential value of public authorities can be circumscribed by their indiscriminate use. Overdosages and misdirected applications of both the miracle drugs and their governmental counterpart, "authoritycin," have resulted in serious side effects. The loss of a sense of equilibrium, encountered by certain patients from medicines, has affected counties and municipalities where these quasi-public agencies have produced awkward relationships with existing local governments. Even anemia, not uncommon as an indirect effect of drugs, is apparent in the case of those municipalities and counties which have divested themselves of control over essential functions for the expediency of the more autonomous public authority. The organisms of Federal and state governments, against whose encroachment on home rule local public authorities are claimed to forfend by circumventing restrictive debt ceilings and meeting emergencies expeditiously from below, are showing signs of developing resistance to them. The Federal government, indeed, has struck up a very lively working relationship with local public authorities, and the state governments increasingly are resorting to the device themselves by establishing state agencies which cut right through local jurisdictions.

An occasional voice of caution breaks through the acclamation for expediency. A Bergen County, New Jersey, Judge, in ruling that the Borough, under State law, has a right to create a municipal utilities authority by ordinance without submitting the issue to the people by referendum, explained, in announcing his decision, that he personally thought that the matter "should be passed on by the voters," but that there is "no legislative provision to that effect." The formation of such a public agency, he advised, "is a very serious event."(5)

The Municipal Finance Officers Association of the United States and Canada, while not warning against their formation, cautions that the "creation and financing of special districts is a rather complex subject, which is full of pitfalls for the uninitiated."(6) It recommends the consultation of competent advisers.

One of the most serious attacks on public authorities has been issued recently from the Commonwealth of Pennsylvania, where, as has been noted, they abound. In 1962 the Standing Committee on Constitutional Law of the Pennsylvania Bar Association recommended that the Pennsylvania Constitution be revised so as to "remove entirely any limitation on the amount which might be borrowed with the consent of the voters at a public election" by municipalities and school districts in order to "discourage the use of the authority device." Municipal authorities, it explained, have incurred indebtedness "to an extent which the electorate scarcely realize."(7)

So potentially damaging was this attack by the Commission on Constitutional Revision considered that Butcher and Sherrerd, a Company that announced in 1960 that it had served as underwriter to 464 separate authority bond issues with a total value of more than $656,000,000, published an answer in pamphlet form, under the title, "Authorities -- Effective Public Servants." "Rather than eliminate authorities," the booklet argued, "taxpayers in Pennsylvania should appreciate the fact that a method has been provided which not only gets the job done economically, quickly, and with flexibility, but adds such a measure of desirable talent in public service as well."(8)

Anonymity

The Commission's charge that authorities had built up total debts "to an extent which the electorate scarcely realize" is easier to substantiate than the relative merits of authority finance, inasmuch as the general public is almost completely unaware of the meaning of the public-authority device.

The term, "authority" itself is unfortunate in this regard, as special agencies so referred to blend into the more general connotation of the term, "authority" and fail, therefore, to attain individual identity apart from other types of government all of which exercise authority. The early public corporations of the mercantile period were chartered with authorizations from the government to conduct certain public functions. With these authorizations they became known as "authorities" for carrying out their purposes. It is in the light of this background that one should read the somewhat apocryphal account of the derivation of the modern term, "authority" as having been suggested by the fact that the Act of Parliament which created the Port of London Authority in 1908 had contained the words repetitiously, "Authority is hereby given," to such an extent that Lloyd George, perhaps on the recommendation of a newspaper correspondent, in desperation for a name for this new agency, decided to call it simply the "Authority."

Perhaps it is not surprising that the authorities, handicapped by such a generic title, have remained unknown to the public when one considers the lack of attention to the local governments of which they frequently are subdivisions. Bollens, in his book on special districts, has compared them with counties as the "new dark continent of American politics."(9) A survey of departments of political science and economics in thirty-five colleges in and around New York City in 1962 revealed that 40 per cent of them did not make any references to public authorities or special districts in their teaching. Of those who said they did include these special agencies in their courses, certain of them added qualifications:

"(T)his topic is only given peripheral consideration."

"(W)e do touch upon them in our government classes...."

"I merely treat public authorities as one more topic within the whole...."

"Although some incidental references are made in our courses on American Government, State and Local Government, Economics, and Urban Sociology, we do not give direct consideration to these independent agencies...."

"There is no special emphasis on the growth of 'the authority concept,'...."(10)

The indifference of college educators to authorities is particularly hard to understand when one considers that education nationwide has been intimately affiliated with the authority system for years. In fact, educators have been one of the most successful groups in the use of authorities. Dormitory or school-building authorities have been established in such states as Georgia, Indiana, Maine, Pennsylvania, and New York, with Pennsylvania alone having 543 municipal-school building authorities.(11) Colleges are now receiving land for campus use from redevelopment authorities.

In fact, earlier in the same academic year in which the survey of the colleges was made, New York State, in which it was partially made, had been through a bitter referendum battle over an issue of $500,000,000 for the State Dormitory Authority which had been defeated on the basis of separation of church and state. On the same ballot, incidentally, had been two other referenda providing for large sums of money to public authorities: one for $100,000,000 to enable the Port of New York Authority to purchase railroad passenger equipment and lease it to various commuter railroads; and the other to enable New York State to lend money to public authorities established to finance the construction of industrial or manufacturing plants, or to rehabilitate existing ones, in areas of unemployment in the State. These two referenda had been passed.

Most public authorities have done little to make themselves known to the public, but have remained satisfied to perform their functions under a cloak of anonymity, or to direct their appeal more to the potential bondholder than to constituents of the area over which the authority has been superimposed.

With the exception of Pennsylvania, where the Pennsylvania Municipal Authorities Association is accepted as "the recognized organization of municipal authorities in Pennsylvania," the striking fact is that officials of public authorities have seemed singularly unaware of the peculiar identity of the unique units of government they represent. In the main, one does not find professional associations of public authorities' officials to anywhere near the extent one might expect for those engaged in pioneering efforts with units of government functioning in an area encompassing both the public and private sectors. Missing are organizations of authorities themselves which could correspond to the National Association of Counties. A beginning may have been made recently in the Conference on Interstate Agencies, the Airport Operators Council and the National Association of Housing and Redevelopment Officials and individual State Associations of Housing and Redevelopment Authorities. However, despite the fact that by 1961 there were 37 port authorities organized as public corporations, 22 as independent commissions, and

10 as government departments,(12) the General Counsel for the American Association of Port Authorities could still say: "I doubt whether it can be said that the Association has any offical position with respect to what you refer to as 'the authorities concept.' I would guess that if its members were questioned individually they would say that there is no hard and fast rule, — that under certain circumstances the Authority form of organization is very desirable, whereas in other cases it is preferable to act through existing departments or boards."(13)

Austin Tobin, Executive Director of the Port of New York Authority, takes virtually the same position when he points out that "an authority should not be created simply to replace the normal function of the established bureaus or divisions of government; nor to lull the public into a belief that the activity is self-supporting when in reality it is subsidized; nor solely as a device to avoid debt limitations."(14) Inasmuch as the greatest number of local authorities are established in order to circumvent state constitutional debt ceilings, Mr. Tobin is indicting the largest group of public authorities and he is the Director of one of the best-known public authorities in the United States.

What becomes clear is that participants in public authorities not only are not ready to recognize the broad spectrum of this type of device, but are critically conscious of the distinctions among types of authorities. Officials of county and municipal governments must differentiate carefully the various kinds of authorities in deciding whether or not to create any of them in the community.

Prototype

Care must be taken at the outset to free one's thinking of authorities in terms of the large interstate ones. Wherever the word, "authority." has come to the attention of the public with any degree of regularity it has been in connection with those multi-purpose, interstate agencies which have dramatized their achievements in monuments of steel and concrete. County and municipal authorities under consideration by local officials bear very few similarities to the super units bearing the same name.

Nathaniel Preston repeats a story sworn to by Julius Henry Cohen, first General Counsel of the Port of New York Authority, of the fiscal officer of a midwestern town who approached a speaker for the Port Authority after the latter had delivered a talk about its functions, and said: "Mr. Speaker, what you just said about the Port Authority hits the nail on the head in my town. You know, ... we have been wanting to build a playground in my city and the taxpayers have opposed it because they don't want to spend any money and raise taxes. But I told the Mayor, ... 'Why don't we have a Playground Authority? The taxpayers have heard all about the wonders of the Tennessee Valley Authority, and even the Port of New York Authority, and if we just call this project the Playground Authority, the taxpayers will fall for it like a ton of bricks.' "(15)

Although in more subtle ways, much of our own thinking about authorities is conditioned by images of those few whose functions are sufficiently spectacular, are used daily by a great many people, or fall within the coverage of large city newspapers. How can one compare the kind of prestige enjoyed by the Port of New York Authority to the relative anonymity within which local authorities operate? The New York Times reflected the one extreme on August 30, 1962, with its account of the ceremonies attendant on the opening of the second deck of the Port Authority's George Washington Bridge: "The hour-long ceremony ended with the cutting by the Governors of two traditional red-white-and-blue ribbons, one for each state. As the tapes dropped, gold-colored curtains parted and the states' seals, with 'Welcome' at the top, were unveiled to 3,000 invited guests .... As Governor Hughes' car moved east toward the speakers' platform, Governor Rockefeller was moving west in another 1931 touring car. The Governors were re-enacting the initial ceremony.... As it ended, the Coast Guard cutter, Campbell at anchor below the bridge roared a nineteen-gun salute and harbor craft blasted foghorns."

The other extreme is illustrated by the report of the establishment of a county authority, the Onondaga (New York) County Water Authority: "It is significant to note that, except for a brief news story dealing with the original recommendation to the Board of Supervisors by the study committee, practically no publicity attended the creation

of the authority . . . . (T)he water authority slipped by without dissent and virtually without notice."(16)

Overlooked in the preoccupation with the relatively few
interstate, or large state, authorities is the fact that within the very jurisdictional boundaries of these large agencies
are literally hundreds of unrelated single-purpose authorities. Accurate records of them are not kept, but some one
hundred separate semi-autonomous authorities can be identified within the twenty-five mile radius of the Statue of
Liberty which roughly constitutes the jurisdictional lines
of the Port of New York Authority. The very fact that
records are not kept of these smaller ones indicates the
general lack of concern for them.

The giant proportions of the Port Authority have served
to blur the perspective of those who should be concerned --
government officials, students, economists, taxpayers --
until they have missed the point that the real problem lies
in the increasingly large number of public authorities which
are being set up independently, each designed to handle
one function of the area, and each expected to act without
coordination with the others. There are, after all, only
three interstate port authorities in the United States; there
are 18,323 special districts, or public authorities. Fasci-
nation for the three, and the relatively few other interstate
units, has blinded most people to the fact that the meaning
of even the big ones cannot be seen in its proper perspective
except in relation to the total complex of all authorities
and their combined overall impact on the area. Victor
Jones emphasizes the point: "The great disadvantage of
special districts and authorities lies in the cumulative effect of their use. One special district may be of no im-
port, but ultimately their use will lead to functional dis-
integration."(17)

The Port of New York Authority came not at the beginning of special districts in the United States, but well
along in their development. Special districts even on
something like a metropolitan scale appeared in the United
States as early as 1790. In that year Philadelphia formed
a special body to combine the administration of the City
and suburban prisons. Six additional metropolitan districts

were organized before 1900 "including a sewage and water district in Boston, sewage districts in Chicago and in New York, a levee district in New Orleans and a port district in Portland."(18)

In 1914, seven years before the Port of New York Authority was established, The American Political Science Review had begun running reports on "Special Municipal Corporations." In the November issue of that year, Charles Kettleborough wrote under that title that during "the past few years there has been a significant increase in the number and diversity of municipal corporations, and the creation and development of interesting political units seems to be only in its infancy." He referred to the "inadequacy" of the standard forms of government to meet the "obligations ... imposed by an increasingly complex community life" and concluded that this difficulty "has led to the creation of special municipal corporations of greater flexibility and with more homogeneous interests."

As illustrations, he cited water districts in New York State and six other States and a number of "exceptional departures in the creation of municipal corporations" in Illinois, Washington, and New Jersey. "In New Jersey," he explained, "two or more townships and boroughs or other municipalities lying within the boundaries of adjacent counties may maintain public parks and pleasure grounds and for that purpose may acquire land, lakes, ponds and rights of flowage, and erect and maintain dams ...." "The affairs of the park," he said, "are administered by an inter-municipal park commission consisting of one member for each 1000 persons resident within the constituent municipalities, the members of which are appointed for five years by the several municipal governing bodies and serve without compensation." New Jersey had gone so far as to authorize "three or more counties on the boundary of the state to form a district for the construction of bridges or tunnels over or under navigable streams."(19)

By May of 1920 the Review could report that special municipal corporations "continue to be a prolific source of legislation. In 34 states legislating in this field in 1919, there were 1096 acts passed directly concerning 82

varieties of districts which are essentially special municipal corporations ...."(20)

The port of Portland, Oregon, had been given an "extra-
ordinary extension of powers" in 1917, four years before
the formation of the Port of New York Authority. The Review of 1918 saw this as "evidence of the utility of this
special municipal corporation and the popular confidence
in it."(21)

Were these early agencies public authorities? They
certainly were special districts, as they had the power to
levy taxes within their boundaries. But they had, also, the
characteristic tool of authority financing, the right to issue
revenue bonds. Authorities depend far more on the bond
issue than do the special districts which tend to lean more
on special tax levies within their borders. These early
municipal corporations had attributes, therefore, of both
the special districts and the public authorities of today.
F. H. Gould, the Review's writer, concluded: "(O)ne fact
now stands forth clearly: namely, that all these districts
for special purposes are one in essential nature, regardless
of the divergence of many of the individual districts from
the standard type, and the designation, 'special municipal
corporation' may be used to indicate every such district
which is a public corporation, with definite territorial
limits, formed for a single local purpose or for a few
closely related purposes, autonomous, with power to elect
its officials, determine boundaries, levy taxes, and issue
bonds to carry out the corporate purpose."(22)

The Port of New York Authority, created by interstate
compact between New York and New Jersey in 1921, added
the interstate aspect and the use of the word, "Authority,"
to the growing application of the special-district device.

It is these "special municipal corporations," as they
were called fifty years ago, rather than the Port of New
York Authority, which should be considered the fore-
runners of the present county and municipal public authorities and studied accordingly. Knowledge of the functioning
of the Onondaga County Water Authority, born unsung in
upstate New York, will prove of far more value to the local

officials than an understanding of the bi-State Port Authority downstate.

The public authority they will be asked to create will
resemble the Port Authority in very few respects:

It probably will not cut across existing governmental
boundaries to form a cooperative district, as the Port
Authority does across two States, 17 counties, and 219
municipalities, but more than likely will have coterminous
boundaries with the county or municipality, as the great
majority of them do. This fact, in itself, sets up an entirely
different frame of reference for the decision as to whether
to establish a local authority.

It will not be able to issue general-obligation bonds, as
does the Port Authority, but will have to float bonds for
the single functional purpose, a much more expensive way.

It will not have a staff of more than 4,000 employees,
many of whom are recruited on college campuses, with
salaries ranging above $40,000 and up to $60,000 for the
Executive Director. Rather, the local authority will have
a small staff with salaries not much better or worse than
those of employees of the local government.

It will not have a public relations department with an
annual budget of $328,000 in addition to a community re-
lations department, as does the Port of New York Authority.
It may well function almost in obscurity.

It will not be required to submit its board minutes to
the county or municipal government for possible veto within ten days, as does the Port Authority to the Governors
of the two States, but will, in most communities, not have
to gain prior approval for its undertakings or for the flotation of its bonds. After a thorough study of controls,
Preston concludes that "a great number of authorities go
substantially unsupervised."(23)

It will not have its offices in the "third largest building
in the world by cubical content" as does the Port of New
York Authority where its offices are combined with its

union railroad freight terminal. The local authority's office more likely will be a single room on the second floor of a wooden house one block from Main Street. "We don't have salaries, secretaries or an office," the Chairman of the Woodbridge, New Jersey, Parking Authority was quoted as having said. "We meet in my [real estate] office to save rental expenses."(24)

It will, in all probability, be single-, rather than multipurpose in character, devoting itself to the one specific function for which it was created, rather than, as in the case of the Port Authority, to a variety of projects designed to foster "a better coordination of the terminal, transportation and other facilities of commerce in, about and through the port of New York ...."

It is in the light of their own peculiar strengths and weaknesses, rather than in the image of the large interstate or even state authorities, that local agencies of this kind will have to be evaluated.

Five Claims for Authorities

A realistic appraisal of their meaning for a community should be based on the claims advanced in their favor:

(1) They make possible the financing of desperately needed capital construction which otherwise would be impossible under the present restrictive ceilings on debt and taxation, set by the states. They do so by floating bonds in the name of the authority, usually without obligation to existing governments, which will be self-liquidating through the collection of charges for the use of the facilities. After the bonded indebtedness has been paid, the facilities and functions are to revert to the parent government.

(2) As agencies each engaged in one particular function of importance to the community, they have a greater attraction to professional persons who think in terms of specialization. They thereby draw into participation in civic affairs the better citizens of the community, and may, in effect, represent interests at the same time that

the existing governments' representation reflects the more conventional basis of population and geography.

(3) They must be "business-like" by the very fact that they do not rely on direct taxation, but must finance themselves through the selling of their bonds and the maintenance of a bond rating. Their projects must meet the needs of the people or the public will not pay the user charges from which the bonded indebtedness is to be liquidated.

(4) They take "out of politics" enterprises that are somewhere in between the private and the public sectors, permitting their operation in the public interest but with the motivations of private business.

(5) They make possible, through their flexibility, the formation of more logical lines of jurisdiction, no longer tied to boundaries established centuries ago, but centering now on combinations of municipalities, or counties, or on a natural factor, such as a port or river valley. In this way they adjust much better administration to area for the effecting of functional needs.

An objective critical assessment of these five factors, in the light of experience to date and their application to the local circumstances that are relevant, should prove constructive for the county or municipal official who is faced with the serious decision as to whether to add to the already complex system of units of local government.

The format of this book is designed to devote a chapter to a consideration of each of these five aspects.

These five criteria are tested against the actual functioning of public authorities on the county and municipal levels in the five States of New York, New Jersey, Pennsylvania, Delaware, and Connecticut. A number of the commonly accepted generalizations about authorities are challenged by such an evaluation.

Although the concern of the book is the local public authority, illustrations are drawn from authorities on all levels in the five States. This is necessitated by virtue of the fact that in a number of ways the presence of the larger public authorities in the area has a marked influence on the smaller county and municipal agencies with the same name. Psychologically, characteristics of the larger ones often are adopted by the others. Subconsciously, at least, many authorities bearing little resemblance to the Port of New York Authority, consider it their prototype.

Furthermore, court cases of importance in the public-authority field have involved the larger authorities, as might have been expected. Decisions concerning the tax-exemption of the large authority will, of course, affect such powers of the smaller authorities.

The evaluation throughout the book, however, is applied to the local authorities. Other criteria, or different appli-cations of the same criteria, would have to be used for those public authorities which have created jurisdictional units not coterminous with the boundaries of existing governments. Indeed, the author's conclusions are that there is far greater justification for the latter-type author-ity than for those which have accepted the same boundary lines as those which demarcate regular governments. The failure in general of explorations into this phase of the flexibility of the public-authority device has lessened its potential value.

REFERENCES

1. May 28, 1955, p. 769, as quoted in A. H. Hanson, Public Enter-prise, (Chicago, Public Administration Service, 1956) p. 40.

2. "Chester Municipal Authority," Pennsylvanian, II August, 1963, p. 10. Emphasis was added by the author.

3. Bureau of Statistics, Department of Internal Affairs, Penn-sylvania Municipal Authorities 1960, (Harrisburg, 1960), pp. 1, 58-60.

4. (New York, 1961), p. 45.

5. Newark Evening News, March 28, 1961.

6. Robert H. Porter, Jr., "Fiscal Administration of a Special District," published by the Municipal Finance Officers Association of the United States and Canada, Special Bulletin 1962B, September 16, 1962, p. 7.

7. Pennsylvania Bar Association Quarterly, "A Revised Constitution for Pennsylvania ('Project Constitution') January, 1963, pp. 314, 313.

8. Municipal Authority Financing in Pennsylvania Communities, revised edition, (Philadelphia, 1960), p. 2; Philadelphia, February 1, 1964, p. 13.

9. Op. cit., p. 1.

10. Robert E. Catlin, Jr., "A Study of the Extent to Which Colleges and Universities in the New York Metropolitan Area Are Dealing with Public Authorities." Unpublished report for the Eagleton Institute Internship in the Port of New York Authority, dated May 25, 1962. In the Fall of 1961 Professor Troy Westmeyer introduced into the Graduate School of Public Administration of New York University a Seminar on "Metropolitan Authorities."

11. Pennsylvania Municipal Authorities Association, 1960 Pennsylvania Municipal Authorities Directory (Harrisburg, 1960), p. i.

12. Marvin L. Fair, "Port Authorities in the United States," Law and Contemporary Problems — Public Authorities, School of Law, Duke University, Autumn, 1961, XXVI, No. 4, p. 714.

13. Letter from Leander I. Shelley, General Counsel, The American Association of Port Authorities, to author, November 6, 1961.

14. Address at Rutgers University, reprinted in part in the Newark Evening News, April 4, 1953.

15. From a lecture, "The Port of New York Authority: The Evolution of the Authority Plan in American Administrative Law," delivered by Julius Cohen at the New York University School of Law, March 13, 1940, as quoted in Preston, "The Use and Control of Public Authorities in American State and Local Governments," unpublished doctoral dissertation, Princeton University, 1960, pp. 19-20.

16. Roscoe C. Martin, et al., Decisions in Syracuse. Metropolitan Action Studies No. 1 (Bloomington, Indiana, Indiana University Press, 1961), p. 119.

17. Quoted in Jane Jacobs, "Metropolitan Government," in Oliver P. Williams and Charles Press, Democracy in Urban America (Chicago, Rand McNally & Company, 1961), p. 212.

18. National Resources Committee, Research Committee on Urbanism, Urban Government, vol. I of the Supplementary Report of the Urbanism Committee, Washington, 1939, p. 32.

19. Vol. VIII, November, 1914, pp. 614-621.

20. F. H. Guild, "Special Municipal Corporations," XIV, May, 1920, p. 286.

21. Vol. XII, November, 1918, pp. 681-682.

22. Ibid., p. 679.

23. Unpublished doctoral dissertation, "The Use and Control of Public Authorities in American State and Local Governments," 1960, p. 261.

24. Newark Sunday News, September 15, 1963.

Chapter Two

Government
by Bond Resolution

Public AUTHORITY OPERATIONS have been characterized as government by bond resolution. Certainly, the most distinctive feature of these agencies is their dependence on revenue-bond issues which are to be amortized by charges for the use of the facilities for which the bonds have been floated. This makes them, as Bollens points out, "the only governmental units in the United States that do not place heavy dependence upon direct taxation." It results in such financing as being "substantially unlike that of any other class of governments in the United States."(1)

It is this feature which must be analyzed with the greatest of care by the local-government official in his evaluation of the merits of the public-authority device. Its implications are startling, when one attempts to weigh them in the context of the traditional concept that he who controls the purse strings controls the government. The purse strings, under the authority device, are now divorced from constituents in the area of the physical location of the project under authority jurisdiction and are in the hands of bondholders not only not living within the area of concern, but residing, perhaps, even in another country. To pay off these holders of the purse strings, moreover, the

facility must be attractive to the users of it, who, themselves, may not be residents of the area of jurisdiction.
This concept thereby challenges the whole theory of representation by population and geography which has characterized American governments. The local government
official, in attempting to balance the relative strengths
and weaknesses of the authority method, must confront at
the outset this factor of control by absentee constituents
either in the form of the bondholder who made the project
possible initially, or of the user who will defray the cost
of its operation and repay the bondholder. The influences
of these two groups — the bondholder, on the one hand, and
the user, on the other — must have paramount consideration in his evaluation of the merits of the authority-device.

Definition

Special districts, or public authorities, being as they
are, ad hoc efforts to meet peculiar contingencies, almost
defy description. The one feature, however, which commonly recurs in attempts at definition is that of the bond-
revenue method of finance.

Governments on all levels of course have relied on their
powers to borrow for capital construction, but none has
evolved into the type of functional autocracy which springs
from the primary dependence of the public authority on
revenue-bond financing. General obligations and taxation
relieve the other units of government of this kind of sub-
servience to the bondholder, whereas in the case of the
public authority its very existence depends upon the success
and continuance of the one function for which the bonds
were floated.

Commentators on special municipal corporations for
The American Political Science Review as early as 1918
complained of semantic problems, and lamented the fact
that they appeared to lie somewhere in "the haze and maze
of that twilight land — the legal concept of a municipal corporation."(2) More recent efforts to delimit their peculiar
features have not cleared the air. How could one define
sharply agencies whose very creation is dictated by the

fact that they require ad hoc flexible organizations to enable them to function outside normal channels?

Still the most generally acceptable definition of public authorities is that used by the study of them by the Council of State Governments in 1953:

> ...corporate bodies authorized by legislative action to function outside of the regular structure of state government in order to finance and construct and usually to operate revenue-producing public enterprises.

def.

The definition gains by an explanation appended:

> Their organizational structures and powers are of the type usually associated with public corporations and like the latter they have relative administrative autonomy. Public Authorities are authorized to issue their own revenue bonds, which ordinarily do not constitute debt within the meaning of constitutional debt limitations, since they are required to meet their obligations from their own resources. They lack the power to levy taxes, but are empowered to collect fees or other charges for use of their facilities, devoting the resulting revenue to payment of operational expenses and of interest and principal on their debts. (3)

Nathaniel S. Preston considers this definition too comprehensive, and insists on confining the definition to include "a non-taxing government agency, having an identifiably separate existence from its parent government, and financially independent to the extent that it determines its own budget and fixes its own prices, subject only to general limitations expressed in law or fixed by regulatory commissions." He reasons that the authority must be visualized as "an adaptable administrative device, and not as a single, unalterable, organizational form."(4)

Attorney Robert Gerwig argues for a "working description of a standard Public Authority," and proposes to refer to it as "a limited legislative agency or instrumentality of corporate form intended to accomplish specific purposes involving long-range financing of certain public facilities without legally or directly impinging upon the credit of the State."(5)

One question persists: namely, the distinction between a special district and a public authority. Woodworth G. Thrombley, in his study of Special Districts and Authorities in Texas, is driven to the conclusion that there is no difference between the two categories which is either consistent or meaningful.(6)

The Bureau of the Census groups authorities under special districts, but now refers by name to certain agencies in the states concerned which use the name, "authority." In its 1962 Census of Governments, it includes as independent units more public authorities than it did in 1957: "This adjustment mainly concerns municipal authorities in Pennsylvania, school building corporations in Indiana, and some municipal authorities in New Jersey . . . ."(7)

Complications in terminology have arisen through the fact that these special agencies have sprung up outside the normal structures of government, and they have been given names without much regard for the significance of the nomenclature. They are referred to variously as special municipal corporations, special districts, public authorities, public corporations, commissions, boards, and the like.

A significant distinction which could serve to divide these agencies into two categories is the one which is the concern of this chapter: namely, one based on their method of finance. Some rely on direct taxation; others depend primarily on revenue-bond issues and liquidation of these bonds by user charges. Two very different frames of reference emerge. Absentee financing by bondholders raises a whole series of questions as to representation, constituencies, and accountability which are more readily resolved in the case of persons in a district paying direct taxes for services which they themselves receive.

Although there is no uniformity in practice, in most parts of the country special districts, so called, include those agencies which employ principally revenue financing. In the northeastern part of the United States, however, it is more common for such revenue-financed agencies to be called public authorities. Exceptions, everywhere, come to mind. In Connecticut, for example, "Improvement authorities" have the power to levy taxes and collect charges for services on beaches and the like, whereas "Transit districts" may of course fix rates but may also issue revenue or general-obligation bonds. As used in this book, public authorities refer to those districts which have the power to issue revenue bonds, depend primarily on such revenue, and repay the bonded indebtedness by charges for services. Whether these be called special districts or authorities, the appellation is far less important than an understanding of the kind of unit under consideration.

This dichotomy was proposed by the Urbanism Committee of the National Resources Committee as early as 1939: "Special tax districts, long in disrepute, were improved by resort to the device of 'authorities' that depend upon their own income-producing capacity rather than general taxation."(8) It is the thesis of this book, based on subsequent experience, that the authorities have created more serious problems for standard local governments than have the special tax districts. At any rate, they demand a whole different frame of reference for their consideration and understanding.

Bondholder's Influence

In everyday practice the fact that public authorities, or independent special districts, if you will, are dependent for their very existence on the successful issuance of revenue bonds has significant implications for the community. Suggestions of the unusual relationships of authority officials and bondholders and brokers, disproportionate to those of other units of government, are to be found for authorities on all levels:

One of the features of good public relations for municipal public authorities, described in an article in the former Authority journal of the Pennsylvania Municipal Authorities Association, is an annual dinner meeting of the board of the authority with "all of the members of our Council, the officers of the Borough, the Trustee, the Brokers, and others."(9)

When a bill was introduced into the State Senate of New York in 1962 to have all the records of public authorities "declared to be public records ... open to public inspection at all times subject to reasonable regulations to be prescribed by such authority or commission," Robert Moses, Chairman of the Triborough Bridge and Tunnel Authority and several other such agencies, opposed the bill in a memorandum in which he asserted: "The general dissemination of information, alleged to be culled from authority files, which distorts and twists the facts in the interest of sensationalism, would necessarily erode investor confidence in authority operations. This could result in an unwarranted decline in the market price of their outstanding bonds and consequent loss to their bondholders. It could also jeopardize the market for future borrowing by authorities."(10)

"Before a workman could lift a finger" on the construction of the 17.6-mile combine of bridges and tunnels from Cape Charles, Maryland, to Virginia Beach, Virginia, explained the Christian Science Monitor, Mr. Lucius J. Kellam, Chairman of the Chesapeake Bay Bridge and Tunnel Commission, "had to persuade Wall Street that the crossing was justified on strictly business grounds. It has neither federal nor state financial backing. 'There's not a penny of taxpayers' money in it,' noted Mr. Kellam." "Consultants," it added, "said the bridge could be built and that a bond issue could be repaid from tolls. Yet Mr. Kellam had to make three trips to Wall Street to finance the project."(11)

The bondholder gains this preeminent role from the very inception of a public authority. Despite protestations to the contrary, the great majority of local authorities are created in order to enable the local government to circumvent restrictive debt ceilings which prevent its fulfilling immediate needs of the community. Inasmuch as these ceilings are based on the assessed valuation of real estate, most municipal governments, particularly those in metropolitan suburban areas, have borrowed to the limit and still have not met the pressing needs resulting from the spill-over of people from the cities who now need all kinds of expensive services in the suburbs. The simple expediency is for the county and municipal governments to create public authorities, or special districts, whose borrowing powers are not nearly so constrained. Authorities are permitted to float revenue bonds in their own names, with or without the underwriting of the parent governments, and with limitations normally of only an interest rate of no more than 6% and a period of years — commonly 20-to-40 — for the maturity of their bonds.

The steps necessary to effectuate this role of the public authority are so disarmingly simple that they cannot be comprehended clearly without a breakdown of the methods involved. No one State could, of course, serve as a prototype for the handling of so complex a situation as the creation of a public authority or special district, but if any one had to be selected, New Jersey would tend to illustrate characteristic principles and practices as well as another. In basic purpose, the policies of New Jersey in this regard are to be found in one form or another from state to state. In the further interest of clarity New Jersey's process for the creation of county or municipal parking authorities is used as an example.

Although New York State requires special acts by the State Legislature to allow for the establishment of public authorities, New Jersey follows the practice of most States in passing enabling acts on the State level to authorize their creation by county and municipal governments. The State Public Authorities Act of New Jersey enables the formation of county or municipal parking authorities by a simple resolution of the county government or an ordinance in the case of municipalities.

By resolution, the governing body then appoints five persons as commissioners of the new Parking Authority, for terms of 1, 2, 3, 4, and 5 years respectively.

In the case of a municipal parking authority the municipal clerk then files with the county clerk certified copies of the ordinance creating the Authority and the resolution appointing the five commissioners. The county clerk sends duplicates of these two documents -- or, in the case of county authorities, copies of his own two documents -- to the Secretary of State.

Through this expeditious method, the county or municipality creates a semi-autonomous agency with broad
powers of government. "Every parking authority," according to the enabling act, "shall constitute a public body
corporate and politic and a political subdivision of the state
with the same territorial boundaries of the municipality
or county creating the authority, exercising public and essential governmental functions, and having all the powers
necessary or convenient to carry out and effectuate its
corporate purposes . . . ."(12)

One of the greatest advantages accruing from this action
is that, instead of being bound by the State debt limit of 4%
for counties and 7% for municipalities of the average assessed valuation of real property — a limit which the local
government may well have met already — the new Authority
is free to "issue its bonds from time to time in its dis-
cretion for any of its corporate purposes" restrained only
by the provision that the bonds are not to bear interest at
a rate exceeding 6% per year. The Authority bonds, according to the recital of the enabling act, "shall not constitute an indebtedness within the meaning of any constitutional or statutory debt limitation or restriction."(13)

The Authority proceeds to authorize the issuance of a
series of bonds through a resolution of its five commissioners. New Jersey requires neither a referendum nor
even approval by the parent government for such bond
issues. Such freedom is common, although the Parking
Authority of New Haven, Connecticut, for example, is
strictly supervised by the Board of Aldermen.(14)

The Authority draws up a prospectus giving relevant
information about the Authority, the community, and the
purpose of the bond issue. The bonds are offered for sale
by the Authority through either an advertised, or public,
sale, or, more commonly, through a negotiated sale. In
the latter case, a large investment concern, or a syndicate,
will buy all of the Authority's issue of bonds and resell
them as the market warrants. A typical syndicate may
include as many as ten major firms, and perhaps 40
smaller participating companies. The majors may be al-
lotted equal amounts of the bonds and the others smaller

amounts based on such factors as their relative capital, customers, and record in selling bonds.

The Authority designates a bank as trustee for the bond issue which is secured by an indenture, or agreement, between the Authority and the bank. As trustee, the bank will carry out the financial transactions under the bond issue. It will receive the bond proceeds, and income from any source of the project undertaken under that issue, such as rentals. It also will pay the bills to contractors, pay the principal and interest to bondholders, invest surplus funds from the project, and, where authorized by the Authority, may call for early redemption of the bonds, if they are callable. To accomplish these functions the trustee bank will set up a revenue fund, debt service fund, sinking fund, and general fund.

The prospectus guarantees that the "Authority shall at all times, to the extent permitted by law, defend, preserve and protect the rights of the Bondholders ... against all claims and demands of all persons whomsoever."(15)

The relative simplicity of this entire procedure is in sharp contrast to the kind of campaigns necessary to the enactment of a bond issue by county or municipal governments, where it has to contest with a great variety of other needs, adjust to state limitations of the debt ceiling, and then gain a place on the ballot as a referendum where it then has to face the critical appraisal of the voter. The record on votes on such bond referenda since World War II, showing some 28% of the bond issues turned down by the voters, further serves to accentuate the advantages inherent in the public authority device.

A government official, in determining fiscal policy, is faced always with the question as to how much of the financial burdens of government should be borne by the present generation, and how much should be proportioned to be paid for by future generations. He must weigh the relative responsibilities of present and future residents of the community particularly in regard to large capital outlays which cannot be paid for in a short period of time. Public authority enterprises fall within the long-term

project category, and, therefore, call for an unusual concern for their meaning not only for existing governments,
but for the impact they may have on future governmental
relationships.

The immediate effect of authority bond-revenue financing is perfectly clear. It gets the job done. Without
public authorities and special districts local governments,
especially those in suburban areas, might well have been
overwhelmed by the unprecedented needs which confronted
them suddenly following World War II. Some have gone so
far as to say that the suburbs would have strangled to death.
This statement, in itself, assumes, however, that had there
not been the easy outlet of the public authority, governmental relationships would have remained the same and
that unrealistic state debt limitations would have prevented
effective action in counties and municipalities. One might
speculate, on the other hand, that the mere fact that the
availability of public authorities made unnecessary a re-
consideration of the role of the local governments in relation to the state delayed, perhaps indefinitely, the facing
up to the facts of that more basic concern. It is one thing to
view authorities as transitional techniques to help local
governments over the impelling requirements of the post-
war period, but it is quite another to perpetuate them until
they become indispensable units of government.

What is the long-view result of authority revenue-bond
financing?

Expense of Bond Issues

First of all, of real importance for both present and
future generations, is the fact that revenue-bond issues
are more expensive than general obligations. They require
higher interest rates because they must be paid for by the
income from the one project itself for which they are issued, rather than have repayment spread over income from
various sources available to the more conventional forms
of government. Success or failure of the one functional
project is a far less certain guaranty than the future of the
total activities of a county or municipal government where
failure in one function may be offset by success in others.

A study of the relative costs was made in 1958 by the Federal Reserve Bank of Philadelphia and published by it under the suggestive title, "Pennsylvania's Billion Dollar Babies, The Story of Our Mushrooming Municipal Authorities." Its conclusions were that interest on the revenue bonds seemed to range from one-eighth of a point to a full point more than that on general obligations. The analysts were aware, of course, that, had there been more general obligations on the market than revenue bonds, the result might have been different and the spread between the two narrowed. Be that as it may, the use of revenue bonds rather than general obligations apparently cost governments in Pennsylvania for the year 1957 "between $5 million and $10 million in extra interest." Even though seen in the light of the fact that the authorities had borrowed about a billion dollars, this is a considerable sum of money.(16)

A study made two years later by W. Marshall Schmidt, of Hornblower & Weeks of Philadelphia, came to almost the same conclusion. "The evolution of the Authority device for financing," he wrote in 1960, "remains the most significant development of the past ten years. By using the Authority method, the job has been done in a prompt fashion, albeit at the cost of higher interest charges." He estimated the difference at 1/2 to 1%. He based his figures on the following evidence; these rely, in turn, on comparisons of Moody's ratings in 1950 and 1960:(17)

A COMPARISON OF MOODY RATINGS – 1950 and 1960

				Specific Type Revenue				
1950								
Rating	Total Ratings	General Obligations	Total Revenues	Water	Sewer	Sch. Auth.	Toll	Misc.
AAA	11 (8.8%)	10	1	--	--	--	1	--
AA	27 (21.6%)	26	1	--	--	--	1	--
A	58 (46.4%)	52	6	4	--	--	1	1
BAA	22 (17.6%)	18	4	4	--	--	--	--
BA	4 (3.2%)	1	3	3	--	--	--	--
B	2 (1.6%)	1	1	1	--	--	--	--
CAA	1 (0.8%)	1	--	--	--	--	--	--
Total	125 (100.0%)	109 (87.2%)	16 (12.8%)	12	0	0	3	1
1960								
AAA	9 (3.3%)	8	1	--	--	--	1	--
AA	49 (18.1%)	37	12	1	3	5	2	1
A	119 (44.0%)	71	48	8	11	28	1	--
BAA	87 (32.1%)	9	78	14	13	49	--	2
BA	7 (2.5%)	0	7	2	--	5	--	--
Total	271 (100.0%)	125 (46%)	146 (54%)	25	27	87	4	3

A COMPARISON OF MOODY RATINGS – 1950 and 1960 (Continued)

		1960		
		10 Year	20 Year	30 Year
AA	General Obligation	3.00	3.15	--
A	General Obligation	3.40	3.75	3.85
AA	Revenue Bond	3.10	3.40	3.60
A	Revenue Bond	3.50	4.05	4.20

One reason for the additional cost of revenue bonds as against that of general-obligation bonds is the fact that the commercial banks in the Federal Reserve system significantly are not allowed to buy the revenue bonds. Even the bonds of the Port of New York Authority, which are based on the total functions of the Authority, are not permitted to commercial banks. Authority bonds suffer, therefore, because of the lack of competitors for them. The smaller authorities, of course, have more difficulty in selling their bonds and, accordingly, have to pay a higher rate of interest. But even the larger issues, from the more powerful authorities, feel the effect of lack of competition for their bonds. Competition would, of course, serve to force the rate down. In the case of the larger authorities the practice of syndicate bidding for them reduces, or eliminates entirely, the possibility of competition. In 1955, for example, the State Controller of New York delayed the sale of $125,000,000 of bonds for the New York State Thruway Authority because he had received only one bid. A syndicate headed by the National Bank of New York and Lehman Brothers made the only bid for the first issue of $150,000,000 New Jersey Highway Authority bonds to construct the Garden State Parkway despite the fact that the bonds were underwritten by the State. The Authority accepted the one offer. When, in 1961, a bond sale for the extension of the Sunshine State Parkway by the Florida Turnpike Authority was delayed, Governor Farris Bryant of Florida was reported to have commented: "Florida people have advised me you just can't fight the current interest rate. You either sell at the current rate or you don't sell. You don't beat the market down. We don't have that kind of power."(18)

Congress refused in 1963 to pass a bill that would have extended to commercial banks the right to buy revenue bonds. Two rulings, however, have served, if nothing more, to emphasize the nature of the problem:

In November, 1962, the Controller of the Currency of Georgia, declared that revenue bonds of Georgia public authorities were general obligations of the State, and therefore that they could be underwritten by commercial banks, both national and state, that are members of the Federal Reserve system. Georgia has laws which prohibit general-obligation bond financing, except to suppress an insurrection or to defend the State in time of war, and had resorted, therefore, to revenue-bond financing by authorities to circumvent the constitutional restrictions.

Almost one year later, October, 1963, the Controller of the United States Government ruled that a series of revenue bonds to be issued by the Pennsylvania State Highway and Bridge Authority could be purchased or underwritten by national commercial banks inasmuch as they were supported by certain types of tax revenue and did not depend entirely on charges for services. There remains, however, a conflict between this decision and the general attitude of the Federal Reserve Board which does not accept revenue bonds as meeting the requirements of general obligations and therefore does not permit their purchase or underwriting by state or national banks that are members of the Federal Reserve system.

In view of the fact that the very raison d'etre of most local public authorities is the circumventing of debt ceilings, their bonds frequently are not underwritten by parent governments. New Jersey, for instance, specifies in the enabling legislation that the "bonds and obligations of an [parking] authority ... shall not be a debt of the state or any political subdivision thereof."(19) The bonds must so state on their face. Connecticut requires its municipalities, on the other hand, to support bond issues for municipal sewer authorities.

Turnpike authority bonds afford a fascinating comparison in this regard.

The bonds of the Pennsylvania Turnpike Authority are supported solely by toll revenues, a most expensive way.

The New Jersey Turnpike Authority was authorized in its enabling legislation to receive advances of funds from

the State of New Jersey to start its construction of the
road, and accepted from the State Highway Department
$100,000,000. In December of 1949, however, the State
Supreme Court ruled that the State could not advance funds
to the Turnpike as this was an independent Authority. This
left the Turnpike without funds. The Governor, Alfred
Driscoll, then arranged for the Authority to sell a ten-year
revenue bond issue of $2,000,000 to the State Fund. The
bonds bore an interest rate of 3-1/4% and could be called
for redemption at any time on fifteen days' notice. They
were called on February 17, 1950, after the Authority had
taken the unique step of arranging for leading insurance
companies to buy its bonds and to make the money available on a "borrow-as-you-build" basis, rather than the
more conventional way of borrowing the money at one time
from an investment broker or syndicate. The bonds were
not backed by the State of New Jersey. It is estimated that
the "buy-as-you-build" device saved the Authority some
$10,000,000 in interest.(20)

Bonds of New Jersey's second large Turnpike Authority,
the Garden State Parkway of the New Jersey Highway Authority, are backed completely by the State. Here the highway is used principally by persons within the State as it
runs down along the coast, whereas the Turnpike Authority
had been built in the corridor of the State to accommodate
traffic traveling through the State between the Southern and
New England States. The New Jersey Supreme Court upheld the right of the State to guarantee the bonds of the
Parkway despite a challenge on the basis that such backing
contravened the State Constitution's provision that the
"credit of the State shall not be directly or indirectly loaned
in any case." The Court explained that this support did
not constitute a loan to private enterprise, but rather, the
state's own debt or liability.

The New York State Thruway Authority was given the
backing of the State for its first $500,000,000 bond issues,
but not issues in excess of that amount. The one Authority
therefore has both State-supported and non-State-supported
revenue bonds.

The underwriting of bonds by the parent government
tends to reduce the interest rate that the authority has to

pay. This advantage, however, has become smaller as authorities have become better known to the financial community. Turnpikes, for example, are so well known today that they have to stand or fall in the bond market on their own cognizance.

Government's Continued Responsibility

There remains a constitutional issue as to whether a government may divest itself of responsibility for a function normally within its province simply by setting up a semi-autonomous agency to operate it. From a practical standpoint, could a government stand by and let an authority of its own creation fail?

The plight of the Jersey City Sewer Authority may serve as a case in point here. It shows how a City was unable ultimately to let the Authority go bankrupt despite provisions of the New Jersey enabling legislation against the underwriting of the bonds by the parent government. It reveals, also, however, that a City may choose to ignore the plight of one of its Authorities until it has deteriorated to a point where its financial condition may impair that of the City itself. It raises doubts as to commonly accepted generalizations to the effect that public authorities have to operate efficiently for the bondholders will watch their operations and insist that the bond ratings not be impaired. The corollary question which emerges is: Where were the bondholders during the four years of retrogression within the Authority?

The Jersey City Sewer Authority had run into difficulties soon after its inception in 1949. Debt-ridden from the start, the Authority reached so bad a condition by 1961 that its Chairman was quoted as having said publicly that an investigation of the Authority had revealed "most shocking conditions...." "We are all stunned," he is quoted as having added, "at the conditions uncovered."(21)

Actually, the revelations should not have been so surprising. As early as 1958 the Authority had been forced to request special appropriations from the City to meet

operating shortages. From then on there had been repeated evidence of basic troubles.

Part of the problem was not the fault of the Authority.
In order to comply with a directive of the New York-New
Jersey Interstate Sanitation Commission, the Jersey City
Sewer Authority had had to construct in 1957 two treatment
plants at a cost of $40,000,000. It had been ordered by the
Commission to do so in order to control better the pollution
of the waters of the Hudson River and Newark Bay. The
State had estimated that these large plants would be necessary to serve Jersey City's population which would be
385,000 by the year 1977. Actually, Jersey City's population has declined, having dropped from 299,017 persons in
1950 to 276,101 in 1960. The system, therefore, was over-
built.

Political conflicts which have plagued the Authority are
more directly chargeable to the administration of the
Authority, but may have been inevitable in the political
upheavals in the City since the Frank Hague machine was
overthrown in 1949. The John V. Kenny group, which succeeded Hague, was replaced in the 1957 elections by Charles
S. Witkowski's faction. These two factions engaged in protracted political warfare in Jersey City, and no segment
of the government was spared. They clashed in the Sewer
Authority through the fact that the Chairman of the Authority was of the Kenny group. The Authority Chairman asked
the Mayor in 1958 for a loan for the Authority from the City
to meet its new obligations, claiming that shortages had
arisen because of confusion over whether the Authority or
the City should be doing the billing for the new sewer
system. The billing, caught in the controversy, had been
delayed. The Mayor complained about the assessing by the
Authority of public and parochial schools, hospitals, private
schools, orphanages, and City buildings.

When an audit of the Sewer Authority's books early in
1959 revealed a revenue loss of $1,332,000 for its first
fifteen months under the new system, much of it from un-
collected bills, the Mayor requested the State Attorney
General to conduct an investigation. The latter announced
that he would undertake the investigation but in so doing
he would have to work through the County Prosecutor of

Hudson County, who happened to be none other than the Chairman of the Authority under investigation. The examination led nowhere.(22)

The Newark Evening News on July 2, 1959, made public details of a "confidential authority report," showing that the Jersey City Sewer Authority "is fast going broke," and that "the authority now lacks sufficient funds to meet either its reserve or operating obligations." The newspaper reprinted from the report by the auditor the following statistics:

> Reserve obligations, including
> amounts due to the operating ac-
> count. $1,719,011
>
> Reserve fund's cash.   986,841
>
> Deficit.   732,170
>
> Operating obligations, including a-
> mount owed City for billing, and the
> current payroll   96,240
>
> Cash on hand   59,982
>
> Deficit. . . . .   36,257 (sic)
>
> Debt reserve fund guaranteed bond-
> holders   1,060,000
>
> Actual amount in debt reserve fund.   566,812
>
> Deficit.   493,188

By the first of the year, 1960, the Mayor had gained control of the Sewer Authority, having been able to replace three members of the five-man board. Consistently throughout that year, however, the City Commission refused requests from the Authority for an investigation. By December, 1960, however, the new Chairman of the Authority reported that an engineering firm had been hired to survey the plants' operations and equipment. He made the statement in reply to a request from the Interstate Sanitation Commission for a schedule of when the Authority would make improvements in the matter of pollution resulting from the unsatisfactory operation of the Jersey City sewerage plants.

Three months later, right in the midst of the campaign of Witkowski for reelection as Mayor, the report of a private concern was revealed, showing "most shocking conditions" which would require some $3,000,000 to repair. On March 18, 1961, Mayor Witkowski dismissed six high-ranking employees of the Sewer Authority, including its chief engineer and superintendent, chief operator, the chief engineer's assistant, the consulting engineer, superintendent of one of the plants, and the superintendent of the intercepting lines. The City's Finance Director summarized the resultant political confusion in the statement: "Everyone is going to blame everyone else for everything that happened."(23)

The defeat of Witkowski and election of Thomas Gangemi as Mayor of Jersey City meant an opportunity for an entirely new Sewer Authority to be appointed, in view of the fact that the electorate also voted Jersey City a new-type government, changing from commission to mayor-council form. Gangemi accordingly replaced all five members of the Sewer Authority.

After a report by the bonding company to the effect that the failure of the City Council to make up the deficit of the Sewer Authority was "damaging to credit," and "in direct violation of the bond ordinance," the Jersey City Council voted in May, 1962, to approve a $3,000,000 bond issue to finance repairs to the four-year-old plants of the Authority.

The City, having relieved itself, so it thought, of responsibility for sewerage needs, by the creation of the Sewer Authority in 1949, had discovered by 1961 that the financial problem, not having been handled effectively by the Authority, was still in the lap of the City Council. The very bond-revenue method which gives the local government an escape from restrictive state debt ceilings may, through its insistence on the rights of the bondholders, make it impossible for the same government to relieve itself of the responsibility in the last analysis.

A less likely remedy, but entirely legal one, is granted bondholders in enabling acts for authorities in one state after another. In the event of default on the payment of principal or interest on the authority's bonds for a period of thirty days, the holders of 25% in aggregate principal amount of the bonds then outstanding are empowered to appoint a trustee to represent them. He in turn may then arrange for the appointment of a receiver who "may enter and take possession of the facilities of the Authority... and operate and maintain the same, and collect and receive all rentals and other revenues thereafter arising therefrom, in the same manner as the Authority or the board might do." There are alarming possibilities here for the conduct of governmental functions of the greatest importance in counties and municipalities, as well as on higher levels. The ramifications of revenue-bond financing by public authorities require the most careful consideration.

Obsession with Single Function

Not only do such bonds prove more expensive than general obligations, but they tend, also, to give to government finance less flexibility. Paradoxically, although useful in enabling local governments to make use of new methods and functions, authorities, through their legal guarantees to the bondholder to continue to operate and maintain the same function to the maturity of the bonds, perhaps forty years later, may bind the hands of the government to perpetuate that activity beyond the time of its usefulness, or to an extent disproportionate to its subsequent need.

The New Jersey Parking Authority Act assures the bondholder that "for so long as any authority has issued and has outstanding bonds ... it shall be the mandatory duty of the authority to fix, charge and collect rents, rates and other charges."(24) And the State of Delaware pledges that "the State will not limit or alter the rights vested in the Authority until all bonds at any time issued, together with the interest theron, are fully met and discharged."(25)

Conditions change rapidly today in all areas -- urban, suburban, and rural — but, notwithstanding the changes, the project of the authority must be continued until the bonds and interest have been paid in full. Because of the commitments to the bondholders, an authority lacks the ability to adjust, which is possible for other types of government through their general obligations and more comprehensive programs and budgeting.

Kirk H. Porter has complained that "the prime evil of the special district is that it grossly decentralizes administration." "It tends," he explains, "to ex alt each little service. It tends to make those who are in charge lose their sense of proportion."(26)

Luther Gulick, who in general takes a somewhat more dispassionate view of public authorities, agrees on this point: "When you set up a function in a single authority, that single authority knows it was designated by God to do a certain job — and its work is the most important task in the world. Nothing can stand in the way of what the authority is planning to accomplish. They don't care if they bankrupt the town — they're going to get their job done because that's the only job they have to do."(27)

The academician would refer to this obsession as "vertical functional autocracy." Bond resolutions earmark the profits of the authority for the specific purpose for which it is designed years into the future. Contracts to implement its functions today may mature in the year 2004, if they are of the customary 40-year kind. The authority thereby has a vested interest in the continuance of the function for which it was established well into the future. This interest may impel it to develop aggressively new programs, which could be of great benefit in a multipurpose agency, but which, in the case of the single-purpose authority serve mainly to aggrandize that one function. That function may, or may not, have lost its relative significance among other more recent community needs before the expiration of the bonds and the conclusion of the contractual commitments.

Symptoms of this tendency may be discerned in the following newspaper report concerning the New Jersey Turnpike Authority:

The New Jersey Turnpike has its own plans for spending any surplus funds.

The authority yesterday outlined a five-year, 60-million-dollar development program that would ready the super highway for the 75 million vehicles expected by 1965.

The pike's announcement came on the heels of three new legislative proposals for spending surplus turnpike funds on education or local roads. The latest plans for tapping the turnpike till are expected to be put before the 1960 Legislature when it convenes Tuesday. Last year a transit aid referendum that would have drawn upon surplus toll road funds was soundly defeated at the polls.

Highlighting the turnpike's predicted money needs are additional lanes in the northern section of the toll road, from the George Washington Bridge to the New Brunswick interchange; more toll collection lanes at several northern interchanges; continuous lighting from Elizabeth to the northern terminus; expanded interchanges at Carteret and possibly at the parkway; development of a modern traffic circle at Newark Airport and the construction of a service area designed to accommodate chartered bus patrons.

. . .

'However, this is not just a case of spending money for the sake of spending, he [Turnpike Chairman] added. 'We just do not feel we can afford to sit on our hands and wait for federal highway development to solve a situation that may force the turnpike into obsolescence.' . . .(28)

A corollary to this single-mindedness may be becoming visible in regard to a possible built-in resistance to dissolution of the authorities, although it is too early to determine this tendency with any degree of certainty inasmuch as the dates of self-liquidation of so many of the plethora of authorities which were created as a result of the depression of the 1930's are still some years in the future. Any such indication should be noted, at least in passing, however, as one of the reassurances to the local government official in creating an authority is that it is being formed to accomplish a specific purpose, such as the construction of a sewer system, housing, recreation park, and the like, and that when the charges from its functions have enabled it to pay off the principal and interests on its bonds, the authority will cease to exist and its powers and facilities will revert to the parent government. The authority, in other words, is considered a transitional device to accomplish some capital construction which will amortize itself in a period of years. If, on the other hand, the self-liquidating principle does not prove true, then the official is faced with the more serious prospect of establishing an agency which may become a permanent part of local government outside its normal structures.

The terminal period for many public authorities is forty years, predicated as a rule on the period of maturity of its revenue bonds. Enabling legislation declares that the authority bonds "shall mature at such time or times ... not exceeding 40 years from their date...." or that the authority, when it "shall have finally paid and discharged all bonds ... may ... convey such project to the city creating the Authority.... A certificate requesting termination of the existence of the Authority shall be filed in the office of the Secretary of State." In its agreement with the City of New York relative to the leasing of airports at Idlewild, LaGuardia, and Floyd Bennet Field in 1947, the arrangement was that the Port Authority "shall not issue any bonds for Municipal Air Terminal purposes maturing later than May 31, 1997 and any bonds so issued and maturing subsequent to May 31, 1997 shall not be taken into consideration in determining the date of expiration of said term."(29)

The possible clue as to what may happen at the terminal date of such an agreement, May 31, 1997, may be found in very recent developments. It may just be that long before the terminal date, set by enabling legislation or agreement, the decision as to the future of the authority will have been made. The question frequently asked as to what will happen at the date of the maturity of the bonds and presumably thereby the dissolution of the authority itself, may prove to be purely academic. To be sure, many authorities have come into existence, served their purpose, and been dissolved, and others, authorized by law, never have come into existence. The fact remains, however, that many now in existence are showing desires to perpetuate themselves. Illustrations include the larger authorities. Whether or not the same tendency may be ascertained in the smaller local agencies must be determined by studies from this point hence toward the period of maturity of their bonds.

The principal reason for the suggestion that in the case of the large authorities, at least, the government official may not be faced with a decision as to their dissolution on the final day of the maturity of their bonds, is based on the fact that almost all authorities are established in the areas of capital construction, and that, therefore, in order to continue to finance such long-term projects, the authority must get extension of its lease or agreement many years in advance of the terminal date. If it fails to do so, the authority will be unable to float bonds after the first issue. In this way, then, the terminal date of the authority may be pushed further and further back, or postponed indefinitely. The authority, therefore, may not come up to its final years, because, long before, it may have found it essential to have obtained extension of its longevity in order to issue new series of revenue bonds to carry out its functions far beyond the terminal date.

In 1962 the Board of Estimate of New York City extended by twenty-five years the ten-year lease under which the New York City Transit Authority operates the subways and certain buses. This extension was made necessary by the fact that the New York State Legislature had authorized the Transit Authority to float $92,000,000 of its own bonds for the purchase of 724 new subway cars. The bonds would fall due between 1965 and 1987 and the former lease would have expired June 30, 1963. The extension protected the right of the City to recapture the subway lines after thirteen years, however.

The same year, the Port of New York Authority began meetings with the Mayor of Newark, New Jersey, to discuss a possible increase in rent for the Newark Airport in return for the extension of the expiration date for the lease of the Airport beyond 1998, the date originally agreed to by the City of Newark and the Authority. Negotiations continued on into 1964 without conclusion.

The continuance of the correlation of airport activities in the New York port district may well be desirable beyond the period of the leases, as there is no other unit of government having the same range of power. However, the self-perpetuation of public authorities with boundaries coterminous with those of counties and municipalities should be viewed from quite a different perspective. Here the problem is one of the fractionating of responsibilities within the one jurisdictional area, the county or municipality.

As bond issues continue to be necessary to finance expansions and replacement of equipment, local governments may prefer to extend the existence of authorities rather than assume the burdens.

Certain local governments which have moved away from authorities and placed their functions under regular government operation have gained not only greater flexibility in their management, but even financial rewards.

Dover, New Jersey, for example, had had a Parking Authority since 1953. Plagued by the characteristic problem of shoring up downtown businesses to meet the threat of new shopping centers, the town complained of the awkwardness of getting approval from an investment firm in Minneapolis, holder of most of the Authority bonds, for even changes in rates for its parking meters, and its inability to swap or sell land for parking lots. The bondholders were receiving an interest rate of 3.6 per cent. The Authority was not permitted to pay back more than $15,000 a year on the bonds.

In 1962 the Board of Aldermen of Dover adopted an ordinance to provide for the issuance of $480,000 in bonds with which to pay off the Authority bondholders, with the help of a cash reserve of $100,000 which had been required of the Authority by law. The new bonds became part of the town's overall bonded indebtedness. Officials estimated that the saving in future interest payments would be at least $80,000. The new utility bonds bore an interest rate of only 3.1% and they would mature in 20 years. The Mayor spoke favorably of this saving and also of the utility's bringing "control of the whole situation to the town instead of the bondholder."

The local newspaper echoed the same thought: "The plan reflects some solid thinking on the part of the administration, and a sincere effort to place control of the parking lots in the hands of local officials who will be able to make changes seen to be needed."(30)

This control reverted to the town through the creation of a Parking Utility, to which the same members of the Authority board were appointed. Changes in the Local Bond Law of New Jersey in 1961 had made the conversion possible. The amended law applied a new definition of municipal public utilities which was much broader than the former one, and provided power to make special covenants in the utility bonds, including those for parking systems and electrical systems which had not been included in the former law, thereby making such bonds more readily marketable. It includes now "water, sewer, electric power, gas works, public parking systems or utilities or enterprises and urban renewal development projects." The law permits any local government to borrow and issue negotiable notes to provide funds for the operation of the utility.(31)

Dover's action was the first time that a major authority bond issue had been called in in New Jersey and the control turned back to the municipality. "Authorities generally insist on maintaining their control," commented George Skillman, Director of the New Jersey Division of Local Government, as quoted in the local newspaper. "There are jobs and other factors to consider that they do not wish to surrender." The conversion in the case of Dover, he added, "has resulted in a better financial position for the community and the taxpayers."(32)

This new power in New Jersey is not quite the same as the "special-fund doctrine" in which debt is defined as "only obligations resting upon the taxing power" which the Public Works Administration had helped the States to adopt in the 1930's. Under that doctrine, revenue acts for water works, sewer systems, and the like, financed by revenue bonds and paid for by charges for the services, provided for local governments exemption from debt limits for such enterprises. In the case of the amended Local Bond Law, used by Dover, the debt limits of 4% for counties and 7% for municipalities still applied.

Not all municipalities and counties, therefore, are in a position to convert from authorities to utilities. Consideration, accordingly, must come before the government creates an authority, because once having done so it may discover too late that it has locked itself out of a potentially profitable enterprise. In order to maintain their bond ratings authorities tend to "pick the plums and shun the prunes" among the needs of a community, and it is the plums that subsequently could produce income for the county or municipal government. This income, when made by the authority, stays within the control of the authority, and must be used for the purposes designated in the bond issue.

The State of New Jersey has found itself in a bind of this kind in regard to the surplus built up by the New Jersey Turnpike Authority. Repeated efforts to find ways to tap this surplus to meet State needs for other highways, schools, commuter railroads, and institutions have failed. On two separate occasions referenda designed to make use of the surplus for these other purposes were voted down by the people of the State.

In 1959 Governor Robert Meyner proposed a plan whereby the State would place its credit behind the $430,000,000 in New Jersey Turnpike Authority bonds then outstanding if the bondholders would agree to permit the State to siphon off the surplus funds from the Turnpike between then and 1988 when the bonds would be retired. It was estimated at that time that the State would thus gain $570,000,000 from the surplus over the eighteen-year period. The funds would be used to help defray the costs of commuter transportation in general, particularly the commuter railroads, but also other highways and distressed bus lines. Specific legislation to that effect would have been submitted to the legislature if the plan were approved. However, in a referendum in November of 1959 the voters defeated the proposal.

The suggestion in the plan that the bondholders of the Turnpike Authority would have to approve the use of the surplus in return for the underwriting of the bonds by the State, raised a complicated mechanical difficulty. The sheer problem of contacting them would have become a major obstacle. Few of the bondholders were registered, as the bonds were of the bearer type and therefore negotiable by anyone. The bondholder did not need to record his ownership of the bonds, but all that was necessary for him to get payment was for him to detach an interest coupon from the bond papers and present it to a bank. The bank, in turn, would cash the coupon with the trustee bank of the Authority. One guess was that it would require some four months, at least, to locate and poll the bondholders who were living all over the world, and two-thirds of whom probably would have to approve.

Governor Richard Hughes presented to the voters of the State a somewhat different proposal in the 1963 election, also designed to make use of the Turnpike surplus. His plan was in the form of two referenda which appeared on the ballots in the Fall of 1963. One of these proposed a $475,000,000 bond issue by the State to finance elimination of railroad crossings at road grade, provide State grants to assist municipalities and counties to construct and improve public roads and highways, and construct and improve State highways. The other referendum called for a State bond issue of $275,000,000 to be used for public building construction and improvement for local school districts, community colleges, State institutions, and State institutions of higher education. This money would be spent over a five-year period during which time the bonds would be amortized from the proceeds of their sale. Then $42,000,000 a year would be diverted from surpluses of the New Jersey Turnpike Authority for repayment of the bonds. The Turnpike revenues could not be diverted until the Authority were debt free, the earliest estimate for which was 1972. The voters rejected both issues.

If, therefore, the function performed by an authority becomes relatively less important to the community, but has to be continued for the period of maturity of its bonds, it may prevent the accomplishment of other functions whose need has since become apparent.

If, on the other hand, the function of the authority becomes more important over the years, and perhaps thereby
more profitable, the community may find that by having
divested itself of this function in favor of the authority-
device it has sealed off revenues which could now be used
to help carry the burden of the whole governmental program.

Total Financial Impact

In deciding on whether or not to vote for the creation
of an authority on the local level, therefore, the local official must be aware not only of the future development of
the particular function which would be handled by the
authority, and what that would mean to the community, but,
even more significantly, what the total impact of the cumulative effect of hundreds of such authorities will mean for
the whole theory of local government.

In the 1920's probably less than 10% of new state and
local indebtedness relied on its own revenues for repayment, and by the 1930's, not more than 20% was so earmarked. Most of it was in the nature of general obligations.
Today the figure may well have reached 50% or more. The
alarming fact is that actually the amount of revenue-bond
indebtedness through the authority-method is not even
known. This debt generally does not show in the accounting
of government debt outstanding on any level. In its "Statements of Financial Condition of Counties and Municipalities"
in 1960, for example, the Division of Local Government of
New Jersey pointed to this fact: "A tabulation will be
found ... setting forth the amount of authority debt. The
Division has no authority over the budgets of these agencies
but does receive copies of annual audits. Thus, the information is only as complete as the reporting thereof.
Furthermore, no attempt has been made to include debt of
certain authorities created by special acts of the Legislature."(33)

Wade S. Smith, Director of Municipal Research for Dun
and Bradstreet in 1961 was quoted by the Wall Street
Journal as confessing "to a certain degree of alarm over
the increasing earmarking of municipal revenue sources

for the payment of specific bond issues."(34) The Federal Reserve Bank of Philadelphia warned: "With authorities there is no concrete limit to the borrowing-spending cycle. Communities still can sink over their heads as they did in the last century.... Just imagine what a wave of defaults would do to our communities today, how it would ruin their future borrowing ability."(35)

As has been illustrated in this chapter, this revenue-bond method of finance imposes on local governments a frame of reference quite different from the more traditional reliance on taxation and general obligations. The major new factor which it introduces is that of the influence of the absentee bondholder upon whom governments now come to depend to an extent never before known in this country. This outside influence must be understood before the local government places control over its functions in the hands of a public authority.

The payment of the bonds by user charges raises further issues for the consideration of local governments. Not all of the concerns regarding the principle of such a method of taxation apply in the case of local county and municipal authorities, but certain ones do. Arguments applicable to the user tax anywhere are to the effect that these are payments for wanted services by those who want them, often forcing a person to pay for luxuries. In this way, they do tend to shift some of the burden of taxation from the property holder, already overburdened, to the user of the special functions. Such a device makes possible facilities not constantly in use, on a "readiness-to-serve" basis; when the person wants them they will be available and he will pay for them accordingly.

General criticism of the user tax method revolves about the thought that such services are unnecessarily expensive, particularly in view of the fact that many such functions cannot actually be considered luxuries but necessities. They do appear to impose double taxation; the motorist, for example pays for the use of the highways, both the gas and other taxes relevant thereto, and the tolls on the turnpikes. It may, also, delay governments' facing up to the more basic problem of the entire tax base. The use of "earmarked" funds, which single-purpose authority funds really are, runs counter to the trend of thought concerning governmental finance.

From the standpoint of local governments, moreover, there are considerations about the user tax other than these economic issues. There is, again the question of the kind of powers the authorities acquire through their ability to fix rates and charges for their services, and the privileged status this power gives them over that of the counties and municipalities. Rate fixing has been considered for years as legally within the public interest and therefore subject to public regulation and supervision. Public authorities rather commonly stand on the principle that their rates and charges are not subject to control by such regulatory agencies as the Interstate Commerce Commission or state public utility commissions. Their reasoning is that, inasmuch as the user does not have to avail himself of the facilities of the authority, he, by the same token, does not need the protection of the government as to the charges for their use. "There's nothing wrong with the principle that roads like the Turnpike and Garden State Parkway are luxuries, for which their users ought to pay. For those who don't want to pay, there are other ways of getting across the state or down the shore."(36)

Overlooked is the fact that most public authorities are endowed by the enabling legislation, or special legislation, with virtually monopolistic rights with regard to their functions. There are some other roads, to be sure, that could be used to get to a destination to which the turnpikes lead. But there may not be other parking lots, or street meters, or sewer systems within a community, in addition to those for which authorities have been established. Enabling legislation affords the authorities this kind of protection: "No municipality the area of which has been included (with its consent) within the area of operation of a parking authority created by a county shall thereafter create a parking authority." "No municipality which shall have created an Authority under the provisions of this chapter shall thereafter create any other Authority serving the whole or any part of the same area"

Private enterprise usually cannot compete because of the tax exemption of the public authorities. The result is a monopoly for the authorities. The thesis, then, that their rates need not be reviewed by a higher agency because these are luxuries, loses much of its force.

The local government is confronted, therefore, in the case of public authorities, with the problem, on the one hand, of the control over local functions by absentee bondholders, and, on the other, the control over necessary functions of the community by authorities themselves who must repay the bondholders solely, or primarily, by money received from user charges which are not reviewable by the normal federal or state utility commissions.

REFERENCES

1. Special District Governments in the United States, op. cit., pp. 44–45.

2. Vol. XII, November, 1918, p. 679.

3. Public Authorities in the States, op. cit., p. 3.

4. Unpublished doctoral dissertation, Princeton University, op. cit., p. 18.

5. Duke University, Public Authorities, op. cit., p. 591.

6. University of Texas (Austin, Texas), p. 2n.

7. Census of Governments 1962, Governmental Organization, p. 17.

8. Urban Government, op. cit., p. 126.

9. J. E. Kuhn, "Authority Publicity and Public Relations," The Authority, XX, No. 3, March, 1962, pp. 8–9. Emphasis was added by the author.

10. The New York Times, February 14, 1962.

11. February 21, 1964.

12. New Jersey Revised Statutes, Cumulative Supplement, Title 40:11A-6.

13. New Jersey Revised Statutes, Cumulative Supplement, Title 40:11A-6, 8, 10.

14. Preston, op. cit., pp. 163, 234n.

15. Butcher and Sherrerd have published a detailed account of the procedure in Pennsylvania, in Municipal Authority Financing in Pennsylvania Communities, 4th printing, (Philadelphia, 1960).

16. "Pennsylvania's Billion Dollar Babies, The Story of Our Mushrooming Municipal Authorities," Business Review, Department of Research, Federal Reserve Bank of Philadelphia, Philadelphia, March, 1958, p. 15.

17. W. Marshall Schmidt, "An Evaluation of Changes of Credits of State and Local Municipal Units and the Development of the Authority as a Vehicle for Financing in Pennsylvania since 1950." Winning essay, second-year class, 1960 Institute of Investment Banking, and, winner of the All-Institute Essay Competition, Investment Bankers Association of America, Forty-ninth Annual Convention, Hollywood Beach, Florida, 1960 (mimeographed), pp. 5, 6, 8.

18. The Miami Herald, December 2, 1961.

19. N. J. Statutes, R. S. Cum. Supp., 40:11A-9.

20. New Jersey Turnpike Authority, Annual Report, 1950, p. 17.

21. The New York Times, March 19, 1961.

22. Newark Evening News, February 25, 1959.

23. Newark Evening News, April 4, 1961.

24. N. J., R. S. Cum. Supp. 40:11A-8.

25. Parking Authorities Act, 48 Del. Laws, 22-512.

26. National Municipal Review, XXII, No. 11, November, 1933, p. 547.

27. Quoted in William B. Shore, "Developments in Public Administration," Public Administration Review, XXI, Winter, 1961, from Scott, Stanley, Metropolitan Area Problems.

28. Newark Evening News, January 8, 1960.

29. The City of New York and The Port of New York Authority, "Agreement with respect to Municipal Air Terminals," dated April 17, 1947, p. 5.

30. Dover Lake Land News, November 1, 1962.

31. Local Bond Law, New Jersey Statutes, R. S. Cum. Supp. 40: Chapter 1.

32. Dover Advance, March 22, 1963.

33. Department of the Treasury, Division of Local Government, State of New Jersey, Twenty-third Annual Report of the Division of Local Government, State of New Jersey, 1960, p. xii.

34. September 6, 1961.

35. "Pennsylvania's Billion Dollar Babies," Business Review, Federal Reserve Bank of Philadelphia, March, 1958, p. 14.

36. Editorial, Newark Evening News, October 31, 1961.

Chapter Three

Government
by Specialists

Bᴇᴛᴡᴇᴇɴ ᴛʜᴇ ʙᴏɴᴅʜᴏʟᴅᴇʀs and the local government stands the board of commissioners of each local public authority. Appointed by the governing body of the county or municipality, the three to five commissioners are plunged into a confusing complex of "constituencies" – bondholders, users of the authority's services who pay the charges therefor, residents of the county or municipality, and members of the parent government.

Their relative responsibilities to these four groups warrant more concern than they have been given, especially when these agencies are recognized not to be mere administrative units carrying out policy established by their parent governments, but policy-making units of government in their own right.

Authority Powers

Public authorities vary from regular governments in that the authorities are restricted to the function or functions they may perform, but are relatively free as to the methods they may employ. Standard governments are not so restricted as to functions, but are less free as to methods of implementation.   One expectation is that

53

A Political Constituency?

NOTICE OF REDEMPTION TO THE HOLDERS OF

COMMONWEALTH OF PENNSYLVANIA TURNPIKE

REVENUE REFUNDING AND EXTENSION	SYSTEM REVENUE 2.90% BONDS
3¼% BONDS, DATED JUNE 1, 1948,	(WESTERN EXTENSION)
DUE JUNE 1, 1988	DATED JUNE 1, 1949, DUE JUNE 1, 1988

NOTICE IS HEREBY GIVEN as provided in Article III of the Trust Indenture dated June 1, 1948, Pennsylvania Turnpike Commission to Fidelity-Philadelphia Trust Company, as Trustee, that $2,793,000 principal amount of the above Bonds described below have been called for redemption from moneys in the Pennsylvania Turnpike System Interest and Sinking Fund in accordance with Section 510 of said Trust Indenture and will be redeemed on June 1, 1961 at the prices stated as to principal amount, plus interest accrued thereon to said redemption date:

$1,737,000 PRINCIPAL AMOUNT OF 3¼% (TERM) BONDS, DATED JUNE 1, 1948, DUE JUNE 1, 1988,
at one hundred and two per cent. (102%) of their principal amount, bearing the following numbers:

```
47017 50059 54284 58907 62917 67612 72080 76152 80965 84597 89105 92881 96128 99693 103920 109565 116528 119239 124556 127096
47033 50110 54305 58947 62945 67639 72114 76396 80986 84622 89156 92958 96132 99825 103967 109590 116549 119261 124585 127110
47064 50179 54326 58894 62972 67686 72134 76422 81017 84650 89190 92978 96171 99828 103975 109612 116565 119287 124611 127132
47090 50226 54353 59021 63006 67724 72163 76759 81048 84670 89217 93083 96203 99875 104004 109637 116592 119332 124640 127146
47101 50319 54381 59065 63034 67749 72192 76872 81073 84689 89252 93124 96257 99901 104144 109658 116612 119353 124641 127163
47123 50419 54414 59097 63058 67780 72430 76989 81093 84702 89281 93202 96357 99922 104192 109681 116789 119413 124689 127181
47138 51228 54452 59133 63088 67813 72476 77015 81124 84737 89285 93227 96454 99983 104220 109701 116815 119444 124735 127229
47167 51272 54499 59202 63111 67868 72521 77040 81150 84763 89419 93280 96488 99985 104288 109726 116848 119484 124767 127244
47191 51327 54611 59251 63134 67909 72557 77107 81182 84788 89443 93297 96617 100025 104345 109748 116870 119511 124801 127260
47223 51395 55559 59290 63156 67961 72592 77127 81199 84811 89487 93356 96818 100079 104415 109763 116893 119550 124837 127282
47244 51483 55592 59372 63185 68004 72628 77161 81216 84827 89530 93374 96925 100832 104490 109793 116901 119586 124888 127298
47277 51542 55749 59491 63210 68005 72665 77193 81239 84845 89557 93408 96936 100893 104550 110801 116926 119650 124922 127312
47327 51608 55820 59822 63439 68049 72689 77222 81268 84870 89590 93458 97033 100938 110596 109818 116955 119676 124964 127326
47349 51689 55876 59959 63470 68069 72711 77251 81298 84894 89626 93473 97080 100971 104637 109839 116991 120174 124986 127346
47382 51751 55934 60016 63507 68091 72734 77267 81332 84921 89655 93489 97140 100100 104706 110854 117018 120192 125015 127354
47442 51800 55986 60070 64244 68134 72761 77307 81369 84949 89684 93505 97152 100192 104737 110955 117045 120219 125072 127440
47479 51998 56049 60106 64366 68173 72780 77333 81429 85004 89709 93552 97255 101188 104794 110905 117069 120319 125072 127459
47501 52153 56078 60176 64468 68197 72734 77361 81465 85396 89728 93555 97268 101206 104881 110959 117095 120445 125121 127495
47536 52184 56108 60227 64552 68251 72841 77375 81494 85426 89760 93591 97343 101270 104926 109799 117121 120475 125153 127511
47567 52215 56148 60276 64609 68278 72872 77396 81524 85448 89773 93618 97371 101288 104926 100979 117141 120519 125186 127526
47625 52250 56184 60346 64700 68312 72889 77419 81549 85476 89833 93621 97409 101335 104975 101015 117162 120540 125213 127542
47659 52283 56236 60439 64759 68417 72909 77456 81582 85498 89822 93675 97466 101386 104978 101038 117184 120610 125252 127559
47686 52320 56292 60495 64674 68474 72944 77504 81616 85507 89881 93685 97524 101454 105229 100077 117221 120641 125298 127623
47723 52356 56329 60536 64699 68633 72975 77531 81722 85529 89932 93766 97524 101454 105229 100093 117223 120673 125300 127650
47747 52402 56390 60574 64965 68702 73013 77568 81767 85559 89955 93784 97604 101539 105422 100117 117228 120710 125353 127691
47768 52445 56444 60612 65002 68788 73094 77611 81789 85869 89976 93848 97604 101539 105422 100138 117243 120757 125360 127692
47794 52480 56516 60649 65036 68840 73187 77650 81852 85895 90001 93852 97612 101465 105548 100537 117266 120812 125389 127818
47823 52522 56564 60698 65069 68949 73253 77676 81870 85917 90018 93915 97646 101568 105738 100187 117288 120842 125435 128245
47838 52573 56610 60741 65096 68991 73325 77717 81897 85946 90131 93940 97694 101593 105960 100187 117320 120842 125467 128283
47858 52600 56644 60779 65138 69038 73390 77742 82005 85977 90227 93952 97719 101635 105960 100457 117337 120871 125543 128291
47866 52631 56690 60818 65191 69084 73455 77771 82003 86011 90281 93976 97820 101683 106049 100644 117357 120873 125482 128317
47910 52663 56720 60855 65231 69400 73533 77798 82075 86029 90329 94010 97845 101684 106194 100887 117378 120973 125520 128338
47959 52700 56753 60913 65270 69454 73617 77826 82143 86049 90352 94014 97897 101694 106301 100994 117433 120048 125522 128374
47987 52728 56968 60945 65326 69520 73676 77800 82200 86085 90380 94047 97913 101775 106132 101415 117445 121002 125610 128401
48014 52743 57007 60981 65373 69538 73725 77971 82232 86123 90444 94071 97946 101847 106189 100891 117449 121100 125668 128422
48041 52769 57039 61029 65421 69591 73795 78094 82266 86100 90478 94107 97970 101891 106256 100905 117475 121212 125642 128459
48055 52792 57074 61073 65468 69671 73864 78161 82287 86191 90515 94128 97988 101924 106414 100937 117503 121271 125643 128482
48067 52833 57099 61119 65521 69726 73926 78254 82444 86213 90569 94155 98002 101924 106414 101353 117526 121316 125713 128510
48110 52875 57125 61160 65554 69801 74042 78270 82456 86237 90586 94178 98063 102027 106471 101381 117558 121355 125754 128541
48140 52906 57153 61223 65690 69833 74078 78360 82540 86287 90616 94199 98124 102068 106511 101332 117577 122200 125769 128587
48162 52958 57205 61272 65726 69871 74124 78441 82561 86322 90640 94241 98140 102073 106642 101358 117611 122250 125856 128607
48176 62902 57244 61302 65776 69889 74170 78501 82577 86534 90665 94253 98170 102110 106646 101366 117615 122385 125908 128630
48210 52995 57269 61325 65812 69935 74220 78569 82659 86378 90696 94286 98195 102189 106806 101373 117630 122396 125928 128676
48229 53019 57292 61354 65848 69979 74261 78616 82687 86401 90729 94330 98240 102266 106716 101391 117706 122325 125970 128693
48250 53047 57327 61377 65872 70030 74336 78666 82716 86414 90751 94316 98258 102332 106411 101394 117733 122312 126005 128721
48282 53064 57366 61398 65919 70081 74398 78689 82771 86459 90778 94422 98294 102339 106811 101415 117746 123388 126041 128714
48309 53069 57402 61422 65956 70152 74441 78748 82783 86494 90803 94445 98311 102378 106689 100912 117777 123411 126073 128783
48332 53103 57423 61439 66001 70207 74478 78815 82799 86521 90841 94490 98368 102379 106912 101426 117729 123405 126089 128846
48358 53122 57471 61481 66021 70250 74519 78843 82843 86561 90871 94647 98392 102445 106938 101405 117829 123463 126144 128871
48397 53147 57509 61505 66057 70295 74550 78928 82967 86597 90898 94687 98495 102485 107002 100447 117863 123483 126173 128901
48460 53167 57535 61695 66076 70389 74639 78991 83018 86631 90912 94748 98490 102448 107047 100448 117891 123490 126238 128923
48621 53179 57560 61718 66112 70428 74698 79045 83104 86665 90941 94773 98536 102528 107129 100451 117947 123548 126246 128973
48669 53219 57662 61776 66184 70527 74731 79133 83201 86773 90903 94924 98647 102924 107212 100463 117958 123586 126265 129009
48703 53249 57606 61800 66203 70580 74792 79163 83328 86773 91053 94925 98669 102625 107243 100476 117988 123626 126299 129018
48727 53258 57687 61833 66236 70635 74792 79240 83391 86821 91073 94955 98669 102625 107243 100476 117988 123626 126299 129018
48761 53281 57710 61866 66276 70695 74834 79299 83437 86884 91109 94990 98706 102890 115449 117997 123642 126342 129062
48187 53299 57731 61890 66306 70735 74888 79331 83468 87000 91125 95038 98725 102985 103021 101494 118019 123667 126392 129084
48221 53320 57763 61920 66413 70787 74893 79378 84195 87067 91155 95053 98742 102762 103389 115579 118074 123707 126393 129097
48250 53336 57791 61950 66448 70822 74926 79444 83554 87145 91174 95087 98796 102836 104174 115465 118081 123712 126431 129129
49279 53378 57832 61984 66502 70873 74949 79490 83577 87232 91200 95125 98799 102924 104773 115477 118000 123762 126425 130425
49309 53389 57863 62011 66543 70909 74993 79545 83625 87977 91245 95141 98841 102974 107535 115718 118143 123802 126470 130444
49353 53421 57893 62051 66545 70943 75046 79587 83670 88047 91277 95180 98859 102919 107550 115716 118178 123837 126626 130456
49380 53458 57913 62098 66570 71005 75106 79648 83694 88093 91311 95208 98910 102903 107659 115763 118195 123874 126556 130504
49406 53502 57944 62146 66621 71039 75106 79680 83723 88152 91355 95209 98947 103046 107659 115859 118222 123904 126531 130531
49421 53531 57972 62179 66672 71084 75141 79739 83762 88250 91387 95354 98974 103066 107659 115874 118295 123886 126557 130576
49466 53576 58026 62252 66858 71163 75196 79860 83893 88359 91455 95405 99003 103180 107726 115928 118266 123970 126600 131180
49493 53769 58046 62280 66997 71196 75228 79893 83947 88411 91484 95450 99087 103261 107752 115973 118287 123991 126600 131188
49516 53773 58084 62307 67031 71231 75250 79942 84093 88451 91572 95501 99141 103319 107828 116011 118312 124000 126658 131722
49547 53802 58109 62347 67068 71278 75283 79988 84162 88523 91616 95530 99154 103379 107828 116069 118480 124132 126685 131769
49575 53845 58132 62381 67095 71405 75316 80006 84258 88574 91921 95580 99187 103466 107855 116111 118515 124161 126743 131950
49602 53869 58175 62430 67127 71447 75351 80068 84369 88575 91964 95631 99201 103380 107841 116186 118527 124181 126766 132429
49627 53892 58208 62463 67174 71487 75372 80191 84233 88598 91800 95627 99336 103447 107877 116233 118615 124216 126791 132461
49658 53926 58232 62483 67208 71523 75400 80257 84256 88634 88675 92221 95706 99368 103508 116396 118685 124295 126825 132616
49690 53960 58260 62511 67246 71565 75436 80325 84290 88657 92277 95814 99314 103508 107930 116426 118703 124214 126833 132671
49714 53992 58283 62528 67271 71694 75455 80374 84438 88709 92465 95768 99358 103580 107952 116316 118773 124321 126873 133007
49732 54028 58316 62590 67293 71636 75476 80431 84429 88747 92480 95798 99679 103527 116401 118616 124369 126896 133077
49733 54071 58336 62632 67321 71661 75668 80502 84562 88777 92407 95799 99398 103937 107952 116330 118889 124349 126939 133313
49734 54094 58363 62655 67351 71682 75712 80550 80667 84810 92533 95867 99445 103668 109146 116366 118927 124399 126955 133464
49761 54106 58398 62711 67382 71712 75550 80617 85038 88882 92539 95894 99392 103677 109191 101854 118399 124447 126986 133694
49793 54128 58414 62738 67405 71738 75582 80665 84709 88907 92640 95941 99453 103733 100116 116440 118840 124445 127015 133760
49821 54150 58437 62756 67439 71770 75738 80707 80409 88941 92669 95971 99544 103771 100271 101418 119017 124482 127038 133863
49854 54155 58463 62787 67470 71959 75648 80728 80820 84533 88996 92763 96049 99606 103851 100142 119071 124526 127072 133944
49891 54214 58498 62820 67499 72007 75722 80867 84559 89036 92814 96059 99606 103851 100442 119011 124526 127072 133944
49933 54245 58826 62849 67550 72038 75885 80871 84559 89036 92814 96075 99665 103904 100474 116504 119099
50002 54262 58871 62877 67578 72055 75913 80935 84576 89066 92875          116504       119099
```

The New York Times, April 27, 1961

authorities <u>will</u> develop new techniques. So long as they confine themselves to the single function for which most county and municipal authorities were created, they encounter little control or supervision by the parent government. Financing themselves through their revenue-bond issues, they escape the check of the annual appropriation characteristic of American governments. In a very practical sense, then, they are the most autonomous units of government in the country.

Enabling legislation contains "necessary-and-proper" provisions:

"Every Authority may exercise all powers necessary or convenient for the carrying out of the aforesaid purposes."

"Every parking authority shall constitute a public body corporate and politic... having all the powers necessary or convenient to carry out and effectuate its corporate purposes and the purposes and provisions of this act...."

"Whenever conditions are such as to require immediate action to protect the public health or welfare, the Authority may take such action as it may deem advisable for summary abatement of the nuisance."

"... any and all powers which might be exercised by a natural person or a private corporation in connection with similar property and affairs."

"To fix, alter, charge and collect rates and other charges in the area served by its facilities at reasonable and uniform rates to be determined exclusively by it ...."

Boards have the additional influential power of naming their own staffs and employees: "An authority... may employ a secretary, who shall be executive director, and technical experts and such other officers, agents and employees, permanent and temporary, as it requires, and shall determine their qualifications, duties and compensation ...."

This is considerable power for the semi-autonomous authority. Through it these agencies outside the normal structure of government furnish most of the services essential to the life of a community today, such as transportation, sewerage, recreation, utilities, buildings for public purposes, transit, housing, and the like. Their power to fix rates, in itself, as has been discussed, is broad in that authority rate fixing commonly is not subject to review by state or federal commissions on the premise that a person does not have to pay the toll, for example, and use the toll-way; but does so as a convenience which he himself chooses to enjoy. The rates often are not reviewable even by the parent government.

A transit authority, by such "a simple matter as the location of the express stops on the rapid transit system decides whether a street will be developed with high rental properties or with modest shops and apartments."(1)

The placing of signs on a limited-access toll-way can affect the businesses of towns along its route. Businessmen from Buffalo, New York, for instance, appeared before the Joint Legislative Committee on Commerce and Economic Development in the summer of 1961 to complain that signs of the New York State Thruway Authority were too specific in directing motorists to motel areas rather than to downtown Buffalo hotels, stores, and restaurants. These latter, they said, were operating at 48% of capacity. The "very nature of limited-access highways," one of their spokesmen pointed out, "reduces the exposure of the visitor to the enticements of the business man."

Decisions as to the placing of interchanges along these thruways will alter drastically the entire social and economic development of the area. The New York State Thruway made possible, for example, the establishment of an Industrial Park in Syracuse. A study has shown that, as a result, park land located near the Thompson interchange (Thruway Exit 35) increased in value from $500-$700 an acre in 1950 to $30,000 an acre.(2)

Even when the law does require approval of new projects it remains the power of the independent board of commissioners to plan, finance, and operate them. Their actions and decisions, therefore, are changing the face of one region after another. Rockland County, New York, enjoyed a building and business boom with a 34% increase in population in the decade of 1950 to 1960 largely because of the construction of the New York Thruway and its Tappan Zee Bridge in 1955, and, more recently, the Palisades Interstate Parkway and the connection with the Garden State Parkway. This construction was carried out under the direction of the public-authority boards of the Thruway and the two Parkways.

Richmond County, or Staten Island, New York, rapidly is being changed from a rural to an urban way of life by the impending thrust of the new bridge across the Narrows to link it with Brooklyn. The bridge is being built by the Triborough Bridge and Tunnel Authority.

Housing authorities, springing up in one municipality after another, have been referred to as "Our New Municipal Landlords."(3) They now have their own police force, as do many of the public authorities. The New York City Transit Authority, with a police force of about 1,000 persons, has advertised that its police staff is larger than that of most towns.

Dover, Delaware, is being changed as the newspaper described it, from a "quiet town" into "a bustling hub of metropolitan area of more than 23,000 population." Instrumental in this changeover it explained, was a "parking authority formed during the 1950's" and "an urban renewal project" just "getting ready to hatch."(4)

Composition of Boards

The composition of the boards of commissioners that direct projects so extensive therefore becomes a matter of considerable importance.

Studies confirm the claim that public authorities are able to attract to their boards those persons in the community who consistently have refused to participate in the more political activities of local government. Statistics compiled from several sources substantiate the statement.

Those revealing characteristics of members of public-authority boards in Pennsylvania, made in 1957 by Paul A. Pfretzschner, of the Government Department of Lafayette College and himself a Vice-Chairman of the Easton Housing Authority, are relevant. His survey covered persons on urban authorities, including 46 water authorities, 40 sewer, 22 parking, 11 general, 11 sewer and water, 10 housing and redevelopment, 5 airport, and 2 promotion-of-industry authorities. His results showed the following characteristics of these board members:(5)

Occupations:	businessmen	28.0%
	merchants	12.8
	engineers	10.1
	bankers	9.7
	laborers	9.6
	educators	3.7
	public officials	3.7
	lawyers	3.6
	retired	2.8
	doctors	2.5
	insurors	2.5
	realtors	1.8
	salesmen	1.8
	clerks	1.0
	accountants	1.0
	others	5.4
Education:	college post-graduate	11.5%
	college graduate	30.4
	college non-graduate	7.6
	high school graduate	38.5
	high school non-graduate	5.6
	grade school only	6.4
Age:	70 or over	4.1%
	61-70	19.1
	51-60	36.1
	41-50	28.0
	31-40	11.8
	21-30	.9

Income: over $20,000. . . . . 14.8%
             $10,000-$20,000. . . . . 29.6
             $5,000-$10,000 . . . . 40.3
             under $5,000. . . . . 15.3

Politics: Republican 79.2%
             Democrat. 12.4
             Unknown. 8.4

Politics of Boards:
             bi-partisan. 55.3%
             All members Republican. . . . 32.6
             All members Democratic . . . 2.3
             undetermined 9.8

A composite description of an authority-board member in Pennsylvania urban areas, according to this survey, would show him to be a businessman, well educated, about fifty years of age, with an income of $5,000 to $10,000, white, and Republican.

In 1962, an official of the Pennsylvania Municipal Authorities Association, estimated that bankers, automobile dealers, lawyers, and doctors were chiefly represented by board memberships. He said that following World War II most people had preferred to serve on boards of water authorities, but that, more recently, sanitary, or clean-streams, authorities had become the most popular.

The findings of Robert A. Dahl concerning New Haven, Connecticut, bear out conclusions of the Pennsylvania analysis. The Chairman of the Political Science Department at Yale University set out to discover who actually governs in a typical American city. To do so, he studied three kinds of decision-making activities in New Haven in 1957-1958: political parties, public education, and urban redevelopment for which New Haven has attracted national attention. The last, of course, is intimately associated with public authorities, inasmuch as redevelopment authorities are being established throughout the country. In New Haven there was not only a Redevelopment Authority, but also a Parking Authority and Housing Authority all involved in redevelopment.

Among the upperclass New Haven society, which Dahl refers to as "Social Notables," he found very little interest in public-office holding, but where such offices were held they were largely in the area of urban redevelopment:

	Polit-ical parties	Public Edu-cation	Urban Rede-velopment	Dupli-cations	Total Less Dupli-cations
Social Notables.	2	2	24	1	27
Others	495	129	411	38	997
Total	497	131	435	39	1024

Business executives, referred to by Dahl as "Economic Notables," participated more in public affairs than did the "Social Notables," but again their office holding was limited rather exclusively to positions in urban redevelopment:

	Polit-ical parties	Public Edu-cation	Urban Rede-velopment	Dupli-cations	Total Less Dupli-cations
Economic Notables . . .	6	- - -	48	2	52
Others	491	131	387	37	972
Total	497	131	435	39	1024

These leaders in a community depend on "subleaders" to "aid in formulating strategies and policies; carrying out the dull, routine, time-consuming or highly specialized work of the eternal spear bearers, the doorbell ringers, the file clerks; recruiting and mobilizing the following; and, in a country like the United States where there exists a strong democratic ethos, helping by their very existence to furnish legitimacy to the actions of the leaders by providing a democratic facade." Dahl discovered that these subleaders who participate in urban redevelopment "are drawn from the upper and upper-middle strata; the subleaders in public education are drawn exclusively from the middle strata; and the subleaders in the political parties are drawn from the lower-middle and the upper working

strata." The chart reflects the total pattern of characteristics of the subleaders in relation to their participation:

| Characteristics | Subleaders in: | | | |
	Rede- velopment	Public Edu- cation	Parties	Regis- tered Voters
Residential Areas	%	%	%	%
Class I.........	26	12	7	5
Class II and III. ...	49	60	30	26
Class IV, V, and VI .	12	27	62	67
No answer.......	13	3	1	2
Total........	100	100	100	100
Occupation				
Major professionals, higher executives, etc...........	32	12	12	5
Managers, adminis- trators, small businessmen	46	59	24	20
Clerks, wage earners........	7	5	42	60
No answer.......	15	24	22	15
Total........	100	100	100	100
Income				
Above $10,000	54	22	12	6
$5,000-$10,000. ...	30	66	34	39
Below $5,000.....	6	2	39	47
No answer.......	10	10	15	8
Total........	100	100	100	100
N	115	120	46	525

A profile of the urban redevelopment subleader concerned with the activities of public authorities, might run:
"an executive in a large or medium-sized firm, a professional man (or the wife of an executive or professional
man), who owns his own home and lives in one of the 'good'
or even one of the 'best' neighborhoods. He earned at least

$10,000 a year in 1958. He is probably either a Protestant or a Jew and was not born in the New Haven area. He came from middle-class parents both of whom had been born in the United States; he went to college; and judged by widely prevailing standards he has moved up in the world since his childhood."(6) Note how closely this description compares with the composite picture of the public-authority board members of Pennsylvania:

Authority Member	Redevelopment Subleader
businessman	executive or professional
well-educated	attended college
$5,000-$10,000	at least $10,000
white	Protestant or Jew

The sociologist, Robert K. Merton, studied two types of persons, the "local" and the "cosmopolitan," in the local community of Rovere (New Jersey). "The chief criterion for distinguishing the two is found in their <u>orientation</u> toward Rovere. The localite largely confines his interests to this community. Rovere is essentially his world. ... He is, strictly speaking, parochial. Contrariwise with the cosmopolitan type. He has some interest in Rovere .... But he is also oriented significantly to the world outside Rovere, and regards himself as an integral part of that world." Merton found the latter concerned politically with the kind of activities "which involve not merely political operations but the utilization of special skills and knowledge (<u>e.g.</u>, Board of Health, Housing Committee, Board of Education)." The "locals," on the other hand, "tend to hold political posts."(7)

The same pattern comes through, then, in these various studies. The person interested in the kind of activities that are conducted by the public authorities, such as urban redevelopment and housing, and willing to participate actively in such matters, is the educated professional or executive. He is little interested in the more conventional political participation.

The reference in Dahl's profile of the urban redevelopment subleader to the wife of the executive is relevant also in that women have fared well on public-authority boards. A number of women head authorities. Mrs. Katherine Elkus White was Chairman of the New Jersey Highway Authority until she was named Ambassador of the United States to Denmark by President Johnson. Other women hold high posts in authorities in the region.

Authority Board members take their responsibilities seriously. In a survey of twelve metropolitan districts and authorities, "chosen to provide a range of agencies, with differing functions and responsibilities, as well as to insure a reasonable geographic distribution" across the country, board members were found to spend from nine to forty-eight hours a month on agency business. The workload for each district or authority follows:

	Hours per Month	
	Range	Median
Bay Area Air Pollution Control District	4-11	9
Chicago Transit Authority.	44-200	48
County Sanitation Districts of Los Angeles County	2-9	4.5
Los Angeles Metropolitan Transit Authority.	25-40	40
Massachusetts Port Authority . .	10-100	16.25
Metropolitan Water District of Southern California.	11-55	25
Michigan Supervisors Inter-County Committee	3.5-18	10.5
Municipality of Metropolitan Seattle	3-20	5
Municipality of Metropolitan Toronto	14-368	40
Port of New Orleans Authority. .	10-36	20.5
San Francisco Bay Area Rapid Transit District.	12.5	30.5

Only three thought the demands on their own time from two such positions was "excessive." Most of them spoke favorably of their responsibilities. A member of an airport commission and a transit authority said: "It is at my own choosing that I do this. ... I retired from active business 2-1/2 years ago with ample funds to keep me for life."(8)

Specialization

The public-authority board provides for the citizen of today a medium for synthesizing two almost paradoxical interests that he has in government, especially on the local level. He expects the government to meet his needs, and he recognizes that to do so it may well have to employ specialists in various areas, but, at the same time, he insists that he must have the opportunity, at least, to have something to say about how the government is run. His confrontation with the heavy burden of spiraling taxation gradually is beginning to evoke more respect for the expertise in government, but he is not quite sure at what point the role of the expert should be restricted, or checked, by him and other citizens. He does not "associate taxes with services," suggests Charles Adrian, "Amateur fire fighters provide enough service to meet his demands -- and a little glamour rubs off on him in the process. He is not sure, either, about professionals in welfare, health, and even sewage disposal."(9)

Sewage disposal does, indeed, seem to be at the center of his concern here. Sewerage Authorities provoke stronger emotional reactions from citizens than any local public authorities. Certainly, one reason for this response is that the sewerage authority actions involve costs readily discernible to the individual, and its decisions vitally affect the health and comforts of the people. Throughout the disputes between citizen and sewerage authority, however, there runs an undertone of fear lest the residents lose control over local affairs.

These ingredients were evident in complaints of The Homeowner's Taxpayers Association of South Plainfield, New Jersey, against the South Plainfield Sewerage Authority early in 1960. Throw-away literature to the taxpayers from the Association urged that the Borough, and not the Sewerage Authority construct the sewer system in South Plainfield. The Authority, it charged, "is NOT required to listen to the wishes of the people and further ... it DOES

Can You Afford Another
Mortgage On Your Home????

CAN **YOU** AFFORD ANOTHER MORTGAGE ON YOUR HOME??????

DEAR FELLOW TAXPAYER:

If YOU can AFFORD ANOTHER mortgage on YOUR home, then don't read any further. BUT....if YOU believe the way WE do, that the PEOPLE should choose their OWN mortgagor, then read on......

It should be apparent to ALL that the "proposed mortgagor" (Sewer Authority) is NOT required to listen to the wishes of the people and further that it DOES NOT INTEND TO!!! This,ONLY ONE of the MANY, MANY REASONS that this ASSOCIATION has BACKED A BORO FINANCED SEWER PLAN!!! Other reasons are:

1. THE FINANCIAL PLAN OF THE BORO IS DEFINITELY CHEAPER!!!!!

2. The DICTATORIAL POWERS of the Sewer Authority IS NOT THE AMERICAN WAY!

3. The Sewer Authority WILL CHARGE only YOU, THE HOMEOWNER, and NOT the VACANT LAND OWNER which is DISCRIMINATORY SINCE VACANT LAND OWNERS WILL BENEFIT by INCREASED VALUATION OF THEIR LAND!!!!

4. YOU WILL PAY FOR FORTY YEARS (40) under the Sewer Authority plan whereas under BORO FINANCING you can pay YOUR share IMMEDIATELY or WITHIN TEN YEARS (10).

5. It IS possible for the annual sewer charges, under the Boro Plan, to be INCOME TAX DEDUCTIBLE!!!!!

6. The Sewer Authority represents a duplication of administration, billing, collecting, legal, clerical, house expenses, etc.

This ASSOCIATION has ALWAYS felt that the construction of sewers is vital to the health and welfare of this community and we would like to see sewers constructed. HOWEVER, we DO NOT feel that for the sake of EXPEDIENCY just ANY LONG RANGE PLAN and ANY TYPE OF SOCIAL OR POLITICAL organization should be FORCED UPON ALL THE PEOPLE OF THE BORO for the sake of this expediency!!!!!

This ASSOCIATION HAS NOT LET YOU DOWN!!!! THE FIGHT FOR RIGHT CONTINUES!! CALL, WRITE or WIRE YOUR ELECTED REPRESENTATIVES in the BORO and EXPRESS YOUR VIEWS!!!! SUPPORT US!!!! DO IT NOW!!!!!

Robert Baldwin, Mayor,	1615 Plainfield Ave.,	PL 5-4028
James Caulfield, Councilman,	1437 Cherry Street,	PL 5-3829
Richard Kennedy, Councilman,	101 Young Street,	PL 4-0766
Charles Lammers, Councilman,	908 Harrison Ave.,	PL 5-7347
Mrs.Pat Lauber,Councilwoman,	3313 Beverly Road,	PL 7-4696
Anthony Mondoro, Councilman,	120 Clifford Ave.,	PL 5-5206
Michael Saverd, Councilman,	231 Manning Ave.,	PL 4-7606

THIS IS YOUR TOWN AND THIS IS YOUR MONEY THEY WILL SPEND
LET YOUR ELECTED OFFICIALS KNOW YOUR THOUGHTS
ACT NOW AND YOU WON'T HAVE TO PAY AND PAY AND PAY AND PAY AND PAY
LOOK FOR OUR NEXT CIRCULAR WITH DETAILED INFORMATION TO FOLLOW SOON

THE HOMEOWNER'S TAXPAYERS ASSOCIATION OF SOUTH PLAINFIELD, INC.
PO BOX 71, SOUTH PLAINFIELD, N. J.
NEXT MEETING, MARCH 9th, 8PM, POLISH HOME, JOIN US & HELP YOURSELVES!!

NOT INTEND TO!!" Further, and even more relevant, was
its caution against the acceptance of "ANY TYPE OF
SOCIAL OR POLITICAL organization ... for the sake of
this expediency!" The distribution of certain of these
sheets on a ·Sunday brought a suit for civil action by the
Authority Chairman on the grounds of false and malicious
misrepresentations.(10)

An even more violent outburst against a Sewerage
Authority had occurred earlier in Keyport, New Jersey,
when a crowd, reported to have numbered 200 persons,
attempted to force the Keyport Sewerage Authority to delay its repair program until a public hearing could be
held. The "shouting and hooting" group, according to a
newspaper account, "pushed and crowded around the small
Broad St. office to demand the dissolution of the authority."
Persons "banged on windows and doors" and Authority
board members had to leave under police protection. Even
with that, the report was that the Authority Vice-Chairman
was "punched in the back as he was escorted to his car."
In answer to the demands that the Authority dissolve, its
counsel explained that it could not do so unless no members
were appointed to the board, or unless the board consented
to do so, but only then "after commitments are cleared" —
commitments particularly to the bondholder.(11)

The building of a sewer system traditionally has been
the privince of the local government. As this function
passes, in one county and municipality after another, into
the hands of an authority board it raises the issue of the
relative role of the expert who can "get things done" in the
name of efficiency as against that of the amateur who has
long cherished the dream that, to the extent at least that he
chooses to do so, he may help direct, if not control, the
actions of his local government which affect him.

The "natural habitat" of the "impartial expert," Edward
Banfield explains, is the special function district or the
public authority: "without the protection it affords from
the electorate (he) could not survive."(12)

The public-authority board provides a congenial outlet
for the resident of the community who believes in the need

for specialization and who, although eschewing "political" involvement, nonetheless desires to express a sense of civic responsibility in the decision-making process. Some experts conceive of the citizens' interest in authorities as a reflection of the American predilection for pluralism. James W. Fesler, for example, sees these agencies as catching up, in government, the "emphasis on specialization, segmentation, functional autonomy, and pluralism" which have developed throughout American life.(13) And Peter Drucker views their new proliferation as a return to that pluralism.(14)

The citizen's preference for service on the authority board is predicated, more than anything, on the professional nature of the authority and its potential for achievement. The industrial engineer, the physician, the lawyer, or traffic manager, by occupation, can meet with specialists, in whatever field of daily endeavor, on the board of the authority and apply to its single function the same kind of technical methodology and knowledge. The turnpike, transit system, housing project, or even sewerage system, is a single highly technical function. Its problems do not require of the board member the comprehensive scope of the generalist which service on a county governing board or town council seems to demand. The gap in ways of thinking between the increasingly specialized private sector and the increasingly broad scope of even local government disappears in the medium of the authority board.

Specialized decisions, once arrived at by the authority board, furthermore, can be implemented directly by it. The restrictive hand of the State government does not reach to the authority, except perhaps for audits or reports. There is not the frustrating period of waiting characteristic of the checks and balances of the federal system between decision and accomplishment. Actions are more direct, or "businesslike," as authorities often boast.

Membership on the board may be remunerative or not. The scale ranges from no salary, frequently on local boards of authorities, to an annual salary of $30,000 on the Board of the New York City Transit Authority. Enabling legislation usually approves "compensation for their services within an annual," although not uniformly so. In Pennsylvania members of the boards "shall receive such salaries as may be determined by the governing body or bodies of the municipality or municipalities," except for members of the board of an authority created by a school district. Salaries of $2,500 for membership on boards of small river authorities and $17,000 for thruways are not unknown.

Attractive to the business and professional man or woman is the fact that he or she does not have to run for office in a political campaign to gain membership on a board, and yet once on it is in a decision-making position of great importance. The non-political nature of the role of the public authority has been overemphasized, however and therefore misconstrued. Politics rather often plays a hand in the very appointment to authority boards. The Delaware River Port Authority suffered for eight years because of a political struggle between the Democratic Governor of New Jersey and the Republican dominance of the State Legislature. During Governor Meyner's two terms in office he was able to get confirmations of only two of his nominees to fill the eight New Jersey positions on the Board of Commissioners of the Delaware River Port Authority. All eight posts had become vacant on July 1, 1954, the year Meyner had become Governor. However, Republican Senate leaders from Southern New Jersey Counties, had blocked confirmation of any new appointees to the Authority in order to keep the Republican Commissioners, whose terms had expired, in a holdover position on the Board. The compact establishing the Delaware River Port Authority, had provided that all "commissioners shall continue to hold office after the expiration of the terms for which they are appointed and qualify...."(15) The result of the "lame-duck" Delaware River Port Authority Board was continued indecision concerning the role of the Authority's Executive Director. When the Authority had been created in 1952, it had taken over as its Executive Director the Executive Director of the Delaware River Joint Commission, inasmuch as the Authority was the successor to the Joint Commission. However, he announced in December, 1958, that he planned to retire as of July 31, 1959, but it was not until April, 1960, that the Commissioners could agree on a successor, some twenty-nine months later, and then only after meeting-on-meeting involving political controversy. During this time, the Governor of one of the States in the Compact, Robert Meyner of New Jersey, continually urged more positive action by the Authority, and held up before it the image of the Port of New York Authority as the desired prototype. In December of 1959, for example, the Governor told a news conference: "This is a propitious time to get the agency to develop policies like the Port of New York Authority by hiring a strong, outstanding executive director." He charged that the Delaware River Port Authority "seems much more interested in patronage," and that politics influenced it in such business relationships as insurance.(16) As early as April, 1957, he had issued a statement to the Philadelphia Evening Bulletin to the effect that "the members of the Delaware River Port Authority were dragging their feet." From time to time during the twenty-nine months of deliberation over the appointment of a director, he repeated the assertions.

The Commission was split by the viewpoints of two of its members. Edward C. McAuliffe, New Jersey Commissioner, who had been the first to serve as Chairman of the Authority, endorsed John McCullough for the position of Executive Director. McCullough had been Assistant to the former Director. His background was in journalism, and he had studied some engineering. James H. J. Tate, Pennsylvania Commissioner, on the other hand, felt strongly that an engineer would make the more capable Executive Director, and advanced the name of John Smallwood, an engineer and Street Commissioner of Philadelphia. A long stalemate ensued.

The Compact for the Authority had stipulated that "no action of the commissioners shall be binding unless a majority of the members of the Commission from Pennsylvania and a majority of the members of the Commission from New Jersey shall vote in favor thereof."(17) As there were only seven members from each State on the Board during this period because of unfilled vacancies in each State's representation, three members from either State could block any appointment, with McAuliffe or Tate.

McCullough's appointment was effectively barred in this way by the votes of three Democratic Commissioners from Pennsylvania.

In December, 1959, one of the Democratic Commissioners went so far as to propose a compromise of splitting the Executive Director's position in two, thereby making a place for both McCullough and Smallwood — McCullough as Director of administrative matters, and Smallwood Director of the more technical activities. The Commission voted against it.

A Republican member of the Pennsylvania State Legislature, among others, suggested in 1960 that the deadlock could be broken by Governor Lawrence of Pennsylvania who could appoint a new Commissioner to fill the Pennsylvania vacancy on the Board. He thought that "no reason other than politics is behind the delay in the choosing of a replacement, and the Governor should tell the Commissioners to place the best interests of the port over personal interests."(18)

The Governor acceded to this suggestion and named John P. Crisconni, a Democrat from Philadelphia; he was confirmed by the State Legislature on March 16, 1960. He had not held public office, and, of interest in relation to the study of characteristics of persons willing to serve on authority boards, he was an automobile dealer. Automobile dealers are among the four leading vocational groups represented on Pennsylvania municipal-authority boards.

At a meeting of the Commissioners on April 21, 1960, Tate, in a surprise move, nominated McCullough for the position, thereby breaking the protracted tie-up. He added that a new position, that of special technical adviser, should be created.

Shortly thereafter McCullough became ill but continued to direct Authority affairs from his home until he died in September, 1961. Two weeks after his death, with contrasting speed, the Commissioners appointed Paul MacMurray, a trained engineer, former Street Commissioner of Philadelphia, as its new Executive Director.

At the depth of the prolonged stalemate, the Philadelphia Evening Bulletin summed up the problem by the simple statement that "you can't expect a bistate body dedicated to the development of the port to be beyond the 'Plimsol line of politics.' "(19) Nautically, this would mean below the "legal limit of submergence." Certainly in performing duties of such significance to a given area and of such great expense, the authority will be subjected to political pressures of severe intensity.

More recently the Delaware River Port Authority has made progress, moving even into the construction of a high-speed rail line to South Jersey municipalities.

In the light of the power and relative autonomy of the board of commissioners of the public authority, the method by which members are appointed to it, and the representation which its members reflect, are of real significance. In the creation of authorities, neither of these factors has been given the kind of careful scrutiny it deserves.

Representation

The importance of the appointment is underscored further by consideration of two recent decisions in Pennsylvania court cases in which the appointing power loses the right to remove those members. In 1955 the Governor of Pennsylvania notified a member of the Pennsylvania Turnpike Commission, who had been appointed to that position by a Governor of Pennsylvania, that he was removing him from it, under the provisions of the Constitution of Pennsylvania which reads: "Appointed officers, other than judges of the courts of record and the Superintendent of Public Instruction, may be removed at the pleasure of the power by which they shall have been appointed." The member so removed brought action in the courts. The Supreme Court of Pennsylvania ruled that the member should be returned to the Commission with full rights to serve out his term of office. It noted the provision that the Turnpike Commission consists of five members with the Secretary of highways ex officio, the appointed members serving terms of four, six, eight, and ten years respectively. The Court reasoned that if the

Governor, who makes the appointments, were to have the power of removal from the Commission, he could effectively nullify this scheme of rotation, and that, therefore, he lacked the power of removal. The case was Watson v. Pennsylvania Turnpike Commission.(20) This case was used in part as a precedent for a similar ruling in one involving the removal power of a mayor of a third-class city in regard to a member of the Urban Redevelopment Authority. The mayor was denied the right to remove him, in Commonwealth ex rel. Hanson v. Reitz, in 1961.(21)

Arthur W. Bromage has made a thorough analysis of methods used in appointing members to boards of the larger multi-purpose authorities in metropolitan areas. He discovered all kinds of methods in use, "so variable that they challenge systematic description." Expediency, he concluded, has been the guideline to meet the pressing demands of everyday services. These practical needs, he writes, "can leapfrog political considerations" and have done so at the great expense of any kind of meaningful representation.

His survey disclosed that members are chosen by direct election, appointment by local units of government, appointments by combined state and local governments, appointments by the Governor only, designation by the probate judge, and appointment by the Governor from nominees submitted by economic associations.

The most common method appears to be appointment by the Governor, with only minor use of the two extreme possibilities: direct election, and appointments on the basis of nominations by functional groups.

"Need we be concerned," Bromage summarizes, "that many of our great metropolitan authorities are not directly responsible to the populations served?" He answers: "Immediacy is important, but primacy may serve political man longer. The issue involves political representation as well as administrative efficiency."(22)

Memberships on local authority boards reflect the same indifference to representation. When queried on methods of selecting and appointing to these boards, local government officials invariably will point to the nonpartisan character of the board and mention choosing the best man or woman for the position.

Professor Pfretzshner, who delineated the characteristics of members of authority boards in Pennsylvania, discussed above, went on to attempt to determine how representative these board members were of the population of Pennsylvania, as based on Census statistics. His comparison, he wrote "firmly establishes that Pennsylvania authority members are thoroughly unrepresentative of their communities in terms of their age, education, income, occupation, politics, and race."

He discovered, for example, that, whereas on a State-wide basis 16.4% of the people in Pennsylvania were engaged in business and clerical activities, 60% of the authority board members were occupied in business activities of some type. Although only 7.1% of the State male work force was in the professional and technical fields, 21% of the board members were. Authorities seriously underrepresented the young persons of the State. Only 2 of the authority members were non-white in the overall group of authority members studied, despite the 7.5% non-white proportion of the population.

There is no doubt, of course, that the commissioners are "thoroughly unrepresentative" on the traditional concept of representation in American democracy: population and geography. Authority board members do not mirror the characteristics of the people of Pennsylvania in the proper proportions. But these may not be the only criteria for representation. As Justice Frankfurter declared in his dissent in the case of Baker v. Carr in 1962,(23) the Tennessee apportionment case: "The notion that representation proportioned to the geographic spread of population is so universally accepted as a necessary element of equality between man and man that it must be taken to be the standard of a political equality ... is, to put it bluntly, not true. However desirable and however desired by some among the great political thinkers and framers of our government, it has never been generally practiced, today or in the past."

The further question in the case of authorities is, of course, whether it is the entire population of the State, or county, or municipality, that should be represented on a board. Rather, might it not be the users of the facilities of the public authority who should be compared to the statistics of board members? They pay the user charges for the services they receive and very logically should have something to say about its operations. Or, should the analogy not have been directed to memberships on the governing boards who appoint the authority members and who, in their own right, had been elected by their constituents? And, in all this discussion, what about the bondholders scattered throughout the country and even the world who have invested in the future of the function being performed by the authority? To whom is the authority board responsive and accountable? How should it be composed?

An impulsive answer would have to suggest the possibilities of functional representation. The very terminology of authorities seems to point to that method. Each authority performs a function; why should functional groups, concerned with the purpose of the authority, therefore not be represented by the controlling authority board?

Certainly, there is the potential for functional representation in public authorities. When the St. Lawrence Seaway Authority, representing an international authority between the United States and Canada, was being considered by the Congress of the United States, a powerful coalition of functional interests lobbied on both sides of the issue.

In opposition to the proposed Authority was "a coalition of 264 organizations in 39 states" referred to as the National St. Lawrence Project Conference. One hundred prominent American businessmen joined in favor of the Authority. In the opposition camp were found the American Association of Railways, the Railway Brotherhoods and the American Federation of Labor, joined, significantly, by the Port of New York Authority. The large bi-State Authority of New York and New Jersey was attempting to prevent the establishment of another large Authority, this one on the St. Lawrence River, which might compete for the commerce then directed through the port of New York.(24)

Despite the possibilities reflected in these combinations, few American authorities have been organized to represent functional interests. One of the exceptions is the Board of Commissioners of the Port of New Orleans for which nominations are made to the Governor of the State by five civic organizations, including the Chamber of Commerce, the Board of Trade, the Clearing House Association, the Cotton Exchange, and the Steamship Association.

This type of representation has something in common with the principle of functional representation, but is not refined to the same extent as the provisions for the selection of the Board of the Port of London Authority, prototype of the New York Port Authority. Members of the London Port Authority are appointed in the following manner: one, on nomination by the Admiralty, two by the Ministry of Transport, four by the London County Council, two by the Corporation of the City of London, and two by the Corporation of Trinity House. Of the remaining 18 members, eight are elected by the shipowners, eight by the merchants, one represents the public wharf-owners, and one the owners of river craft.

The Public Parking Authority of Pittsburgh has a Technical Advisory Committee representing interest groups: two city planners from private agencies, the City Traffic Engineer, the Director of the City Planning Department, and the Executive Director of the Authority.(25)

The Richmond-Petersburg Turnpike Authority represents on its Board members of the counties and principal cities along its route, and one representative of the entire State. One member must be a resident of Dinwiddie County, one a resident of the City of Petersburg, one of the City of Colonial Heights, one of the County of Chesterfield, one a resident of the City of Richmond, one of the County of Henrico, and the one resident at large who may not be a resident of these counties or cities unless he is a member of the State Highway Commission.(26)

The Port of New York Authority, with six Commissioners appointed to its Board by the Governors of New York and New Jersey respectively, consciously has

eschewed functional representation on its Board in favor
of Commissioners who reflect the interest of the generalist rather than the specialist. Its reasoning has been that
the twelve Commissioners, each with general interests in
the development of the port and port district will serve
better to reflect the overall interests.

The mechanics, in themselves, of attempting to represent functional interests associated with the project of
an authority on a small board of five members, are disturbing. The role of one or two persons on such a board
may have a profound influence on its decisions, and their
interests may thereby gain priority, for good or ill, over
other interests concerned. An illustration of the nature of
this kind of influence is seen in the construction of the
underground garage by the Newark (New Jersey) Parking
Authority in 1961, the completion of which had an immediate constructive effect on Newark's downtown business
district. Kresge-Newark, large downtown store in Newark,
New Jersey, advertised in January, 1962: "now 1030 extra
parking spaces - - - use the new Military Park Garage."(27)
The Military Park Garage was constructed by the Newark
Parking Authority. The Chairman of the Newark Parking
Authority was the President of Kresge. Vice-Chairman of
the Authority was a lawyer; Secretary-Treasurer was
Vice-President of the Prudential Insurance Company. A
union official, and a dentist were its other members.

Certain members of the Municipal Council of Newark
thought that the Authority was weighted in favor of the
downtown interests, but said that they could do nothing
about it. A Councilman from an outlying Ward, said that
perhaps there should be someone on the Authority other
than a downtown interest man, but that the Council may
only accept or reject appointees by the Mayor. Another
echoed the same opinion in that the appointment of a small
businessman to the Authority to represent other than downtown interests would be impossible for the Council to do
in view of the Mayor's power of appointment. Furthermore, he said that there would be the problem of knowing
which of the many small businesses to represent. He
pointed out that the Council had been blamed for not getting
more parking lots in the outer sections of Newark, but that

it had had to fight the Authority to get these neighborhood lots. A Councilman-at-large, had favored a plan of five parking places for one million dollars each rather than the one parking garage for five million dollars in the one location. He conceded, however, that the Parking Authority had done a good job and had met with representatives of citizen's groups, and others.

The Chairman of the Authority, long had been a civic leader in Newark and an exponent of saving downtown areas in all cities. He had been on record to this effect long before his appointment to the Newark Authority. The underground Garage is an asset not only to Kresge but to its rival department stores located in the downtown section as well. Its construction by the Authority was part of a "New Newark" movement ("Another giant step toward our New Newark") under the direction of Mayor Leo Carlin.

Neighborhood parking areas were not neglected. By 1961 outlying parking areas were in operation at: Commerce Street, 350 spaces; Franklin Avenue, 296 spaces; Clinton Hill, 110 spaces; Vailsburg, 61 spaces; Ferry Street, 38 spaces; and Webster Street, 35 spaces.(28) Nonetheless, the principal project of the Newark Parking Authority from 1957 to 1961 was the subterranean garage so essential to the rehabilitation of the downtown area. As in the case of public authorities in general economic and political issues were determinants. Land for the underground garage was owned by the City of Newark, and the Authority need pay for it only $1 for fifty years. Its use does not remove tax ratables from the City for it is underground. Bonds for the $5,600,000 garage were backed by the City of Newark through action of the City Council. When, on the other hand, the Parking Authority turned to the construction of neighborhood parking lots, which probably would not be profitable, it was unable to propose a bond issue of its own. The appropriation had to come from the Council itself.

As one Councilman pointed out, the people are going to hold the elected Council responsible for parking whether or not there is a parking authority, for, people are unfamiliar with the authority and they do not know how to voice their opinions to it. With the Authority handling only certain aspects of a problem, such as parking, and mostly those projects which will prove profitable, the Council is placed in the unenviable position of dealing directly only with the unprofitable part of the problem but being held responsible in the eyes of the public for anything that goes wrong anywhere even in those areas under the jurisdiction of the authority over which it has no control. Banfield discovered the same thing in Chicago. There the Mayor had no responsibility in a purely legal sense for the Chicago Transit Authority, except to appoint four members as Commissioners. "Nevertheless, in the general view, the Mayor of Chicago had some responsibility for the way the system was run. If everything went smoothly, probably no one would give him credit.   But if something went wrong — he would be blamed more than anyone else."(29)

The Military Park Garage was referred to as "Newark's boldest civic venture since the creation of Newark Airport." It is not without significance that both the Garage and the Airport were built by public authorities. The Garage bade fair to achieve its purpose of rehabilitating Newark's downtown area as soon as it opened. The day it opened, August 1, 1961, the Newark Evening News congratulated it editorially on "the changes already taking place around Military Park which promise to generate much patronage for the garage. New office buildings are under way or planned in the neighborhood and work has begun on an addition to the Robert Treat Hotel."

Despite the collapse of a section of the garage during its construction, which had cost the project three-months' delay, and a dispute between the Authority and City Council over the right to appoint management for it, the $5,600,000 project had been brought to completion in good order.

Even if functional representation could be worked out mechanically so as to represent equitably the various interest groups concerned with public authorities, the paramount weakness of the functional representative system would still not be overcome. The whole person would be subordinated to the one special function of the authority, or his representation would have to be fractionated to a

number of authorities whose activities affect him daily.
If a principal purpose of government is to lend unity to
community activities and give them direction, then the
fragmenting of the powers of government, and the interests
of persons in such powers, into innumerable authorities
may be leading in the wrong direction.

Another suggested system of representation for public
authorities, which tries not to fractionate responsibility
but to join the authority more closely to the parent government, is based on the appointment of the elected officials
of the parent government to the authority board. If the
jurisdictional boundaries of the two are coterminous, as
they often are for local authorities, then the same persons
comprise the local governing body and the authority board.

As a generalization the proposal appears to have merit.
It does seem to return a measure of responsibility from
the authority to the parent government which in itself is
more accountable to a defined consituency. In so doing,
however, it plunges the authority back into the political
nexus from which it is supposed to offer escape. One
illustration of the resulting ambiguity between the "nonpartisan" and political forces is afforded by an Authority
in which the County governing body and the members of
the Authority board are one and the same.

In 1958 the five-man County Board of Chosen Freeholders of Morris County, New Jersey, created the Morris
County Municipal Utilities Authority, and appointed themselves to it as its sole members. The State enabling legislation, the "Municipal Utilities Authorities Law" of 1957,
had stipulated that "the holding of any office or employment
in the government of any county or municipality or under
any law of the state ... shall (not) be deemed as a dis-
qualification for membership."(30) The argument for incorporating an elected board, such as the Freeholders, into
a public authority is that their dual role thus gives the
electorate some measure of control over the authority.

In this instance, however, members of the Board of
Freeholders were all Republicans, elected from the County
at large, and the Authority became embroiled from the

outset in political controversies. Crystallizing the fight
was a personal dialogue between the Director of the Freeholders Board (and, by virtue of that position, Chairman
of the Utilities Authority), who was also running for his
fourteenth term as Mayor of Dover, New Jersey, in the
County, and the newly elected Democratic Mayor of
Morristown, the County seat, which traditionally had been
a Republican stronghold.

The Resolution by the Freeholders creating the Morris
County Municipal Utilities Authority had referred to the
agency not only as "a public body corporate and public"
but as "an agency and instrumentality of the County."(31)
It was formed ostensibly for the provision and distribution
of an adequate supply of water," but actually to prevent
Jersey City from building a reservoir in the County.
Jersey City had filed with the State an application for the
reservoir to be located in Longwood Valley, Jefferson
Township, Morris County, even though Jersey City is in
Hudson County. It had applied under a contract first effected by Alexander Hamilton with the Society of Useful
Manufacturers who had had the legislature give that Society
the right to use the waters of the Passaic River and its
tributaries forever. The Society eventually had sold the
rights to one Patrick Flynn and he in turn in 1898 had sold
his rights to Jersey City. One reservoir already had been
established in Morris County by Jersey City under this
right, and the City now sought a second. The Authority
was created to fight "that water snake, Jersey City," as
the Chairman put it.

Although the County as a whole was alarmed over the
further intrusion of Jersey City, some of the municipalities
were also disturbed over the possible power of the County
Utilities Authority over their own municipal utilities. Five
municipalities, Wharton, Riverdale, Florham Park, Par-
sippany-Troy Hills, and Hanover Township, withdrew from
the Authority right away. They exercised the option provided for in the enabling Act which gave any municipality
a period of sixty days after the creation of the County
Authority to file papers of non-membership with the
Secretary of State.

Less than a year after its formation, in June, 1959, four other municipalities in the County withdrew, and these were key ones in the County: Morristown, Madison, Chatham, and Boonton. They complained of the lack of positive action by the Authority, of a possible compromise by the Authority with Jersey City, and of the political composition of the Board. The Democratic Mayor of Morristown led the fight of withdrawal. There was a legal question as to whether a municipality could withdraw after the sixty-day grace period. One of the Freeholders argued: "We cannot see how any municipality can logically request a withdrawal from the authority at this time." The Mayor reasoned almost the same way: "If you didn't file within 60 days you're hooked — you're on the team whether you want to be or not." He termed the Authority, moreover, "Un-American and dictatorial." The Town Counsel was directed to "get us out from under this thing" and to send copies of the proposed withdrawal ordinance to other municipalities so that they could use it to get out.(32)

Verbal political attacks by the contenders appeared regularly in the local newspaper. An editorial on October 7, 1958, accused "opportunistic politicians" of making "political hay" out of the Jersey City fight.(33) A Freeholder answered the editorial by saying that "it was the greatest disservice by any newspaper to the County in all his years of government life." The Chairman of the Authority added that it would appear that the local newspaper "has gone into politics about as deep as they can go."(34) When Morristown refused to submit its plan for the expenditures of $160,000 for water department improvements to the County Utilities Authority, the Mayor of Morristown characterized his action as "the first shot of open warfare insofar as the County taking over municipal service is concerned." When the Morristown Counsel appeared before the Board of Freeholders with papers of withdrawal from the Authority the Board's Director told him that he was before the wrong board and would have to appear before the Authority Board, which had the same membership. He took the occasion to say that "the Morristown Board of Aldermen has been a pain in our side in the whole case. We're not married to Jersey City, the town of Morristown is, through its politics."(35)

Even though the Utilities Authority did eventually allow the four towns to withdraw, the Authority did carry its fight ultimately to the State Water Policy Division in three years of hearings and subsequently to the Superior and Supreme Courts of the State. Chief Justice Weintraub, of the Supreme Court, finally worked out a compromise for the two parties whereby two reservoirs would be built in Morris County by Jersey City, but Jersey City would agree to sell surplus water from the reservoirs to meet possible future needs of Morris County. The agreement finally was approved, but not until January of 1962.

This practice of having authorities formed on a county level to include municipalities within it automatically unless they withdraw officially within a given period of time, is quite common. The incorporation of the existing governing board as the board of the public authority is less normal, but not unknown, in various parts of the country. The ambivalent position in which this places the person who is cast in the dual role too long has been overlooked. To be at one time a politically elected official and, simultaneously, a "nonpartisan" member of an authority, poses a paradox that may bring into question the whole purpose of separate authorities, divorced from elected governments.

Is it illogical to ask why the utilities of a county should be separated from the supervision and overall coordination of the regular governing body? Is it unrealistic to recommend that the answer to the involved problem of the representation of public authorities whose boundaries are coterminous with those of counties and municipalities is more simple than may have been anticipated -- as simple as returning their functions as soon as possible to the elected government bodies?

The whole philosophy of independent boards of this kind, said Clarence C. Ludwig, "is fatal to the city council as the central governing body for the city." When one insists that these boards are better equipped to handle the multitude of functions they are performing in a municipality today, he says, the "implication . . . is that the city council is an appropriate governing body to handle only matters which are purely local, unimportant, inexpensive, non-controversial, only tax-supported, well-established, or easy and simple of operation."

When, in the same process, one encourages the best people in the community to participate in agencies outside the normal structure of government by divesting the government of functions and methods which might attract them, it not only siphons off their potential contributions to the government, but, as Victor Jones emphasizes, "it weakens the general government for its most important function of bringing the complementary and divergent interests of a locality together into a community."(36)

Where it is not feasible to subsume the functions of the authority under the regular government, the small board of the authority can gain a degree of representation only through the executive who appoints it. The problem here, however, has been that once the executive has made his appointments he then loses effective control over them or close association with them.

In New Jersey, Joseph E. McLean has pointed to the inconsistency of the State's having adopted a new modern Constitution which centralized responsibilities in the hands of the Governor, but in the same year having established the New Jersey Turnpike Authority as a unit of government divorced from his supervision.(37)

Governor Robert Meyner of New Jersey vetoed the first bill to establish the Expressway Authority for South Jersey for the construction of a highway from Camden to Atlantic City because the legislation would have restricted appointments to its board to one person each from Camden, Cape May, and Gloucester Counties, and two from Atlantic County. The Governor was reported to have complained: "I don't wish to take responsibility for this legislation unless I have the counterpart power to determine who will govern it in its formative years."(38)

Effective relationships to enable the executive to be held responsible for his appointees must be carried beyond the initial act of appointment.

REFERENCES

1. Luther Gulick, "Authorities and How to Use Them," The Tax
    Review, November, 1947, pp. 50-51.

2. Roscoe C. Martin, et al., Decisions in Syracuse (Bloomington,
    Indiana, Indiana University Press, 1961), pp. 265-266.

3. Morris B. Schnapper, United States Housing Authority, National Municipal Review, June, 1939, XXVIII, No. 6.

4. Evening Journal, Wilmington, October 18, 1961.

5. The American City, LXXII, No. 8, August, 1957, pp. 189ff.

6. Robert A. Dahl, Who Governs? (New Haven, Yale University
    Press, 1961), pp. 123, 65, 70, 96, 176, 177-178.

7. Robert K. Merton, "Types of Influentials: The Local and the
    Cosmopolitan," in Edward C. Banfield, Urban Government
    (New York, The Free Press of Glencoe, 1961), pp. 390,
    396.

8. Stanley Scott and Willis Culver, Metropolitan Agencies and
    Concurrent Office-Holding: A Survey of Selected Districts
    and Authorities. Bureau of Public Administration, University of California, Berkeley, April, 1961, pp. 6-11, 14-15,
    16, 17.

9. "Metropology: Folklore and Field Research," Public Administration Review, XXI, No. 2, Spring, 1961, p. 151.

10. A crowd estimated at 500 persons turned out for a public
    hearing on the proposal to have the Florham Park Sewerage
    Authority construct a sewer system for that Borough of
    some 7,000 residents in 1961. Persons registered to speak
    at the hearing and 32 did speak at the meeting. All comments were recorded on tape.

11. Newark Evening News, July 22, 1958.

12. "The Political Implications of Metropolitan Growth," quoted
    by William B. Shore, "Developments in Public Administration," Public Administration Review, XXI, No. 1, Winter,
    1961, p. 48.

13. Area and Administration (University, Alabama, University of Alabama Press, 1949), p. 120.

14. "The Breakdown of Governments," quoted in Public Administration Review, XIX, No. 4, Winter, 1959, p. 64.

15. "Agreement Between The Commonwealth of Pennsylvania and The State of New Jersey," Art. II, par. 5.

16. Newark Evening News, December 11, 1959.

17. "Agreement Between The Commonwealth of Pennsylvania and The State of New Jersey," Art. III.

18. Evening Bulletin, Philadelphia, February 21, 1960.

19. Editorial, December 18, 1959.

20. 386 Pa. 117 (1956).

21. 403 Pa. 435 (1961). Cf., William H. Markus, "Removal of Municipal Authority Board Members," The Authority, XVIX, No. 9, September, 1961, pp. 8-10.

22. "Political Representation in Metropolitan Areas," The American Political Science Review, LII, No. 2, June, 1958, pp. 407-413.

23. 369 U. S. 186 (1962).

24. Wilfred Binkley and Malcolm Moos, A Grammar of American Politics (New York, Alfred A. Knopf, 1949), p. 10.

25. Preston, unpublished doctoral dissertation, op. cit., pp. 249-250.

26. The Richmond-Petersburg Turnpike Authority, "Richmond-Petersburg Turnpike Plan of Operation," (undated), p. 3.

27. Four-page pamphlet, "Kresge-Newark January Storewide Sales!" for January, 1962, p. 4.

28. Municipal Council of Newark, "Report to the People — 1954-1961," undated pamphlet, p. 4.

29. Edward C. Banfield, <u>Political Influence</u> (New York, Free Press of Glencoe, 1961), p. 93.

30. <u>N.J.R.S. Cum. Supp.</u> 40: 14B-15.

31. Resolution, Board of Chosen Freeholders, County of Morris, September 24, 1958.

32. <u>Newark Evening News</u>, March 10, 1959.

33. <u>Morris County's Daily Record.</u>

34. <u>Ibid.</u>, October 9, 1959.

35. <u>Ibid.</u>, February 25, 1959.

36. Victor Jones, "The Withering of the City," City Management, XXXII, December, 1950, p. 272.

37. "Use and Abuse of Authorities," <u>National Municipal Review</u>, XLII, No. 9, October, 1953, p. 441.

38. <u>Evening Bulletin</u>, Philadelphia, January 9, 1962.

Chapter Four

Quasi-Public
Agencies

THE TWO MOST FREQUENTLY repeated arguments proffered in favor of the creation of public authorities are: that they afford for the management of public enterprise a more "business-like" efficiency than would be possible in a more conventional unit of government, and that they do so, in part, by taking the control of these enterprises "out of politics."

The reasoning is advanced persuasively by Harold F. Alderfer: "In the municipal authority all the sound practices of a private corporation can be utilized in the interest of the public. On the other hand, the municipal authority preserves some of the advantages of a public body, for its bonds and property are not taxable, and it is generally more free from state regulation as to rates, audits, and financial procedure than private utilities."(1)

Alfred E. Smith, who, as Governor of New York State was responsible for getting approval of the State for the establishment of the Port of New York Authority, referred to the Port Authority as "the modern agency for progress in public works."(2)

The President's Committee on Administrative Management in 1937 summarized the advantages of the government corporation as "freedom of operation, flexibility, business efficiency, and opportunity for experimentation."(3)

Franklin D. Roosevelt had this combination in mind when he referred to the Tennessee Valley Authority, on the interstate level, as "clothed with the power of government but possessed of the flexibility and initiative of private enterprise."

The legal technicality lies in the use of the "quasi," in that the public authority is described as "quasi" public and "quasi" private.

Critics of the authority device counter by admitting that authorities do seem to have the advantages of both government and business, but that, by the same token, they have the restraints of neither. What authorities lack, say the opponents, is a loyal opposition — some group organized to check their activities and bring to the attention of the public their failures. Drawing on the analogy of both public and private institutions, the public authorities, according to this viewpoint, do not have the opposition party organized to attempt to unseat those in power at the next election, nor do they have, as in the private corporations, a group with controlling shares of stock to challenge their management and policy.

The theory of both proponents and opponents does not seem to imply that there is a third area, quite distinct from the other two, between public and private. Rather, the assumption seems to be that any enterprise falling in between the two is partly one and partly the other. The dichotomy is preserved by the creation of a synthetic institution, the public authority, to cover the interjacent field.

A good part of their advantageous flexibility derives from the fact that authorities have this role in between public and private which has consciously not been carefully delimited. The corresponding problem for the community, however, arises from the same fact that, not being in an area distinct and separate in itself, authorities have a necessary interplay with both the public and private sectors which invokes the problem of relative responsibilities. In their ever increasing relationships with local governments, for example, the still unanswered question is: In what respects are authorities public and a part of the American system of checks and balances, and in what respects are they quasi-public and thereby more independent of governmental regulations?

Judicial decisions are of little help in attempts to clarify the distinctions between the authority's public and quasi-public nature. Judge Desmond, of the Court of Appeals of New York State, in dissenting in the case of the New York Post v. Robert Moses, George V. McLaughlin, and William J. Tracy, comprising a Board known as Triborough Bridge and Tunnel Authority in 1961, lamented the confusion of laws concerning public authorities. "The legislation," he wrote, "is mostly ad hoc, a 'wilderness of special instances,' so policy considerations to some extent control us in deciding whether particular statutes which do not mention authorities do or do not apply to them."

The majority ruling in that case had been to the effect that the Triborough Authority "is not an arm of the City of New York nor an arm or agency of the State."

Judicial opinions vary to the extent of the one by the United States Supreme Court which referred to the Port of New York Authority, a bi-State agency, as one of the "state instrumentalities," to that of a New York State Court involving the New York Thruway Authority, which declared that "a public authority enjoys an existence separate and apart from the State, even though it exercises a governmental function."(4) On the local level the Superior Court of New Jersey recently defined a parking authority as "an agency or instrumentality of the municipality in the sense that if performs a governmental function within and for the municipality, but it is not an arm or alter ego of the municipality in the sense that its offices are municipal and its officers or employees are municipal employees."(5)

These citations indicate that the courts are accepting a definition of public authorities as public, rather than private — but as public in a different sense than regular governments. This concurrence was not always universally recognized. In 1925, for example a court in Arizona went so far as to rule that "irrigation districts and similar public corporations, while in some senses subdivisions of the state, are in a very different class. Their function is purely business and economic, and not political and governmental. They are formed in each case by the direct act of those whose business and property will be affected, and for the express purpose of engaging in some form of business, not of government."(6)

The conclusion today, however, is that authorities are instrumentalities, agencies, and arms of the states which have created them, that they normally are endowed with certain specific sovereign powers, and that they are entrusted with the performance of essential governmental functions.

The thought is that the authorities are to be governed by special laws, rather than those which pertain to regular governments. New York State, for example, has the "Public Authorities" Law and special provisions for agencies such as the Port of New York Authority.

In many States these special laws have not kept pace with the increasing complexities of the operations of the authorities. Frederick L. Bird, in a study of local special districts and authorities in Rhode Island in 1962, pointed to a "hodge-podge of special laws under which these districts operate." "Many of the laws," he found, "are slipshod in their drafting; their grants of taxing and borrowing powers not only fail to follow any reasonably uniform standards but often lack necessary precision ...."(7)

More Businesslike?

The fact, then, that the authorities move in and out of the private and public sectors without being a part of one or the other per se, might justify equally the asking as to whether they are "business-like" or, indeed, whether they are "government-like." Efficiency is but one test of any unit of government; it must always be weighed in relation to the sensitivity to the will of its constituency. The problem of assessing authorities in this kind of balanced way is unusually complicated in view of the fact that they are established to perform generally a single function and, in doing so, they have various "constituencies," if you will, such as the bondholders, the users of their services, residents in the area of their functioning, and the parent governing body — or, in another sense, no meaningful constituency.

The generalization that authorities are more "business-like" than a department of government in the handling of similar functions, although a most relevant one, involves so many additional variables that probably it defies comparison. The same function being performed by two units of government, one an authority and the other a department, would seem to provide a basis for comparison. The attempt to evaluate the one as against the other, however, leads to endless frustration.

One must develop, first, a taxonomy of public authorities, for, as has been discussed, there is no "authority concept" as such but wide variations in the application of the use of revenue-bond financing and user charges to divergent degrees of autonomy. Even the segregation of the local public authorities from state, regional, interstate, and international, authorities, requires further refinement. Preston, for instance, divides them into six classes on the basis of administrative devices such as whether they finance, acquire, and operate their projects, or whether they lease them to private builders.(8)

Even as an elementary start, one must dispel the image of the Port of New York Authority and the few larger agencies, and think, instead, of the municipal Sewerage Authority which admitted frankly, albeit apologetically, in its annual report that it had experienced a difficult year because, as it explained, it was "shifting from promises to realities," and, in so doing, had encountered "unknown factors and items" which "become known after the doors are opened for business." The latter conjures up quite a different image, and one which is a much more reliable frame of reference for the local government official.

The comparison would then have to discriminate between the efficiency of the function, such as the toll road, and the efficiency of the authority device in having constructed and now operating the highway. If it is the charge to the users that leads to the efficiency of the turnpike, this is one thing, but the comparer would then have to determine whether the authority device alone is responsible or whether the same kind of income-producing method in the hands of the standard government department, as in the case of the Connecticut Turnpike, would result in the same sort of efficiency.

The authority's dedication to a single goal when placed beside the government's complementary role of balancing the variety of functions necessary locally raises in itself so many variables that the comparison begins to lose all meaning. The almost unrestricted freedom of the authority in methods of operation when compared to the government's more limited means of implementation of even the one function serves further to dissuade the comparer.

The unfortunate conclusion seems to be that there is no significant way to evaluate in a comparative sense the relative efficiency of the authority-device and the performance of such functions in the more conventional government department.

Advantages Enjoyed by Authorities

The advantages enjoyed by the public authority in this regard, can, however, be delineated and discussed. This approach may prove more fruitful. It is undertaken here without regard to the theoretical question of the role of government in the general welfare, as that issue is beyond the scope of the book. The intent is to shed some light on the relative efficiency of the authority and the government department by an examination of advantages the authority has.

The authority, first of all, has been found to be an expedient instrumentality for the invasion of the private sector to a far greater extent than the regular government. This is done in a number of ways:

(1) Through the creation of a public authority to handle a function once considered private enterprise to the extent

that government might have attempted only to regulate it but not own and operate it;

(2) Through the leasing of parcels of its property, or its facilities, to private business;

(3) Through the creation of public authorities, such as development credit corporations, to provide long-term credit and equity capital to private enterprises;

(4) Through the guaranteeing of the financing of new plants and the purchasing and development of land for industrial use, by the creation of authorities specifically for this purpose.

In operating these business and industrial enterprises, the authority-device has, as has been described above, the advantages of flexibility of methods and freedom from state supervision. It may use, moreover, four broad powers of government to aid private business that most state constitutions reserve for public activities. The powers are: eminent domain, tax exemption, public credit, and the establishment of monopolies.

The temptations of county and municipal governments to turn to the authority-device to avail themselves of these advantages, uncommon to local governments, to lure industry, should be tempered by consideration of the very same reasons that the use of these powers by an authority is alluring to industry. Not only will industry be much freer of controls by the local government, when under an authority, but its property will be immune from taxation. Furthermore, the local government should observe the shambles into which any attempt at coordinated planning can be thrown by fractionating its land use in numerous independent authorities for industrial development.

The experience of Delaware Township and Camden County officials in a venture of this kind is revealing.

The financial interests involved were those of the Philadelphia Baseball Club of the National League, known as the "Phillies." Collaterally interested was the City of

Philadelphia in which the team played its home games, drawing some $5,000,000 a year into the Philadelphia area.

In 1950 the "Phillies" won the championship of the National League and played in the World Series, losing in four games to the New York Yankees. But in succeeding years its fortunes declined. The attendance for the first-place Club in 1950 had been 1,217,035 for the season and 196,009 more saw Philadelphia in the World Series. In 1951, however, the team fell to fifth place in the League and attendance to 937,658. A fourth-place finish in 1952 attracted only 755,417 persons, but a third-place in the next year raised the attendance to 853,644. Fourth place again in 1954 meant only 738,991 at the box office. At the end of the 1954 season, however, the other big-league team in Philadelphia, the Athletics, moved to Kansas City, and, despite poor finishes of fourth, fifth, and fifth, in the next three years, attendance climbed to 922,886, 934,798, and 1,146,230 respectively. When the team dropped all the way to last, however, in both 1958 and 1959, attendance fell off proportionately to 931,110 and finally to 802,815 in 1959.

One of the factors blamed for the plight of the team and attendance was that Connie Mack Stadium, in which the Phillies played their games was located in a congested section of Philadelphia with limited parking facilities, and an interior which lacked the comforts of the more modern stadia. Richard Dilworth, Mayor of Philadelphia, warned of the consequences in 1957: "Connie Mack Stadium is out-dated, and unless something is done, both the Phillies and the Eagles (National League Football Team) will move. Other cities have attracted new clubs with new parks and Philadelphia must have a new park too. The loss of the Phils would cut into the city's business and prestige."(9)

The most imaginative plan for a new stadium was one prepared by the Pennsylvania Railroad. It projected the idea of a 60,000-seat stadium to be constructed on the air space over the Railroad's tracks at the 30th Street Station. It would comprise a fifteen-acre platform on stilts.

The concept of a stadium to be built by a public authority crept in at various points in the long discussions of various plans. As early as 1953 Philadelphia's Recreation Commissioner mentioned that a new stadium could be financed through a bond issue by a "public authority."(10) In 1958 a Citizen's Council on City Planning recommended the airspace stadium over the tracks to be constructed by an "authority."(11) Mayor Dilworth thought as late as April, 1959, that the plan to have an authority to build the stadium over the railroad tracks might be worthy of further study.(12)

There was some precedent for the creation of a public authority to build a baseball stadium, although the constitutional issues of a quasi-public agency's constructing a ball park for a private profit-making baseball organization had not been resolved. In an effort to keep the Dodger Baseball Team from leaving Brooklyn, a public authority had been established in 1956 with powers, among others, to erect a sports and recreation center which the Dodgers would use. The "among others" had clouded the constitutional issue, as had been its intent, as this made it possible for the ball stadium to be included as only one part of a comprehensive redevelopment plan for Brooklyn, even though it was clear that the main purpose of the new authority was the construction of the stadium. The value of the public authority device for the Brooklyn team was not only that the authority was empowered by the State Legislature to issue $30,000,000 worth of bonds for the redevelopment program, including the ball park, but, perhaps equally important, it could condemn property for the stadium in the crowded Flatbush area through its powers of eminent domain. This right, of course, could not have been used by the Brooklyn baseball organization as a private corporation.

The $7,000,000-$9,000,000 stadium for Brooklyn had been couched in overall plans for a new subway concourse at Flatbush, Fourth, and Atlantic Avenues, to tie in subway lines and the Long Island Railroad for the stadium exit; a new terminal for the Long Island Railroad in the Atlantic Avenue-Pacific Street location; construction of a housing development and commercial buildings on the existing Long Island Railroad terminal; and the relocation of the old Fort Greene meat market; the development of two parking garages, one on either side of the new stadium; and a small redevelopment project at Flatbush and Sixth Avenues.

The president of a realty company and a Governor of the Real Estate Board of New York, had been named Chairman of the Authority, known as the Brooklyn Sports Center Authority, and he had had as his two colleagues on the Board the Vice-President of Abraham & Straus Department Store of Brooklyn, and the President of the Kings County Trust Company. Robert Moses, Construction Coordinator for the location of the stadium, had termed these three "excellent appointees," but had asked the public to be patient with them as "they have a tough job ahead of them"(13)

They did have a tough job; for one thing, inasmuch as the Authority property would be tax-exempt, the rehabilitation and redevelopment of the Flatbush section would remove $109,069,775 of assessed real estate valuation from New York City's tax rolls at a tax loss of some $5,000,000 annually, at least until real estate values rose under the new development. The obstacles did prove too great, however, and the Brooklyn Dodgers moved to Los Angeles after the 1957 season.

The Philadelphia City administration was trying to prevent a similar loss of its ball team. The most serious threat in this direction came from across the River in Camden, New Jersey. Officials in Camden were taking steps to entice the Phillies to move from Philadelphia to Camden County. In their plans at the very core was a public authority. The attempt to have a public authority construct a stadium in a Township of Camden County set in motion a chain reaction involving interstate, state, county, and township, relationships. The reaction was set off on January 13, 1959, when the State Senator of Camden introduced into the State Senate of New Jersey legislation known as the County Improvement Authorities bill. General legislation applying to all counties was necessary inasmuch as the State Constitution forbids any "special act conferring corporate powers."(14) The immediate purpose of the bill -- to enable a Township in one County to build a stadium for the Phillies without having it charged against the

Township's debt ceiling -- was not readily apparent from the wording of the bill:

> The purposes of every authority shall be the provision within the county (a) of public buildings for use by the state, the county, or any municipality in the county, or any 2 or more or any subdivisions, departments, agencies or instrumentalities of any of the foregoing, (b) of structures and facilities for public transportation or terminal purposes, and (c) of structures or other facilities used or operated by the authority or any governmental unit in connection with, or relative to development and improvement of, aviation for military or civilian purposes, including research in connection therewith. (15)

It was known, however, that recreational facilities were paramount, and the newspapers referred to it as the "Recreational Authorities Bill." The bill was passed by the Senate with only one Senator voting against it, and in the Assembly 45-4.

Camden County created the Camden County Improvement Authority just five days after the enabling act had been signed by the Governor. Named to the Authority were: a United States District Court Judge; a former Assistant United States Attorney; the Chairman of the RCA Conference Board of the International Union of Electrical, Radio and Machine Workers; a member of the County Board of Freeholders; and a former State Senator who was also the New Jersey Counsel for the Delaware River Port Authority.

That same month, February, 1959, the owner of the Phillies, Robert Carpenter, met with the Authority. He said he would make identical bids for leasing a stadium to both Camden and Philadelphia. Camden County officials were encouraged. The Mayor of Delaware Township, in which the stadium would be built, was quoted on the day the Governor signed the Act, as exclaiming: "They say no one wants the Phillies. Well we want them, and now I hope I'm not too old to throw out the first ball."(16)

In a surprising move on March 14, the Mayor announced that he was opposed to the construction of the stadium by the Authority in Delaware Township and that two other

Commissioners would vote with him against it. He said that he had favored the stadium because he had thought that it would mean some $100,000 a year in taxes from parking and seat taxes at the stadium. More careful study of the State enabling Act had convinced him that this would not be possible. If, he added, the Phillies would want to discuss a separate agreement for payment in lieu of taxes, some of the opposition would be removed.

The careful reading by the Mayor apparently had revealed the last section of the provision whereby the Authority was given the right to "enter into agreements with respect to the payment by the authority to such municipality of annual sums of money in lieu of taxes on such property." But it added: "provided, however, that no such annual payment with respect to any parcel of such property shall exceed the amount of taxes paid thereon for the taxable year immediately prior to the time of its acquisition by the authority."(17) The 72-acre plot for the stadium had been standing idle for years and had been paying only about $1,000 a year in taxes. The Camden stadium for the Phillies was a dead issue — "torpedoed," said the Senator who had introduced the enabling legislation.(18)

It is of parenthetical interest to note that two years later Mayor Dilworth of Philadelphia urged the creation of a Municipal Stadium Authority to build a new park for the Phillies in Torresdale in Northeast Philadelphia. The ordinance for it was defeated in July, 1961, by the City Planning Commission by a vote of 4-3 in which all public members of the Commission voted against it, and all three City administration members for it. One of the Committee, a Vice-President of The First Pennsylvania Banking and Trust Company, gave as his reasons for voting against it the fear that the authority plan would take the "planning, development and operation" of the stadium out of the hands of the City, and that it was merely a way of circumventing the requirement for a referendum on the proposed indebtedness. This might well set a precedent, he said, to circumvent both planning and popular referenda, and would place government officials under "increased pressure of special interest groups to make wider use of this device."(19)

Two months later the City second in size to Philadelphia in Pennsylvania, Pittsburgh, was to dedicate its new $20,000,000 Auditorium for sports, opera, exhibitions, conventions, and the like, built by the Public Auditorium Authority of Pittsburgh and Allegheny County. This Auditorium seats up to 13,640 persons, is circular in shape, and is believed to have the largest dome ever built and "certainly the largest movable roof ever designed," enabling it to be an open-air stadium or an indoor auditorium. The Authority had been constituted as early as February 3, 1954, pursuant to the Public Auditorium Authorities Law of 1953. Its Board consists of two members appointed by the Commissioners of Allegheny County, two by the Mayor of Pittsburgh, and one appointed jointly by the County Commissioners and the Mayor. As had been contemplated for Brooklyn in 1956, the plan for the Auditorium was tied in with an urban redevelopment program. The Auditorium occupies twenty acres in the middle of a ninety-five-acre redevelopment project of the Urban Redevelopment Authority of Pittsburgh, known as the Lower Hill Redevelopment Project. The Public Auditorium Authority executed contracts with the Urban Redevelopment Authority to bring to fruition "years of dreams and plans of the civic leaders, the entertainment world and the public officials of both Allegheny County and the City of Pittsburgh."(20)

The County Improvement Authority Act of New Jersey remained on the books, of course, after it was clear that it would no longer be implemented in Camden for the Phillies. Its latent use for other purposes throughout the State caused apprehension among county park officials. County Park Commissions had been set up by County governments to develop and maintain park and recreational facilities. As part of County government, they are, to be sure, subject to County debt ceilings and to the provision for referenda on bond issues. The fear of the County Park Commissions was that the Counties would by-pass them, and, instead, turn to the public authorities which could be created under the County Improvement Authorities Act. A member of one County Park Commission explained: "Even if we are appointed by the freeholders too, we are really at the voters' whims, because if we need a new appropriation, we have to go back to the voters, where these people (authority members) wouldn't have to." She added, "The park commissions know what they are doing," and expressed objection to "the interference of these 'big laws' from the state."

Early in 1960 the State Legislature repealed the Improvement Authorities Act. "It's a good thing the bill was repealed," said a representative of the park commissions, "before someone found out about it."

Tax Exemption

One year later the Superior Court of New Jersey rendered a decision in favor of the Borough of Moonachie over the claim of the Port of New York Authority for tax immunity for a building on its property at the Teterboro, New Jersey, Airport, which it had leased to private industry. The decision cast grave doubts on the constitutionality of the extension of tax exemptions by authorities to private industry conducted on their property for profit.

Teterboro had been a private airport and had been used by the United States Air Force during World War II, and subsequently had been used by commercial concerns such as Standard Oil Company. By 1948 it had become a busy fourth-class airport used by private planes, training ships, and nine non-scheduled airlines. In August of that year the Port of New York Authority had arranged to purchase it with its 450 acres from its private owner for the sum of $3,115,000. The Authority began operating it on April 2, 1949. In the next eight years the Port Authority purchased more land for the Airport in neighboring boroughs of Hasbrouck Heights and Moonachie. It lies now in the three boroughs, Teterboro, Hasbrouck Heights, and Moonachie, and contains 900 acres.

An "In Lieu of Tax Agreement" was approved in 1952 by the Port Authority and the Borough of Moonachie and Bergen County, to the effect that the Authority would pay to the Borough and County the amount of taxes that had been assessed against the last private owner of the property. This was carried out each year.

Newark Evening News, December 23, 1961.

The Teterboro Airport operated at a loss, and the Authority sought means of helping to finance it. One method used was effected in February of 1959 when the Authority agreed to a twenty-year lease for the Jersey Screen and Storm Window Co., Inc., for a ten-acre plot of Teterboro Airport on which the Port Authority was to build a single-story general-purpose building to be used by the Company for the "manufacture of metal windows, doors, sidings, panels and other building materials." The Company was to pay the Port Authority a rental of 12-1/2 per cent of payments to contractors for the design and construction of the building. This clause could be cancelled by either the Authority or the tenant if the proposed construction contracts were to exceed $1,143,800. If after five years the property were to be needed for airport purposes necessitating the demolition of the building the Port Authority could terminate the lease. The building was constructed, at a cost of $890,000 and was completed in June, 1960. The Company began operation with the proviso that if the Port Authority gave 365 days' notice, it could terminate the lease at any time after the five-year period, for the purpose of using it for airport development. To break even in its investment in this building the Port Authority would have to allow the Company to lease it for twelve to fourteen years.

The Assessor for Moonachie in assessing the new building came to the conclusion that it was not tax exempt, as the property was now being used by a profit-making corporation. Accordingly, he levied taxes in the amount of $10,441.08 for 1960 and $21,248.91 for 1961. The Authority had been paying $183.77 in lieu of taxes for the plot. The Assessor did not tax the land on which the building was located, conceding that the land was still covered by the "In Lieu of Tax Agreement."(21)

The Port of New York Authority "denied any liability for taxes other than as contained in the 'In Lieu of Tax Agreement.'" The Authority based its claim in part on a decision in the New York Courts involving the Port Authority's Inland Terminal Building in 1940. The Inland Terminal Building had been constructed by the Port Authority so as to occupy the entire City block between West 15th and

16th Streets and 8th and 9th Avenues. The Authority had entered into an agreement with eight railroads to lease to them the "basement, portions of the ground floor ... to be used and operated by them as a Union Inland Freight Station through such organizations as may be formed by said Carriers for such purpose." The ground and basement floors of the building serve as the Freight Terminal for the railroads, five of whom now use it. Individual shippers drive their trucks in there and unload their less-than-carload freight which is then pulled across the platform by tractors, loaded on trailers for the respective railroads and delivered to the railroad station. The building, in addition, houses offices, stores, and lofts in its sixteen stories each one of which covers four acres. The Port Authority itself has its central offices in the building.

Prior to the opening of the building the Port of New York Authority had offered in 1931 to enter into a "In Lieu of Tax Agreement" with New York City in which it would pay the equivalent of the taxes on the property prior to the time the Port Authority had acquired it, an amount of approximately $60,000 annually. After the construction of the new $16,000,000 building there the taxes of course would have jumped to many times that figure.

Bush Terminal Company, owners of large buildings using space for similar purposes and therefore in competition with the Port Authority, sought to restrain the City from entering into the agreement with the Port Authority.

The New York Courts had held that the use of the basement for the Union Railroad Freight Terminal was within the meaning of the purpose for which the building had been built and the agreement with the railroads. The New York Court of Appeals reasoned:

> Property held by an agency of the State is ordinarily immune from taxation only while it is used for a public purpose. Property used primarily to obtain revenue or profit is not ordinarily immune from taxation, but property held by a state agency primarily for a public use does not lose immunity because the state agency incidentally derives income from the property.... There is here no purpose to make a profit and without the use of the upper

stories of the building for revenue the public purpose could not be carried out. (22)

The Port Authority has, therefore, continued to pay New York City in lieu of taxes only the amount that had been levied before the Authority had acquired the property.

The Port Authority Counsel in the Moonachie Case argued that this decision in the Bush Terminal Co. v. City of New York, at al. case, should be followed in the Moonachie decision. Francis A. Mulhern, Attorney for the Port Authority, told the Jersey Court that the Compact which had created the Port of New York Authority required uniformity of treatment for it in the two States. "Bush has been the law of New York since 1940," he urged, "a date long prior to the enactment of the Air Terminal legislation and is still the law of New York. That legislation then should be read and interpreted in New Jersey in the light of Bush. The law in New Jersey is not contrary to Bush." (23)

The Superior Court of New Jersey, however, found what it considered significant differences between the Bush and Moonachie cases. It cited another section from the Bush opinion:

> Of course, the power to construct terminals which incidentally contain 'storage space and space for other facilities' might be transcended if, under cover of that power, the Port Authority assumed to construct an office or loft building intended primarily for revenue and only incidentally for terminal purposes. The factors involved are often relative, not absolute, and the test may be one of degree. (24)

The Port Authority had argued that the fact that it had made the lease with the Window Company flexible and subject to termination at the end of five years or thereafter, was evidence that the property was being held for purposes of airport development, and that, in the meantime, it was being used to attempt to reduce the deficit at the Airport and make possible the continued operation of the Airport.

The Court decided, however, against the Authority's contention, saying that the "Port Authority in erecting the building at Moonachie had as its sole object the collection of revenue. It was not to serve an air terminal purpose." It held, therefore, that "both land and building are subject to taxation" by Moonachie. "When the Port Authority voluntarily put these ten acres to a use entirely foreign to 'air terminal purposes,' " ruled Judge Charles W. Broadhurst, "it was required in good faith to eliminate those ten acres" from the schedules under the "In Lieu of Tax Agreement."

The result of this decision has been, as might be expected, a rush of other municipalities to assess such property of the authorities. Newark, New Jersey, has been particularly interested in prospects of taxing certain businesses at the Airport operated there by the Port Authority.

The Port of New York Authority had been given permission by the States of New Jersey and New York to make payments in lieu of taxes under the Terminal and Air Terminal statutes relating to inland, marine, and air terminals.

The government concerned must weigh carefully the relative value of the authority as a whole to its community as against the loss of income through the tax-exempt provisions of authority facilities.

Attempts at a form of compromise between the two factors — the value of the authority as such and the loss of tax ratables to the community — have taken various forms, one of which is the use of air-rights over authority property by taxable enterprises. Although experimented with in other parts of the country for a longer period, there have been recent uses, and proposed uses, of the principle in the region under consideration in this book. Governor Nelson Rockefeller, of New York State, suggested in 1961 the construction of middle-income housing by using the air rights over tax-exempt property. He reasoned that this would mean that properties "that are now tax-exempt can be put onto the tax rolls to yield the city millions in new revenue. No existing dwelling will have to be torn down to make room for these new units. The new housing will be a complete gain in our supply of housing."(25) In December of that same year work was started on the first such middle-income housing project spanning the air space over the George Washington Expressway. The air rights over this public-authority approach had been purchased for this 920-family development from the City of New York by the realty company. Simultaneously, the Board of Estimate of New York City appropriated $50,000 for a study of a project for a thirty-acre campus for the Bronx Community College over subway storage tracks. The estimated cost was $10,000,000.

In Massachusetts, however, Governor John A. Volpe vetoed a bill in the 1961-1962 session of the Legislature which would have allowed the Massachusetts Turnpike Authority to lease air space over the extension of the road into Boston. The Governor had approved the extension's being a toll road, rather than free, from Weston to Boston a year before. In his veto message, Governor Volpe gave as his reason the fact that he could not allow a "vested interest of this state to be turned over lock, stock and barrel to one agency that doesn't even reveal the pertinent facts relative to its position."

On the local level the use of air rights over authority property is meeting with favorable reaction. In 1964 the Morristown Parking Authority in New Jersey approved plans for the construction of a half-million dollar four-story office building over one of its parking lots.

Competition for Personnel

There is another matter of concern to local officials in the creation of such agencies, almost entirely overlooked: namely, that they become competitive not only for tax sources, but for competent personnel, also in short supply. Authorities may prove attractive not only to certain of the best citizens for their board positions, but they may well siphon off from local governments trained technicians and personnel all down the line. If there is something in the kind of functions performed by the authorities that strikes the imagination of employees, then thought might be given to the keeping of those functions within the government itself.

A paper on "Careers in the Rebuilding and Management of Cities," issued in 1962 by the Pittsburgh Graduate School, advised, that, in addition to the usual positions in regular governments, "there are thousands of public authorities which offer some of the most challenging employment opportunities."(26)

It may be unreasonable to blame authorities for paying the kind of salaries that other levels of government should pay. Who can say, for example, that Austin Tobin is not worth to the Port of New York Authority his $60,000 annual salary, and who is really at fault if this gives him, as it does, a higher salary than that of the Mayor of New York City or the Governors of New York and New Jersey respectively? Is it wrong to pay the head of the New Jersey Turnpike Authority $29,500, or is it wrong to pay the Governor of the entire State only $500 more? Is the sewer authority to be faulted for paying its board members $2500 annually in a municipality where the members of the municipal council are being paid nothing? If the more competitive salary scale does continue to drain off capable officials and employees from the more traditional units of government it may have the desirable effect of causing the latter to reconsider their policies.

Indeed, if public authorities are to reflect, as they are, certain attributes of private corporations, such salaries as those mentioned for the directors of these authorities is not at all commensurate with the corresponding salaries of officials in private corporations who bear this kind of responsibility.

On the other hand, if the disparity of conditions of employment between a public authority and another government results from preferential treatment through the circumvention of constitutional principles, then there are justifiable grounds for complaint. The Constitution of the State of New Jersey, for example, provides that persons "in private employment shall have the right to organize and bargain collectively," but that persons "in public employment shall have the right to organize, present to and make known to the State, or any of its political subdivisions or agencies, their grievances and proposals through representatives of their own choosing."(27) In other words, public employees are denied the right to bargain collectively and to strike; they may organize and petition. On the federal level, the Taft-Hartley Act stipulates: "It shall be unlawful for any individual employed by the United States or any agency thereof including wholly owned Government corporations to participate in any strike."(28) When employees of a public authority claim the right to strike and to bargain collectively, the question quite naturally is raised as to whether a public authority, and not any other governmental unit including a Government corporation on the federal level, has the right to claim such exception.

Employees of the New Jersey Turnpike Authority have had grievances since its inception. They are not covered by civil service, as public-authority employees often are. Their unions failed to provide security for them inasmuch as various unions claimed to represent not only different categories of workers in the Authority, but even different geographic sections of the Turnpike itself. In 1954, for example, Local 1511, Government and Civic Employees Union, CIO, claimed to represent toll collectors in the Southern division of the road, whereas Local 10, Highway Maintenance Workers, AFL, seemed to represent the toll collectors in the Northern part of the Turnpike from New Brunswick to the George Washington Bridge.

The two union groups, Local 1511, Government Civic Employees Union, CIO, and Local 10, Highway Maintenance Workers, AFL, joined in 1955 in a union called Local 1511, AFL-CIO, the American Federation of State, County and Municipal Employees. After threatening strikes against the New Jersey Turnpike Authority in 1957 and 1958, Local 1511 struck the Turnpike on March 17, 1959, a Tuesday. The strike lasted five days.

Was such a strike unconstitutional? The State Constitution gave public employees the right to "present . . . their grievances . . . through representatives of their own choosing" to "the State, or any of its political subdivisions or agencies . . . ."(29) Was the New Jersey Turnpike Authority a political subdivision or agency of the State? The New Jersey Turnpike Authority Act of 1948 had defined the

Structure of the Labor Unions Organizing
Employees of the New Jersey
Turnpike Authority

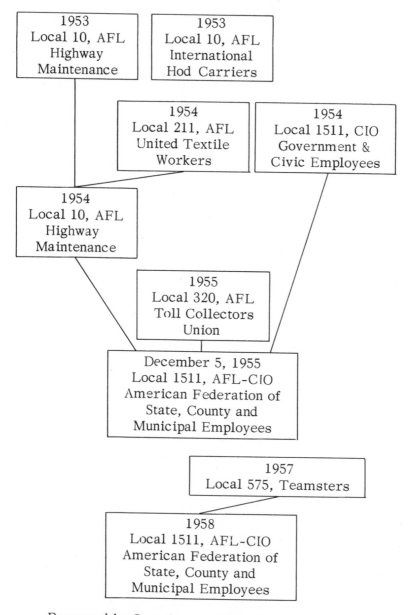

Prepared by Jane Spence Fink, Drew University

Authority as "an instrumentality exercising public and essential government functions," whose operations "shall be deemed and held to be an essential government function of the State."(30)

Only a skeleton force of supervisory personnel and other non-union persons kept the Turnpike functioning and, then, with four of the interchanges, at Swedesboro, South Camden, Mount Holly, and Hightstown, not serviced. No tickets were used, rather, instead of the toll range of 10 cents to $1.75 for passenger cars and $5.00 maximum for trucks, passenger cars were assessed only 25 cents and trucks 50 cents. One employee was hit on the head while collecting tolls and required ten stitches in the wound. An "essential government function of the State" was thus crippled by a strike.

"The strike of the toll collectors and maintenance workers...is illegal," editorialized the Newark Evening News. "No amount of rationalizing by the Union, 1511, can make it anything else." "The Turnpike Authority's erroneous labor policy is primarily responsible for the inconvenience and loss of revenue caused by the strike," the newspaper charged. "... The Turnpike Authority should have stood firm, as the Parkway Authority has done and fought out the collective bargaining issue when it first arose in 1957."(31)

The Turnpike Authority did not fight out the issue even then, in 1959. In telegrams and letters the strikers were warned that if they did not report by 3 p.m. of the second day they "will have separated themselves from employment with the Turnpike Authority." In the letter the Executive Director of the Turnpike promised them wages, benefits, and working conditions which would "either equal or exceed those found in similar Turnpike operations or in similar jobs throughout the state." He reminded them that the three-year agreement the Authority had signed with Local 1511 in 1957 had contained a "definite no-strike provision."(32)

The head of the Union, 1511, said that the strike had been called not only over the right of the collectors to wear a union button, of which the Executive Director disapproved, but also "job reclassification, the study and negotiation of a contract for 50 'senior men,' ... heaters in toll booths, recognition of the union's right to bargain for employees in the Toll Audit Department and an end to letters of warning that have been sent to toll collectors concerning overages and shortages in traffic counts."(33)   "Our men," a Union representative was quoted as having admitted, "have actually been wearing buttons for about 4 years and nobody complained about it until we asked for formal approval of it."(34)

Here again the weakened position of an Executive Director of an Authority seemed crucial. He himself was in a compromised position in view of the fact that just prior to the strike he had been embroiled in a struggle with the Governor of New Jersey and the Authority to have his five-year contract renewed. He was then the only employee in the Authority with such a contract, and not thereby subject to employment at the will of the Authority. Although his contract was to expire on April 12, it was not until the day before the strike, Monday, March 16, after weeks of speculation, that he was given a new contract, and then only for one year rather than five.

On the fourth day of the strike the Authority went before the Superior Court of the State to ask an order to restrain the strike and to order the men to return to their jobs. The restraint was granted to be effective the next Wednesday, when it would be decided before the Chancery Division of the Court whether the injunction should be continued. The Union was not represented in Court, but its Counsel commented: "There is a big question whether the State Court has jurisdiction in this matter and there is a bigger question as to whether these employees are public or private employees."(35)

After meetings among Joseph Morecraft, Jr., Chairman of the Turnpike Authority; representatives of Union 1511; and State Highway Commissioner, D.R.G. Palmer, who represented the Governor, the strike finally was settled. The agreement reached was to the effect that negotiations on existing and future grievances would be held between the Union and the Authority with a terminal date of five days. In regard to the issues of the present strike, they were to be arbitrated.

Despite this settlement, the Superior Court extended the injunction two weeks. Subsequently, Superior Court Judge, Mark A. Sullivan, Jr., criticized the Authority for having entered into a settlement without awaiting the Court hearing on the return of the injunction. The Authority, he said, had put the order in its pocket, despite the fact that the injunction was supposed to be served within 24 hours, thus "undermining" the power of the Court.

The Executive Director agreed with the employees and Union that the settlement was made on the basis of no reprisals, and wrote the men to this effect:

> To make certain that there is no misunderstanding, I want again to state that every employee's position and status in the Turnpike Authority organization is, and will continue to be, based solely upon his or her job performance. Membership or nonmembership in an organization will not affect that position or status.(36)

In November, 1959, the Authority workers, both toll collectors and maintenance men, were granted the right to wear union buttons on their Turnpike uniforms.

Immediately after the strike settlement, April 8, it was announced that the Turnpike Authority had agreed thereafter to have the State Commissioner of Labor serve as arbitrator in grievances between the Authority and the Union. The Authority Chairman explained that this action could be justified on the basis that "it has never been legally determined if the Authority is a state agency" and for that reason "it would be out of order to have an outside arbitrator decide what the Authority should be permitted to do."(37)

The inconsistency is apparent: If, as the Authority was contending, only the State could arbitrate because it might well be declared that the Authority is an agency of the State, then, by the same token, the whole agreement was illegal because no employees of an agency of the State may strike or bargain collectively.

"The only possible conclusion to be drawn from the settlement," claimed the Newark Evening News, "... is that by an unconstitutional use of force the workers got what they wanted." "There isn't much to admire," it admitted, "in the labor policies of the Authority. There is evidence that it failed to redress legitimate grievances and that its working conditions left much to be desired." But, "the Union's resort to a strike remains unchallenged and unpunished. The New Jersey Turnpike Authority is storing up trouble not only for itself but for other state agencies."(38)

The Turnpike Authority published a "Statement of Employee Relations Policy" for the Toll Collection Department, and another one for the Maintenance Department. Open recognition is made throughout these two mimeographed booklets of the fact that Local 1511, American Federation of State, County and Municipal Employees Union, AFL-CIO is "the employee organization representing the Authority employees," and, as a matter of fact, the statement of policy is that agreed to by the Union with the Turnpike Authority. It is certified as being "in accordance with the results of an election held on December 21, 1960, as certified by the Honest Ballot Association, and Municipal Employees Union ...."

A strike against the Massachusetts Transit Authority in March of 1962 was handled summarily. Governor John A. Volpe called the Massachusetts Legislature into an emergency session to grant him power to seize the Transit Authority. The power was granted, and he seized the Authority at once. Eight members of the Boston Carmen's Union who defied an injunction of the Superior Court not to strike against the seized Transit, were arrested and jailed. They were held in contempt of the court and given thirty days for having defied the injunction which had been issued because the Authority was now under the control of the government. The strike had lasted only two days. When the strikers, some of them apparently pawns in a move of the Boston Carmer's Union against the Authority, apologized to the Superior Court Judge, they were released. The Massachusetts Supreme Court had upheld the Superior Court's action in holding the men in contempt. Justice John V. Spalding ruled: "That the employees of the Authority are public employees we have no doubt."

A New Year's eve strike has become a perennial threat against the New York City Transit Authority since its creation in 1953. The New York State Condon-Wadlin Law appears to forbid strikes by all state, local, and governmental authority employees, but it is not so clear as the New Jersey provisions. Despite the Law, Michael Quill, representing the Transport Workers Union, has threatened walk-outs if the Union's terms are not met by the Authority in the alternate years when the two-year contracts expire on December 31. The threats have been most effective, although no actual strike has materialized.

The prototype for public authorities to adopt labor policies not permitted standard governments is, of course, the Tennessee Valley Authority. That Authority had been exempted from the beginning from the federal civil service, and was the one government corporation whose employees were not authorized to be placed under civil service by the Ramspeck Act of 1940. The Authority was free from the first, therefore, to develop its own merit system and labor policies. It has worked out enviable relationships: It "encourages unionization, maintains machinery for negotiation, and readily enters into written agreements with its organized employees." From the time the policy was announced in 1935 TVA employees have had the right to organize with the understanding that exclusive recognition would be given by the TVA "to the majority union to represent its group, craft, or unit." On the other hand, no employee was to be forced to join a union. There was to be no discrimination on the grounds of union membership, sex, or race. Under a "force-account" policy, the TVA takes responsibility for conditions of work of even labor under contract firms.

The Tennessee Valley Trades and Labor Council meets annually with officials of the TVA to work out a written agreement. This is recognized as a form of collective bargaining without benefit of strike.

The Port of New York Authority has taken a position contrary to that of the Tennessee Valley Authority in regard to the "force-account" principle. The Port Authority does not involve itself directly in labor-management relations of the companies under contract for its vast construction projects. In its relationships with its own personnel, the Port Authority states that it "does not recognize any organization as the exclusive representative of Port Authority employees, or of any group of employees in the Port Authority." It will "recognize and deal with any and all accredited organizations of Port Authority employees or with individual employees who do not belong to an organization." There are three such groups: the Police Benevolent Association; the Port Authority Employees Association, for maintenance workers; and the Port Authority Associates, for office and clerical employees. "Major changes in personnel policies are discussed with the principal officers of these organizations," the Authority explains. "The Personnel Director asks them to participate in the formulation of personnel policies, and discusses with them various personnel matters, including grievances, that cannot be settled by department supervisors." A person presenting grievances is permitted to do so personally or to "enlist the assistance of his accredited representative in one of these organizations."(39)

The large number of public authorities in Pennsylvania have recently come under the provisions of the Pennsylvania Prevailing Wage Act of 1961, which became effective on February 1, 1962. It applies to contracts entered into by Pennsylvania municipalities and municipal authorities. Under this Act the Authority or other public body awarding a contract in excess of $2,000 has to ascertain from the Secretary of Labor and Industry of the State the prevailing minimum wage rate in the area for each craft necessary to carrying out the project for which the contract is being granted. The specifications for the contract must set forth the minimum wage rate that must be paid. The contractors and subcontractors then have to post a notice as to what the general minimum wage rate for each craft involved is, in a place where it can be seen by the employees. Before the treasurer or responsible officer of the authority or other public body shall make final payment to a company the contractor is required to file statements in writing as to the amounts of wages outstanding and owing to his employees for the project. William H. Markus, Counsel for the Pennsylvania Municipal Authorities Association, urged "authorities entering into any contracts to be placed on the mailing list of the Secretary of Labor and Industry for the wage rates for all crafts."(40)

Actual strikes against the New Jersey Turnpike Authority, the Jersey City Sewer Authority, and the Jersey City Incinerator Authority, and threatened strikes against the New York City Transit Authority, have gained for authority employees labor benefits unavailable to government workers.

This is but one illustration of the many variables in the functioning of the authorities as against that of normal governments that serve to make comparisons of their relative efficiency meaningless.

One assumption in the authority-device is that, for the most part, the normal constitutional provisions which apply to local governments are not binding on these more recent agencies.

Accountability

In addition to the effects that this kind of privileged position is having on the standard governments, there is the further concern as to where, if not in constitutional safeguards, the accountability of the authorities lies.

The core of the problem of accountability rests, paradoxically, in the authority's greatest asset: namely, its ability to operate entrepreneurial projects of public interest with something of the motivation of private business. In moving between the public and private sectors, as this theory requires them to do, they are almost forced to seek that sector which will provide them the greater freedom in the question of the moment. At one time, authorities will stress their public image; at another, their quasi-public characterization. They are designed to take advantage of the two possible designations. Even enthusiasts for the

Newark Evening News, December 15, 1961.

authority potential have to admit "that a certain sleight of
hand is involved," commented the London Economist, "Public Authority's bonds carry on their face a denial that the
'full faith and credit' of the state .... is pledged; yet they
are considered sufficiently governmental to be tax-exempt."(41)

The ambivalence is illustrated by a comparison of the
role of the authority, as seen in the reasoning of the Port
of New York Authority in the Moonachie case, discussed
above, and the role of the authority as seen by the Wilmington (Delaware) Parking Authority in a case involving its
responsibilities for property that it rented to private business. The disparate size and responsible functions of the
two authorities must, of course, be noted, as must the difference in the kind of rights involved. Both cases were
concerned, however, with the issue of the private business located on a lease-arrangement on authority property.

In the Moonachie case, the Port Authority took the viewpoint, as it had consistently, that the private business on
its property was sufficiently a necessary part of its operations to make it tax-exempt along with all property of the
Authority. The Wilmington Parking Authority, on the other
hand, argued that the private business of a coffee shop did
not become the responsibility of the Authority by the mere
fact that the company rented property from the Authority.
The Port Authority explained that, inasmuch as it was
merely trying to reduce the Airport deficit by renting space
pending the eventual use of that property for Airport development, provisions which normally would apply to authority property as that of a governmental unit, should
apply here. The Wilmington Parking Authority, to the contrary, was using the same base for reasoning that the very
fact that the property was rented to the Eagle Coffee Shop
to get additional revenue for the Authority meant that provisions which would apply to use of the property as a governmental unit now should not apply. The determining
factor in the authority's concept of its own role seems to
lie in the question as to whether its public image, or its
private image, will enable it to perform better the function
for which it was created.

The Wilmington case not only offers this interesting comparison, but it indicates as well the kind of constitutional issues facing the public authority boards as they become more and more involved in the social and economic development of communities. The case was brought in 1959 under a charge of racial discrimination. William H. Burton sought a declaratory judgment to prohibit the Eagle Coffee Shop from operating its restaurant in a structure leased from the Wilmington Parking Authority in a "racially-discriminatory manner." Burton charged that he had been denied service there because he was a Negro.

The Court of Chancery of New Castle County agreed with Burton that "the Authority is performing a public or State function ... and, as an instrumentality of the State, is required to insure that the operation of the public facility shall not be in a racially-segregated manner." The Court invoked the equal-protection clause of the Fourteenth Amendment as the basis for its ruling.

On appeal, the Supreme Court of Delaware reversed the judgment of the lower Court and found that the Authority's "sole interest in the Eagle lease is the deriving of rent therefrom in order to defray the expense of operating the parking facility, an otherwise unprofitable operation required, however, to be self-sustaining." It concluded that "Eagle, in the conduct of its business, is acting in a purely private capacity."(42)

The case reached the United States Supreme Court where the judgment of the Supreme Court of Delaware was reversed.(43) The reasoning of Justice Clark for the Court developed points which indicated the unique position of a public authority:

(1) The significance to the Authority of bond revenues: "(T)he bonds were not expected to be marketable if payable solely out of parking revenues. To secure additional capital needed for its 'debt-service' requirements, and thereby to make bond financing practicable, the Authority decided it was necessary to enter long-term leases with responsible tenants for commercial use of some of the space available . . . ."

(2) The governmental role of the Authority: "As an entity, the building was dedicated to 'public uses' in performance of the Authority's 'essential governmental functions.'

(3) The tax-exemption of Authority property: "Should any improvements effected in the leasehold by Eagle become part of the realty, there is no possibility of increased taxes being passed on to it since the fee is held by a tax-exempt government agency."

(4) The 'involvement' of the State in the Authority transactions: "Addition of all these activities, obligations and responsibilities of the Authority, the benefits mutually conferred, together with the obvious fact that the restaurant is operated as an integral part of a public building devoted to a public parking service, indicates that degree of state participation and involvement in discriminatory action which it was the design of the Fourteenth Amendment to condemn."

(5) The responsibility of the Authority: "By its inaction, the Authority, and through it the State, has not only made itself a party to the refusal of service, but has elected to place its power, property and prestige behind the admitted discrimination. The State has so far insinuated itself into a position of interdependence with Eagle that it must be recognized as a joint participant in the challenged activity, which, on that account, cannot be considered to have been so 'purely private' as to fall without the scope of the Fourteenth Amendment."

"Public authorities," argued the Triborough Bridge and Tunnel Authority in a brief before the Court of Appeals of New York State in a different case, "obviously are created to perform governmental functions .... However, the legislature did not want the performance of the governmental functions vested in public authorities to be subject to the burdens and limitations which usually hamper action by boards, officers or departments of the State."(44)

The Court of Appeals agreed with the Authority in the case which had involved a petition from the New York Post to inspect contract files and other records of the Triborough Authority for the previous ten years. The Court sustained the reasoning of the State Supreme Court that "the Authority is a legal entity, separate and apart from the state which created it and the city and counties which it serves," and that, in the absence of special legislation to that effect, the Authority did not have to reveal the information to the newspaper. The Court pointed out that this did not leave the Authority entirely immune from scrutiny, but that the Triborough Authority, similar to authorities in general in New York State, was checked in the following ways:

(1) The investigative and auditing processes of the State Commission of Investigation, the Comptroller of the State of New York, the Comptroller of the City of New York;

(2) The requirement that it submit a detailed report of its operations, receipts, and expenditures, its assets and liabilities, and a schedule of its bonds and notes outstanding, at the end of its fiscal year, to the Governor, the Chairman of the Senate Finance Committee, the Chairman of the Ways and Means Committee, and the City Comptroller;

(3) The right of the bank, serving as the trustee of the bond issues, to investigate its financial operations;

(4) The investigative power of the holders of not less than 5% of the principal amount of the bonds then outstanding into the financial affairs and operations of the Authority.(45)

In addition, the Act creating the Triborough Authority had been more specific than most such legislation in outlining its functions.

These are more carefully defined checks on authorities than most states have. They stress, obviously, the administrative functions of the Authority and in particular its financial operations. They place in a key role the bondholders and the trustee bank for bond issues.

The problem remains that authorities are not merely administrative units of government, but, in addition, are policy-making. State enabling legislation justifies their creation on the basis of the essential governmental roles they are to fulfill: The Delaware Housing Authority Act, for instance, declares the powers it confers on local housing authorities to be for "public objects essential to the public interest." The same State declares in its laws that parking authorities "will promote the public safety, convenience, and welfare." Its Water and Sewer Authorities, Delaware asserts, are created for "exercising public and essential governmental functions."(46)

Despite this governmental attribution, however, public authorities have found difficulty in involving the public in their decision-making processes.

REFERENCES

1. "Is 'Authority' Financing the Answer?" The American City, LXX, February, 1955.

2. Horace A. Davis, "Borrowing Machines," National Municipal Review, XXIV, June, 1935, p. 334.

3. Report with Special Studies, (Washington, 1937), pp. 43–44.

4. Helvering v. Gerhardt, 304 U. S. 405; Matter of Plumbing Ass'n v. Thruway Authority, 5 N. Y. 2d, 420, 424.

5. Broadway National Bank of Bayonne v. Parking Authority of City of Bayonne, 76 N. J. Super. 139, 183 A 2d 873 (1962).

6. Day v. Buckeye Water etc. District, 28 Ariz. 466 (1925).

7. Frederick L. Bird, Local Special Districts and Authorities in Rhode Island (Kingston, Rhode Island, Bureau of Government Research, University of Rhode Island, undated, but probably 1962), p. 30.

8. Unpublished doctoral dissertation, op. cit. See Table 6, p. 103.

9. Evening Bulletin, Philadelphia, June 16, 1957.

10. Evening Bulletin, May 24, 1953.

11. Evening Bulletin, January 30, 1958.

12. Ibid., April 1, 1959.

13. The New York Times, September 12, 1956.

14. Art. IV, Sec. VII, par. 9.

15. N.J.R.S.Cum. Supp. 40:37A-54.

16. Newark Evening News, February 3, 1959.

17. N.J.R.S.Cum. Supp. 40:37A-83.

18. The New York Times, March 20, 1959.

19. The Philadelphia Inquirer, July 22, 1961.

20. Prospectus for the Public Auditorium Authority of Pittsburgh and Allegheny County, "Official Statement in regard to $15,000,000 Auditorium Bonds, series A," to be offered for sale October 26, 1961.

21. The facts are drawn principally from the "Findings of Fact" in the opinion of the Superior Court of New Jersey, Law Division, by Judge Charles W. Broadhurst, November 1, 1961.

22. 282 N. Y. 306, 321.

23. "Brief on Behalf of Defendant The Port of New York Authority," The Borough of Moonachie, Plaintiff, vs The Port of New York Authority, Defendants. Superior Court of New Jersey Law Division, Bergen County, Docket No. L-1654-60, p. 23.

24. 26 N. E. 2d, p. 273.

25. The New York Times, October 19, 1961.

26. Donald C. Stone and Robert L. Brown, "A Work Paper for Discussion Purposes Prepared for the Municipal Manpower Commission," January 2, 1962, p. 23.

27. Art. I, par. 19.

28. Sec. 305.

29. Art. I, par. 19.

30. N.J.R.S.Cum. Supp. 27:23-3.

31. March 19, 1959.

32. The New York Times, March 20, 1959.

33. Newark Evening News, March 17, 1959.

34. Newark Star Ledger, March 17, 1959.

35. Newark Evening News, March 20, 1959.

36. Ibid., May 21, 1959.

37. Ibid., April 8, 1959.

38. March 25, 1959.

39. The Port of New York Authority, Guide for Port Authority Personnel, New York, March, 1959, pp. 74-75.

40. William H. Markus, "Pennsylvania Prevailing Wage Act," The Authority, XX, No. 1, January, 1962, pp. 2-3.

41. May 28, 1955, as quoted in A. H. Hanson, Public Enterprise (Chicago, Public Administration Service, 1956), p. 40.

42. The Wilmington Parking Authority and Eagle Coffee Shop, Inc., v. William H. Burton, The Supreme Court of the State of Delaware No. 38, 1959 (January 11, 1960).

43. Burton v. Wilmington Parking Authority, 365 U. S. 715 (1961).

44. "Reply Brief on behalf of Appellants Triborough Bridge and Tunnel Authority" (argued by Samuel I. Rosenman). New York Post v. Robert Moses, George V. McLaughlin, and William J. Tracy, comprising a Board known as Triborough Bridge and Tunnel Authority, Court of Appeals State of New York, pp. 19-20.

45. "Public Authorities Law," Consolidated Laws of New York, chapt. 43-A, Art. 3, Title 3, section 553.9.

46. 48 Del.Laws, Code 1935, 1951 Amend., 31-4302.
    48 Del.Laws, 22-501.
    49 Del.Laws, 1953 Amend., 16-1406.

Chapter Five

"Out-of-Politics"

T HE STRESS on the non-political composition of
the authority board, and on the need for efficiency in its
operations, has resulted in a certain insulation between
board and public.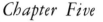

A good share of the responsibility for this gap must be
borne by the indifference of the public to government in
general. Public authorities do advertise their public
hearings and board meetings:

PUBLIC NOTICE

THERE WILL BE A PUBLIC HEARING on the
Annual Budget of Operating Expenses for the
fiscal year ending November 30, 1962, of the
PARKING AUTHORITY OF MORRISTOWN, at
the Authority's offices, 22 Maple Avenue,
Morristown, N. J. at 7:30 p.m., Tuesday,
November 14, 1961.

A typical week's listing of meetings of the smaller
authorities would show: "Wednesday, Jan. 3 ... Boonton-
Housing Authority, 8 PM, Authority Office, Chestnut St. ...
Dover-Parking Authority, 8 PM, Authority Bldg. ...

Morristown- . . . Housing Authority, 8 PM, Authority office."

Attendance by the public is negligible.

Political Identity

A further handicap to the public's interest in authorities lies in the kind of activities conducted by these agencies. In the forefront in performing functions necessitated by the spread city in metropolitan areas, for instance, they bear the brunt of the criticism for those factors which have given rise to the very need for the function itself.

Edward Banfield explains this confusion: "Many riders hated CTA (Chicago Transit Authority) bitterly. The system was a symbol, perhaps, of all that was most wearisome and aggravating in their lives: it stood for the tyranny of the routine, the too-intimate contact with fellow men, the indignity of being one of the mass."(1)

The frustrations of the riders of the Massachusetts Metropolitan Transit Authority subways have been memorialized in song by the Kingston Trio until every teen-ager knows of Charlie, "the man who never returned," and the fact that "he may ride forever 'neath the streets of Boston" rather than pay the increased fare.

The nature of the functions, in addition to the poorly defined nature of the public authority as an institution somewhat private and somewhat public have made it almost impossible for the public to become interested in their normal activities, or for the authorities, conversely, to assume a political identity. In less academic terminology, public authorities lack "political sex appeal." "The Democratic party favors genuine home rule," said a New York politician, "but it does not regard a garbage district as 'home.'"

An attempt to praise the service functions of the Jersey City Incinerator Authority, in the Hudson Gazette serves to illustrate the incongruities:

We would feel recreant to our moral obligation of con-
structiveness if we did not editorialize on the magnificent
Jersey City Incinerator Authority having contributed so
constructively, efficiently and effectively to all the people
of the City of Jersey City. . . .

In all metropolitan cities where the population rises to
the million mark an incinerator is not a luxurious procedure or mere comfort, it is a necessity of first magni-
tude. . . .

Jersey City is indeed fortunate that it has civic consciousness and progressive Authority members inherently
vigilant and on the alert always to catch any new innova-
tion of inventive genius that can improve and better the
general efficiency of this creditable and commandable
(sic) civic service.

They do not relax in a rut of good enough stagnation. . . .

The future of Jersey City is radiant with a militant vibrant
sense of civic consciousness. The administrative conduct
of the public servants has captured the faith and the confidence of the rentpayers and taxpayers of the City of
Jersey City. They know that the members of the Jersey
City Incinerator Authority are trying to give them the
best and most perfect service and they have justly earned
and merited all these accolades of commendation. We
thank God for their vision of progress. (2)

This is about as much as anyone can say for a garbage-
disposal unit.

Thurman Arnold, a specialist on government symbolism,
has stated the public attitude toward government corporations in more general terminology, pointing out that the
government corporation involves "so many ideological con-
traditions:"

Everybody 'saw through' the device of a government
corporation and said that it was just a method of conceal-
ed 'taxation.' This was when the government corporation
'did not make money.' When it did 'make money' it was
'governmental interference in business.' (3)

The perspective may have something to do with it. In the case of the Port of New York Authority the "beneficent corporate image of public service" may well be assigned it by those users, for the most part in the core city, who use and even enjoy its bridges and ports.(4) In certain of the suburbs, however, the characterization of the Port Authority as the "giant" reaching out to control functions in the small towns arises as proposals and actions of the Authority affect them. The New York Herald-Tribune caught this attitude after the courts had awarded the Borough of Moonachie the tax decision against the Port Authority in 1961: "The Little Fellow Scores Against P.A." The lead for the article began: "The victory...makes news because of the David-and-Goliath aspects .... (W)ho can doubt where the public sympathy rests? With the little fellow, of course."(5)

Least adversely affected by the problem of functional symbolism are the turnpike authorities. They tend to conjur up in the minds of the users pleasant thoughts of vacations and travel. "Your Personal Guide to the Pennsylvania Turnpike" points to that road's advantages for the motorist as a "four-lane highway without crossroads, rail crossings, stop lights or interference from pedestrian traffic or livestock crossings." The Garden State Parkway reminds its travellers that it is "the safest superhighway in the nation," and the New York Thruway, under the nostalgic motto, "The Main Street of the Empire State," goes New Jersey one better with the claim of being the "safest superhighway system in the world."

The turnpikes have become personified, with distinctive "personalities." One motorist describes "the intense Pennsylvania Turnpike, the motherly Ohio Turnpike, the sensible Maine Turnpike, the changeable Massachusetts Turnpike, and the self-confident New York Thruway." The New Jersey Turnpike is "the establishment of a successful merchant." The Garden State Parkway is, on the other hand, "a gently beautiful road, very feminine in its personality."(6) Perhaps it is not without significance that its Chairman has been a woman, Mrs. Katharine Elkus White. She has made a special point of service to women drivers on the parkway. It is even tactful with children. Indeed, this Authority has even organized a Garden State Parkway Stork Club consisting of all the children born on the Highway since it opened in 1955. At a meeting of the Club in 1960 seventeen of the eighteen children eligible were present. The Authority also provides special accommodations for the elderly and disabled.

Many authorities, on the other hand, have been content to function anonymously, at least until recently. Annual reports of the authorities were printed expensively, often in color, and with illustrations of authority projects, but were geared largely to the bondholders or potential bond purchasers. The Annual Report to the Governors and Legislatures of The State of New Jersey and the Commonwealth of Pennsylvania, published by the Delaware River Joint Toll Bridge Commission for 1956, was typical. After eleven pages of description of its functions the Report became a financial accounting under the categories: "Maintenance and Operation of Free Facilities, Revenue and Expenses and Bond Retirement for 1956, Comparison of Traffic Volumes, Comparison of Vehicular Traffic, Accountant's Report, Balance Sheet, Statement of Operations and Fund Equities, Statement of Investment in Facilities, Notes to Financial Statements, Investments, Toll Bridges Traffic and Revenue, and Report of Consulting Engineers."

The Port of New York Authority invested heavily in public relations, but centered it on the development of an image of financial affluence. With almost tiresome repetition headlines picked up this focus from the news releases and rarely was the dollar sign absent from Port Authority stories:

"$125,000,000 Plan For Bridge Ready"

"Bus Projects Due for Fall of '62 — Midtown Addition Will Cost 20 Million and One Uptown 13 Million"

"P.A. Opens Sixth Dock In $90-Million Project"

"Millions For Port — PA May Double Investment in Newark"

"Assets of PA Soar To $1,116,100,000"

The role being performed in so many aspects of community affairs today by the authorities, however, has
brought the term, 'authorities,' to the attention of not only
the prospective bond buyer but to persons concerned with
their service functions. Authorities have been placed in
decision-making positions in ways that affect the lives of
most persons in the community, and these decisions have
divided residents who thereby have come to identify with
the judgment of the authority or in opposition to it. Although
still confused as to the meaning of the word, persons concerned have become increasingly aware of authorities and
curious as to their place in the area of service.

As might be expected in the handling of vast capital-
construction projects evidences of corruption by employees
of certain public authorities began to be presented to the
courts and thereby to find their way into newspaper accounts. For the first time, a share of what people were
reading about authorities was unfavorable. The stories
came from varied authorities: the disclosure of the mis-
use and waste of thousands of dollars by toll collectors and
two leading officials of the Delaware River Joint Toll
Bridge Commission in 1956; the conviction in the following
year of three former officers, and two members of the
consulting engineering firm, of the Pennsylvania Turnpike
Commission of "conspiracy to defraud the commission of
$19,500,000 in a Turnpike contract"; the awarding of the
Pulitzer Prize for local reporting in May, 1962, to George
Bliss for some 80 accounts in the Chicago Tribune of
scandal in the Metropolitan Sanitary District of Greater
Chicago which had resulted in the discharging of more than
100 of its employees; the indictment the same month of
six persons in Suffolk County, Massachusetts, on charges
of larceny and conspiracy in connection with the construction of the under-Commons garage in Boston by the Massachusetts Parking Authority, including the Chairman of the
Authority, a consultant engineer, and two Andover law
partners; the filing in the summer of 1962 of eighteen
sealed indictments charging grand larceny, forgery, and
collection of illegal fees in the construction of the New
England Thruway; the State investigation into the State
Liquor Authority (which does not fit the definition of an
authority used in this book, but uses the term) continuing

from 1962-1964 and featured by <u>Life</u> magazine, involving the suicide of a former top investigator of the Authority; the charge by the State Controller's Office of New York that the Adirondack Mountain Authority according to its audit report, had diverted $90,000 from facility improvements, for which it had been appropriated, to meet payrolls; and the awarding of the Pulitzer Prize gold medal for public service to the St. Petersburg (Florida) <u>Times</u> in 1964 for its investigation of spending by the Florida State Turnpike Authorty.

These revelations affected not only the bondholder, but now as well persons living in the service areas of the authorities. The authorities were confronted, therefore, with the dual task of reappraising their public relations in regard to both factions. This is by no means an easy undertaking. Early attempts have offered little encouragement.

The most imaginative job of what he refers to as the improvement of "our public relations acceptance"(7) for a public authority has been done by Sylvester V. Pointkowski, Director of Public Relations for the New York City Transit Authority. The Authority carried 1,796,000,000 passengers over 365,000,000 vehicle miles in the fiscal year 1961. Its annual report for that year, however, did not dwell on such statistics or on matters of finance. Rather, it contained sections on "Data Processing, Personnel, Labor Relations, Training Activities, Safety, Medical, Public and Passenger Relations, Employees Suggestion Program, Employee Activities, Secretary's Office Serves as Host," and other service items of interest to the general public. The Report explained the approach as consisting of a "variety of new programs ... planned for the two-fold purpose of providing information to the public directly" and "advising potential passengers of these improvements in an effort to obtain greater use of its facilities...."(8) In other words, the general public in the area of the functioning of the Authority, as well as the users of its functions, were being considered. And the problem of meeting the desires of the two "constituencies" became apparent.

On January 17, 1962, the New York Transit Authority's campaign reached a climax with the running of a so-called

"dream car" from the Times Square subway station of the
IRT Broadway-7th Avenue line, in which guests and press
were to sip champagne to the background of music by Musak.
Attractively printed blue and red programs explained the
occasion:

> The Young Men's Board of Trade — N.Y.C. Chamber of
> Commerce is sponsoring a Clean Subways Campaign for
> the New York City Transit Authority.
>
> This is the first time that a civic conscious group of
> young businessmen has volunteered to seek the cooperation
> of the public in order to improve the appearance and
> cleanliness of the New York City rapid transit system.
>
> Some indications of the unusual effort that is entering this
> campaign is reflected in the ceremonial inaugural train.
>
> The sponsoring committee and the press will enter the
> second car of the train from a red-carpeted station plat-
> form. The first car has been carpeted completely. Flowers
> are much in evidence. Curtains and draperies, colored
> lights and a bar have been installed.
>
> Volunteering their assistance as receptionists are a group
> of girls who have been selected as Miss Subways. Be-
> cause the occasion is spirited, refreshments will be of-
> fered in the form of champagne. For canapes, there will
> be pretzels (the same as those sold at subway stations).
>
> The carpeting, the flowers, the beverages, pretzels, dec-
> orations, gowns and music have all been donated by civic-
> minded business groups.(9)

The prosaic nature of the function of the Transit Authority reared its head above the tinsel, however, and, as the
New York Times put it, the "Champagne Hour" was "Flat."
"It might have seemed like any other suffocatingly crowded
rush-hour," said the reporter, "but it was compounded by
champagne, pretzels, fresh flowers, window curtains, wall-
to-wall carpeting and beauty queens posing for photog-
raphers. ... The paying public, locked out of the midmorn-
ing festivities ... reacted with puzzlement, indignant glares
or 'so what' attitudes. ... A rider who had been aboard a

'common folks' car peered at the empty champagne bottles, splintered pretzels and wilted carnations after it was all over.   'Give me serivce,' he said.   'Don't give me flowers.' "(10)

"Sic Transit . . . ."(11)

The Port of New York Authority has been concerned in this same regard that the first person to represent it to the public is the toll-collector, who is performing an unpopular task. So unpopular is his job in fact that not infrequently the motorist will hand him coins which have been heated red-hot by the car's cigarette lighter. The Authority, as do most turnpike, bridge, and tunnel, authorities, uses uniformed policemen as collectors, but takes care never to photograph them from their holster side. In the summer of 1962 the Port Authority joined such other authorities as the New York State Thruway, the Southern State Parkway, and the Baltimore Harbor Tunnel, in employing women as collectors. The thought is that, by nature, they can be more friendly and effective in this repetitive-type of work. One newspaper dubbed the woman agent, "Tilly the Toller."(12) The New Jersey Highway Authority has experimented successfully with the use of older men, retired from other jobs, as collectors.

Pennsylvania has been more successful than most states in giving political identity and considerable prestige to public authorities. They are very frankly recognized in that State as distinct political entities. The municipal authorities have their own statewide Association, the Pennsylvania Municipal Authorities Association, with a full-time Executive Director and offices in the modern 2415 Local Government Building in Harrisburg, the State Capital. The color, green, is recognized as its own symbolic reference for its letterheads and publications. Until 1962, the Association published its own journal, The Authority; at that time the Association joined with the League of Cities, the State Association of Boroughs, the State Association of Township Commissioners, Local Government Secretaries and the Munnicipal Assessors Association, in a new official magazine to be known as the Pennsylvanian.

Detailed and accurate records of municipal authorities
in Pennsylvania are kept and made readily available. The
Pennsylvania Municipality Authorities Act and Related
Laws, 1962 edition, was compiled by the Association, and
a Directory of Pennsylvania Municipal Authorities, 1960,
by the Department of Internal Affairs. The brokerage concern of Butcher & Sherrerd, of Philadelphia, has published
a booklet, Municipal Authority Financing in Pennsylvania
Communities, which spells out financial procedures for
authorities. First published in 1957, it was reprinted in
1958 and 1959, and issued in revised form in 1960. In a
foreword Butcher and Sherrerd pay tribute to authority ac-
complishments: "Pennsylvania is in the forefront of those
states which have met the problem of providing needed
public facilities for an expanding and dynamic population.
The largest part of this improvement program has been
accomplished by local municipal authorities, which represent uniquely practical vehicles for the accomplishment of
the purpose."(13)

The Municipal Authorities Act of 1945 provided the
official recognition of these Pennsylvania entities. Under
it, any municipality, or combined municipalities, may form
public authorities "for the purpose of acquiring, holding,
constructing, improving, maintaining and operating, owning,
leasing, either in the capacity of lessor or lessee, projects
of the following kind and character, buildings to be devoted
wholly or partially for public uses, including public school
buildings, and for revenue-producing purposes; transportation, marketing, shopping, terminals, bridges, tunnels,
flood control projects, highways, parkways, traffic distribution centers, parking spaces, airports and all facilities
necessary or incidental thereto, parks, recreation grounds
and facilities, sewers, sewer systems or parts thereof,
sewage treatment works, including works for treating and
disposing of industrial waste, facilities and equipment for
the collection, removal or disposal of ashes, garbage, rub-
bish and other refuse materials by incineration, land fill
or other methods, steam heating plants and distribution
systems, incinerator plants, waterworks, water supply
works, water distribution systems, swimming pools, playgrounds, lakes, low head dams, hospitals, motor buses for
public use, when such motor buses are to be used within

any municipality, subways, and industrial development projects." Authorities for schools have the power "only to acquire, hold, construct, improve, maintain, operate and lease public school buildings and other school projects acquired, constructed or improved for public school purposes."(14)

Under this broad enabling legislation Pennsylvania municipalities had established by 1960 1,364 public authorities, more than 150 of them since 1959. 643 of these were school authorities, known as "lease-back" authorities because they construct the school building and then lease it to the school district. The next largest numbers were sewer authorities, followed by water authorities, multipurpose, and parking authorities.(15)

Lease-back authorities are authorized also on the State-level, as of a Law of 1949 which had provided for the organization of the General State Authority of Pennsylvania. Under this Authority a Department of the State Government, with the approval of enabling legislation by the General Assembly, requests the General State Authority to plan, finance, and carry out the project. The Department of the Government, in the name of the Commonwealth, then leases the completed project from the Authority. By 1959 the General Assembly had approved the fixing of the borrowing capacity of the General State Authority at $621,431,400.(16)

Pennsylvania has made strides, therefore, toward the achievement of "an authorities concept" in which a public authority is aware of its interdependence with other such constituted authorities. "A Code of Ethics for Authorities," adopted by the Pennsylvania Municipal Authorities Association October 5, 1954, recognizes this mutuality: "(T)he reputation of all Municipal Authorities must be of a high order to continue the excellent reputation of the bonds of Municipal Authorities of the Commonwealth of Pennsylvania as a medium of investment. ... [Note again the influence of revenue bonds.] Authorities must recognize that the action of any one Authority may be prejudicial to many, and it is imperative that the conduct and operation of all be above reproach and strictly in accordance with applicable laws and governing resolutions and indentures."(17)

NUMBER AND BONDED INDEBTEDNESS OF MUNICIPAL AUTHORITIES
IN PENNSYLVANIA BY TYPE, 1960

Type of authority	Total number of authorities[1]	Total number of projects	Amount of original bond issues[2]	Amount of bond issues[2] outstanding
Total	1,364	1,459	$1,430,363,040	$1,293,105,347
School Authorities	643	658	824,208,000	759,185,486
Water Authorities	199	280	236,886,175	194,466,663
Sewer Authorities	238	322	319,492,965	294,267,000
Multi-Purpose Authorities[3]	93	---	---	---
Parking Authorities	80	83	42,203,300	38,248,598
Airport Authorities	21	21	1,050,000	790,000
Miscellaneous Authorities[4]	42	47	6,522,600	6,147,600
No Known Purpose Authorities	48	48	---	---

(1) Number of authorities as of October, 1960.

(2) Bond information as of December 31, 1959.

(3) Includes such authorities as buildings and land; parking, sewer, and water; sewer and water; and school and water. Of the 188 projects in this group, there were 15 school, 81 water, 84 sewer, 3 parking, and 5 miscellaneous authorities represented. The bond issues amounting to $127,108,000 were allocated as follows: school $26,696,000, water $43,876,500, sewer $54,317,500, parking $1,198,000, and miscellaneous $1,020,000.

(4) Includes such authorities as: Auditoriums, Factory Buildings, Flood Control, Incinerators, Municipal Buildings, Parks, and Swimming Pools.

PENNSYLVANIA MUNICIPAL AUTHORITIES ASSOCIATION

A CODE OF ETHICS FOR AUTHORITIES

I. Obligations of an Authority.

1. To the Public.

A. There is an obligation on an Authority to make its service available to the greatest number of persons, subject to the limitation of applicable laws, ordinances, and sound operating practices.

B. Rates. An Authority is obligated to render its service and operate its projects at the lowest cost to its customers, consistent with a high quality of service, keeping in mind its obligation to maintain the project in good repair, build adequate reserves and discharge its financial obligations.

C. A Municipal Authority is bound to apply all rules and regulations to the same class of customers equally without preference.

D. Every Authority member, officer and employee should maintain at all times a courteous and respectful attitude in dealing with customers and the public generally.

2. Public Officials.

A. Municipal Authorities recognize their obligation and duty to cooperate with all public officials and public bodies to increase the service to customers and the public and to improve the efficiency and economy of authority administration.

B. Municipal Authority officers and employees at all times recognize a duty of respectful cooperation in their relations with other public officials and agencies which By law have official duties requiring them to work with Authority officials.

C. Authorities recognize the need of supplying to the Congress of the United States, the Legislature of Pennsylvania, to all local government units and other interested parties, information of help and benefit to these groups.

(1) The Legislature of Pennsylvania and the Congress of the United States, Authorities owe a high obligation to these legislative bodies to make available information regarding authorities in order that the public may continue to secure the benefits of Authority operation.

(2) Communities not now sponsoring an Authority but desirous of so doing should have available to them information which is accurate, unbiased and impartial so that these communities may determine if they desire to have incorporated an Authority for the operation of a project or projects in their territory.

3. Incorporating Municipalities.

A. Municipal Authorities recognize an obligation to perform the task assigned to them by their incorporating municipality or municipalities when they were created as an Authority. The Authorities recognize that the conducting of their project affects the lives of all residents of their home community. They will discharge their duties with fidelity.

B. Municipal Authorities recognize their obligation to assist the sponsoring municipality or municipalities in any projects which they are authorized by statute to operate which will result in community betterment and which are financially feasible.

C. Municipal Authorities recognize the statutory right of the sponsoring municipality to appoint board members and will not attempt to influence their selection. Authorities will, however, when requested by a municipality make recommendations based upon a consideration of the best interests of the Authority.

4. Bondholders.

A. Authorities at all times recognize that projects usually are financially possible only by the issuance of revenue bonds and that great trust has been placed in Authorities by the Legislature of the Commonwealth of Pennsylvania in giving to Authorities the right to issue such bonds. Therefore, the reputation of all Municipal Authorities must be of a high order to continue the good reputation of all bonds of Municipal Authorities and of the Commonwealth of Pennsylvania as a medium of investment.

B. Authorities must recognize that the action of any one Authority may be prejudicial to many, and it is imperative that the conduct and operation of all be above reproach and strictly in accordance with applicable laws and governing resolutions and indentures.

II. Conduct of an Authority.

1. Authority members, officers and employees should be constantly aware of their great responsibilities in the administration and operation of Municipal Authorities so that the public may enjoy essential services at a minimum cost.

2. Authority members shall at all times fully discharge their public and contractual duties without fear or favor, and shall be governed by high ideals of personal honor and integrity in all of their work, and shall conduct the business of the Authority in the public interest.

3. Authorities recognize that they must conduct their operations in a business like manner and should employ the most advanced techniques in the management of their projects in order to best serve their customers, their sponsoring municipality and the general public.

4. The best interest of Authorities can be served only by the employment of persons because of skill, ability and merit, and therefore, political considerations shall not enter into the selection of Authority employees or the operation of the Authority.

5. Authority members, officers and employees realize that high personal qualifications for their position are necessary and they will strive diligently at all times to improve and develop their qualifications for the position they hold.

6. To function efficiently, Authorities must be free of politics, but members, officers and employees of authorities may take part in politics as individuals but not as representatives of an Authority.

III. Authorities Association Committee Created.

There is hereby created a committee to be called the **Authorities Association Committee** of the Pennsylvania Municipal Authorities Association, whose duty it shall be to actively foster the practising of such conduct, by Municipal Authorities, their members, officers and employees, as is set forth in this Code of Ethics.

1. Creation.

A. The Board of Directors of the Pennsylvania Municipal Authorities Association is hereby authorized and directed to appoint the members of the **Authorities Association Committee**. The said committee shall consist of three members who when first appointed shall consist of three members who serve for a term of 3 years. Their terms shall be staggered to the end and effect that the term of one member shall expire each year.

2. Powers.

A. The said committee shall have the power to assemble data from the membership which may be required to properly perform its duties.

B. The committee shall be authorized to utilize existing facilities of the Association including, but not being limited to, secretarial services, legal services and publications.

C. The committee shall make available information, advice and data to all proper bodies including the Congress of the United States, the Legislature of Pennsylvania, local government agencies, and communities in need of a project which can be served by operating Authorities, an Authority.

D. The committee shall be empowered to hear charges and complaints filed with said committee by any individual, corporation, Authority, government official or any other interested person alleging that a member or associate member of the Pennsylvania Municipal Authorities Association has violated this Code of Ethics, except as to complaints under Sections A, B and C of Article I-1, the hearing of which are vested in other designated tribunals and shall have power to make rules regarding the filing of said complaints and the hearings had thereon.

E. In the event a charge or complaint is filed against a non-member of this Association, or a non-member, the said Committee shall bring the charges, complaint or information to the attention of the violator with an offer of consultation in regard thereto and suggested corrective action.

F. After Advisory Committee acquires knowledge of a violation of this Code of Ethics by a member or associate member of the Pennsylvania Municipal Authorities Association, the said Committee shall, after hearing to recommend to the Board of Directors proper discipline for any member or associate member of the Pennsylvania Municipal Authorities Association which discipline may include a recommendation of expulsion from membership, and any other proper legal action.

Adopted October 5, 1954

The attitude is reflected in practice. J. E. Kuhn, Secretary-Treasurer and Office Manager of The Municipal Authority of Belle Vernon, Pennsylvania, writes: "(W)e believe that the relationship between our Authority and its consumers, our Authority and its incorporating municipality, our Authority and the governing bodies of municipalities within our service area, and our Authority and public news facilities... ought to be carefully considered and developed."(18)

The Port of New York Authority has organized an elaborate network of community relations which brings together representative groups to discuss problems related to the development of the Port District. This system involves two types of community meetings, which are held regularly: the Community Contact Meeting, and the Progess Report Meeting. In the first type, the Community Contact Meeting, members of the Port Authority meet with the Mayor of the municipality, or the Freeholders or the Commissioners of the County to see whether they have problems with which the specialists of the Port Authority staff could help them. In the second, the Progress Report Meeting, officials of the Port Authority meet with government and business leaders in some 200-300 communities within the Port District in a program planned to present to that community what the Port Authority is doing of concern to it. A progress report is made on what the Authority has accomplished in the past eighteen months or so since the last such meeting in that community.

In 1954 the Port Authority began publishing a monthly bulletin, <u>Port Community Re:Port</u>, "to keep community leaders informed about the activities of The Port of New York Authority as they concern the people of the New Jersey-New York Port District."(19) The circulation list includes more than 10,000 civic leaders. In a questionnaire addressed to this mailing list in 1961, concerning the effects of <u>Re:Port</u>, some 1,709 responses brought a clear indication of interest on the part of the Port District 'constituency' in this kind of communication from a Public Authority. Of the proportionately large number who replied 1,141 reported that they read the monthly bulletin always, 456 frequently, 62 infrequently, and 13 never. When asked if they wished to continue to receive the bulletin, 1,588 replied affirmatively and 121 negatively.

The frank recognition of authorities by the State of Pennsylvania, and the strengthening of the concept of the Port District by the Port of New York Authority, are exceptions to the lack of identity of these agencies by the general public. The resultant blurred image of the authority, on the one hand, and on the other, the diffusion of its accountability among bondholders, users, residents in the area, and parent government, have combined to divorce the authority from the public in the normal sense of responsible government.

The boast by authority advocates that the agency takes the construction and operation of essential functions "out of politics," even if it could be substantiated, must be evaluated in the light of what alternate checks have been established to replace that of the party system. Freedom from political involvement is, of course, a matter of a degree of freedom, rather than absolute detachment, for any unit of government responsible for the making of decisions on public policy. There is no way to take such decisions "out of politics." The claim would have to be phrased as an assertion that partisan considerations play less of a role in the making of decisions by an authority board than they do in policy formulation by the municipal council or county board.

The question of the distinction, at least in the case of county and municipal authorities studied in the given area of five States for this book, may be academic. Although one of the attractions of service on an authority board is the supposed "non-political" nature of an authority, the board member may unwittingly be involved, through his duties with the authority, in the politics of the community to a degree that he cannot even imagine. Rather than being "out of politics," as is the common generalization about an authority, it may be becoming, as Robert Wood has suggested, "a meeting ground for competing political factions within a locality."(20) And these factions may represent not only the traditional party alignments, but the more recent representations of professional, technical, and business interests. The functional service of the authority, in addition to its attraction to the latter representative groups, may have conspired to bring into the decision-making processes of this agency a curious combination of political factors.

Because of the unawareness of the board members of the political involvement of their role, the political influence may be more effective and more intense even than in the acknowledged political institutions. This danger was emphasized in an editorial in The American City, in 1956, which quoted a statement by Dennis O'Harrow, Executive Director of the American Society of Planning Officials, to the effect that by the use of special districts or authorities, a city "exchanged one set of intelligent politicians, sensitive to the citizens' wishes, for a group of inept politicians who, because of their amateur standing, didn't give a damn about the citizens."(21) The statement goes further than do the conclusions of this book, but the two would be in agreement on stressing, even to the authority-board member, that the thought that semi-autonomous units of government with powers to plan, construct, and operate facilities for most of the services of the communities, and to finance them independently, could -- or should -- be taken "out of politics" is far too disarming. They are subject to political involvement of at least three kinds:

Party Politics

(1) Studies for this book show, to a surprising degree, the impact of the regular party politics on the functioning of public authorities. The Delaware River Port Authority, as has been discussed, was seriously handicapped through the refusal of the Republican-dominated legislature of New Jersey to permit the Democratic Governor to appoint new members to its Board of Commissioners. The deterioration of the plant of the Jersey City Sewer Authority was the result, in part, of a factional fight within the Democratic Party of Jersey City. Cooperative effort by the Morris County (New Jersey) Municipal Utilities Authority was made less effective through the withdrawal of Morristown, the County seat, from it because the Authority Board members were all Republican, and the Mayor of Morristown was a Democrat.

An extreme illustration of the inroads of party politics into authority operations is provided by another Jersey City Authority, the Incinerator Authority, in which employees in 1960 were caught in a party power play between followers of one City Commissioner who was a Republican, on the one side, and the Democratic leader, on the other.

At an organization meeting of the Jersey City Incinerator Authority on February 10, 1960, at which it was expected that the Republicans under the Commissioner would gain control of the Authority for the first time, one of his appointees to the Authority was offered the position of Vice-Chairman of the Authority by the Democrats and, in a surprise move, accepted that offer rather than vote with the other two followers of the Commissioner to give the Republicans control of the five-man board. Some two hundred jobs in the Authority are involved in control of it. A Democrat was renamed its Chairman, and another Democrat, Treasurer.(22)

Undaunted, the Commissioner's group called a reorganization of the Incinerator Authority one week later, February 19, and this time the Republicans held together and named one of the Commissioner's followers Chairman. The Democratic Chairman, however, refused to recognize this reorganization, and insisted that he was still the Authority's Chairman. Two separate factions of the Authority each continued to function in the name of the same Authority, with two Chairmen, two Executive Secretaries, and two Counsels. In the resultant patronage play some seventy-three Authority employees lost their jobs.

Local 825 of the International Brotherhood of Operating Engineers called a strike and set up pickets. The Plant Superintendent prevented serious damage to the fire-brick walls of the incinerator chambers by firing them up himself.(23)

The Authority was powerless to act, despite the obvious health hazard that could have ensued. The Commissioner's faction claimed to speak for the Authority, but the dismissed Authority Counsel of the Democratic group which also claimed the leadership of the Authority, had obtained a

restraining order to prevent the opposing group from functioning in the name of the Authority until a Court hearing
was held. Technically, then, the Republican "Chairman"
of the Authority could not even enter the building, and he
was in no position to talk with the strikers. The Democratic "Chairman" himself could not do so effectively because he was now outvoted on the Authority, 3-2.(24)

This impossible situation was relieved when the employee for whom the strike ostensibly had been called was
rehired, but the overall question of patronage remained to
plague the Authority. Another strike was called in October
of 1960, and further trouble ensued during the summer of
1961.

Party patronage possibilities in the authorities are extensive. A semi-autonomous agency, little recognized by
the public, handling large capital construction contracts,
obviously has positions on various levels of ability to fill.
A Republican local leader in Nassau County, for example,
will tell you that the post of general counsel on an authority
is not infrequently used as a political reward. "Who knows
anything about authorities, anyway," he explains. And the
Chairman of the Democratic County Committee in the same
County charged that the special district permits the Republican Party to "wield power and patronage without responsibility."(25)

Edward Banfield and Martin Meyerson found in a study
of how decisions were made in the Chicago Housing Authority that most of the "considerations which finally governed
the selection of sites and of the type of projects were 'political' rather than 'technical'." This result was contrary
to their expectations, as they had thought that this agency,
with a reputation as one of the best administered in the
United States, would have established a process for rational
decision-making with use of the best scientific and administrative techniques.(26)

The authority has difficulty, therefore, in insulating itself from regular party politics. Not only may party politics
invade the very functioning of the authority itself, but it may
influence authority decisions also through the authority's

getting caught in the cross-currents of party politics of other levels. The Port of New York Authority encountered this web of party politics when it proposed the construction, under its supervision, of a large jetport in the so-called 'Great Swamp' in Morris County, New Jersey. The suggestion was fought by an organization calling itself the 'Jersey Jetport Site Association;' however, much of the credit for blocking the jetport was accorded another group, the 'Great Swamp Committee,' which, in the name of the preservation of a wildlife refuge on the proposed site of the jetport, was successful in collecting enough money through donations to enable it to give more than 1,000 acres of the Great Swamp to the Fish and Wildlife Service of the Department of the Interior which then constituted the area a Wildlife Preserve.

"It is ironical," mused the local newspaper, "that a small group of dedicated nature-lovers have been able in a quiet but steady way and without much money to do what all the jetsite associations have been unable to do -- block the Port of New York Authority."(27)

The Great Swamp Committee certainly had played a major role in opposition to the jetport. The local characterization of the jetport opponents as the 'underdog,' however, could not erase the hard facts of politics. The David characterization of the Great Swamp Committee had to be seen on a backdrop of politics in which the Goliath had become involved. The year, 1961, was to witness a gubernatorial campaign in New Jersey; the Port Authority proposal for the jetport had been contested since 1959. The most talked-of substitute site for the jetport was one in Burlington County in South Jersey. A candidate for Governor could not risk alienating voters in North Jersey by supporting the Port Authority's Great Swamp suggestion, for he would, at the same time, lose the votes of the South Jersey voters who wanted the jetport established in Burlington County. The "miracle man who can defy both ends of the state and win hasn't yet been exhumed," said the Newark Evening News editorially.(28)

Governor Robert Meyner, denied a chance to run for a third term by New Jersey State Law, did dare defy the

political omens, and, at a Governors' Conference way out
in Hawaii in June of 1961 suggested his support of the Port
Authority's proposed jetport in Morris County. The political impact on the gubernatorial campaign was immediate.
Under the headlines, "GOP Joyous Over Meyner Jetport
OK -- Own Party Is Struck With Consternation," the New
York Herald-Tribune recognized the intricacies of politics
into which the Port Authority had been drawn: "An obviously concerned Mr. Hughes [Democratic candidate for Governor to succeed Meyner] hastily disassociated himself from
Gov. Meyner's stand today and insisted that the issue was
being 'inflated out of proportion.' Mr. Hughes said he would
stand by the party's platform but at the same time he had
a 'high regard' for Gov. Meyner. 'Divergence by its
leaders won't hurt the Democratic party,' Mr. Hughes insisted."(29)

Interest Pressures

(2) It is less surprising, in view of their functional purpose, to find public authorities embroiled in political differences of interest groups, rather than the standard political parties. A rather characteristic illustration of this
kind of dispute is one involving the Parking Authority of
Woodbridge Township, in Middlesex County, New Jersey,
which was to become so bitter that the Authority's Chairman and three other members resigned. The politics of
this dispute was not a party, but an interest-group contest, with the merchants opposing the Authority on the in-
stallation of traffic meters. The Authority had been created
in 1957 and, as one of its first acts, had purchased 400
meters for Woodbridge, Fords, and Iselin, in the Township.
Under pressure from the merchants the Township Committee had refused to adopt an ordinance approving the
meters. The Authority had been forced to disconnect the
meters and place them in storage, at a loss of some $28,000.
By 1960 the Authority was $40,000 in debt and was again
being rebuffed on attempts to install the meters.

The frustration of this kind of opposition, in the face
of the mounting deficits, was too much for the four non-
salaried members of the Authority, and they resigned. One
of them, who had been a member of the Authority for less

than a year, complained: "I stepped into a hot potato. It got so there's no cooperation with the Township Committee or the merchants." "You try to do something," he concluded, "and all you get is your brains kicked in. So you yell uncle. That's what we did."(30)

As Horace Davis points out in "Borrowing Machines," the ideal of taking issues "out of politics" works all right for awhile, "but the inevitable result is that the commission is soon subjected to political pressure.... As for the central administration, it soon recovers from its chastened mood, and sets out to make the best of what is left."(31)

Middle-Class Politics

(3) A peculiar brand of politics may have developed within the authority-device itself. Concerned in the decision-making process of the authority are members of the authority board who often are leading professional, business, technical residents of the community; the executive director of the authority; the general counsel of the authority; the representative of the trustee bank which manages the financial operation of the authority project; the engineer and other technical employees on the project; and, in the case of the larger authorities, the public relations and even community relations directors.

The emphasis on the professional and technical experts reflected in this combination in the persons of the director, banker, lawyer, and engineer may well be representative of what Edward Banfield has referred to as "the logical fulfillment of the middle-class ideal." "We may see in ... the exalted position of Robert Moses," he adds, "portents of what is to come."(32) Mr. Moses has held simultaneously such positions as: New York City Commissioner of Parks, Chairman of the New York State Power Authority, Chairman of the Triborough Bridge and Tunnel Authority, member of the City Planning Commission, City Construction Coordinator, Chairman of the Mayor's Committee on Slum Clearance, Director of Planning and Construction for Civil Defense, Chairman of the State Council of Parks, President of the Long Island State Park Commission, and President of the Jones Beach State Parkway Authority. The

power he has wielded through these Authority chairman-
ships and positions of the like, may well be more than he
would have had had he been elected Governor when he ran
against Herbert Lehman in 1934.

Instead of personifying the public authorities he has
directed to give meaning to them for the public, as so
colorful a man might have done, Mr. Moses has stood de-
fensively between the two, protecting the efficiency of his
agencies from intrusion by the public. Such a role would
seem strange for a public leader except in the case of the
public authority. There it is consistent with the peculiar
nature of the authority which is designed to place efficiency
in the public service against sensitivity to public involvement.

Moses berates critics, and brooks no opposition. "Who
are these pundits," he remarked of critics, "to say we have
neglected our problems or that others might solve them
better?"(33)

In quite a different way, something of the same concept
of his role as a buffer between an efficient Authority and
the public meddling with it is seen in the case of Austin
Tobin, Executive Director of the Port of New York Authority. In answer to what he considered to be unfair attacks
on his staff during the Congressional hearings on the Port
Authority under the Chairmanship of Congressman Emanuel
Celler, Mr. Tobin wrote: "The reason I spoke up at Mr.
Celler's incredible hearings was that I had the responsibility, so far as my conscience was concerned, of standing
between him and members of my staff who were being
abused."(34) The United States Court of Appeals, in re-
versing Tobin's conviction for contempt of Congress as a
result of those hearings, questioned the need for this role
of the Executive Director: "Especially where the contest
is between different government units, the representative of
one unit in conflict with another should not have to risk jail
to vindicate his constituency's rights."

The respective decision-making influences within a public authority of the executive director, the general counsel,
the director of public relations, the chief engineer, become

of great importance in a new kind of politics evolving within the authority device itself.

Rather than taking authority functions "out of politics," therefore, the agency seems to be involved in a strange combination of the more traditional party politics, which impinge on its operations and cut through it as the authority is imposed over all existing governments and political organizations, and, in addition, of the new middle-class interests of technical, business, and professional people in the community.

The difficulty of establishing and maintaining relationships to take into account the will of diverse groups concerned with the operation of a public authority each for a different set of reasons -- the bondholders, the users of the facilities, the residents in the area of jurisdiction, and the parent governing body -- remains as yet unresolved. The further question as to how sensitive to the public -- or publics -- an agency such as this one which is engaged in highly technical activities and engages for their accomplishment specialists and professional persons in general, should be, confronts one who is disturbed here by the representative problem involved. Any attempt to weigh the efficiency of the public authority, accordingly, must be done with the realization that such efficiency may be attributable in part to the relative freedom of the authority from the kind of electorate or constituency to which regular governments are responsible.

REFERENCES

1. *Political Influence* (New York, The Glencoe Free Press, 1961), p. 96.

2. North Bergen, New Jersey, July 1, 1960.

3. *The Folklore of Capitalism* (New Haven, Yale University Press, 1937), pp. 315-316.

4. Gerald Krefetz, "Larger Issues Ignored at Port Authority Hearings," *The New Leader*, XLIV, No. 6, February 6, 1961. Wallace S. Sayre and Herbert Kaufman, *Governing New York City* (New York, Russell Sage Foundation, 1960), p. 255.

5. November 6, 1961.

6. Katherine Lynch, "Profiles of the Turnpikes," The New York Times, May 6, 1962.

7. Letter, Sylvester V. Pointkowski to author, February 28, 1962.

8. Annual Report for the Year July 1, 1960 to June 30, 1961, pp. 26-33, especially p. 31.

9. "Clean Subways Special, Sponsored by The Young Men's Board of Trade (N. Y. C. Junior Chamber of Commerce) for the New York City Transit Authority," January 17, 1962, Times Square Station, IRT Broadway, 7th Avenue Line.

10. The New York Times, January 18, 1962.

11. Heading for an editorial in another regard, The New York Times, December 29, 1961.

12. Newark Evening News, May 10, 1962.

13. Revised edition (Philadelphia, 1960), p. 2.

14. Sec. 4.

15. 1950 Pennsylvania Municipal Authorities Directory (Harrisburg, 1960), pp. iii, 1. Compare the types of special districts in California:

   There are 5 Air Pollution Control Districts in California; 1 Airport; 239 Cemetery; 41 Community Services; 24 County Area Services; 26 Drainage; 449 Fire; 64 Flood; 17 Garbage Disposal; 1 Grade Separation; 6 Harbor; 1 Health; 12 Joint Highways; 1 Bridges and Highways; 427 Highway Lighting; 51 Hospital; 263 Improvements (Act of 1911); 112 Irrigation; 11 Levees; 10 Library; 45 Mosquito Abatement; 62 Park, Recreation and Parkways; 4 Regional Parks; 12 Parking (Automobile); 7 Pest Abatement; 2 Citrus Pest Control; 1 Placer Mining; 15 Police; 5 Port and Riverport; 9 Protection; 69 Public Utilities; 5 Municipal Utilities; 8 Reclamation; 20 County Recreation; 8 Road (Acquisition and Improvement Act of 1925); 2 Joint County Road; 182 Supervisorial Road; 129 Sanitary (Act of 1923); 106 County Sanitation; 91 Sewer; 40 Soil Conservation; 3 Storm; 55 Storm Drain Maintenance; 1 Transportation; 19 Veterans Building and Memorial; 19 Water Conservation; 139 County Water; 3 County Water Authorities; 76 County Waterworks; 28 Metropolitan and Municipal Water. There are no boulevard, horticulture or public service districts at the present time. Information supplied by the State Controller, correspondence dated February 28, 1957.

Richard Bigger, Evan A. Iverson, Judith Jamison, James Kitchen, Edward Stamford, County Government in California. Bureau of Governmental Research, University of California. Published by County Supervisors Association of California, third edition (Sacramento, 1958), p. 98.

16. The General State Authority, Annual Report 1961, p. 6.

17. Sec. I, par. 4A, B. (Adopted October 5, 1954).

18. J. E. Kuhn, "Authority Publicity and Public Relations," The Authority, XX, No. 3, March, 1962, pp. 8-9.

The City of New York adopted a code of ethics in 1959 for City employees which includes certain City public authorities as institutions, but not their employees. The Code is concerned primarily with conflict-of-interest. Two sections refer to the authorities:

> Representing private interests before city agencies — No Councilman or other officer or employee whose salary is paid in whole or in part from the city treasury shall appear in behalf of private interests before any agency, including the New York City Transit Authority, the New York City Housing Authority, and the Triborough Bridge and Tunnel Authority. . . .

> Representing private interests before courts — No Councilman or other officer or employee whose salary is paid in whole or in part from the city treasury shall represent private interests in any action or proceeding against the interests of the city, in any litigation to which the city, the New York City Transit Authority, the New York City Housing Authority or the Triborough Bridge and Tunnel Authority is a party . . . .

Less than a month later the New York City Transit Authority adopted a similar code of ethics for its employees.

It deals with conflict–of–interest of employees while working for the Authority, and bars Transit employees from representing an enterprise before the Authority or the City for two years after they leave the employ of the Transit Authority.

19. Vol. VIII, No. 6, June, 1961, p. 1.

20. 1400 Governments (Cambridge, Massachusetts, Harvard University Press, 1961), p. 75.

21. "Downgrading the 'Authorities'." Vol. LXXI, No. 11, November, 1956, p. 5.

22. Newark Evening News, February 11, 1960.

23. Ibid., February 24, 1960.

24. Ibid., February 25, 1960.

25. Republican leader to author; The New York Times, April 25, 1960.

26. Edward C. Banfield, "Ends and Means in Planning," in Sidney Mailick and Edward H. VanNess, Concepts and Issues in Administrative Behavior (Englewood Cliffs, Prentice Hall, 1962), pp. 74–75.

27. The Madison Eagle, December 7, 1961.

28. January 20, 1960.

29. June 30, 1961.

30. Newark Evening News, June 21, 1960.

31. Davis, Horace A., "Borrowing Machines," National Municipal Review, XXIV, June, 1935, p. 331.

32. "The Political Implications of Metropolitan Growth," Daedalus, Winter, 1961, p. 74.

33. The New York Times, January 7, 1962.

34. Letter to Dr. E. G. Stanley Baker, Drew University, December 21, 1960.

Chapter Six

Form and Function

PUBLIC AUTHORITIES, or special districts, have
come in large numbers in default of action by existing
governments. They have undertaken functions, especially
proprietary enterprises, within the jurisdictional boundaries of these governments which the latter have hesitated
to assume or have been prohibited from doing by constitutional limitations. The great majority of public authorities
therefore have the very same boundary lines as existing
governments, and have merely been superimposed over
municipalities, counties, and states.

Kirk Porter labels this kind of authority, with boundaries coterminous with those of other governments,
"disguised."(1) Its use has resulted, as has been discussed,
in awkward relationships with existing governments, and
its cumulative impact on a given area has served further
to fractionate planning and cooperative efforts at the very
time that coordination is of greatest concern.

The flexibility of the authority, which has given it
advantages unavailable to local governments, or not
realized by them, could have been used in another direction
to encourage joint actions of existing governments through
its ability to form new lines of jurisdiction geographically

151

which, at least in transition, could be of great value.
"There is virtually nothing an authority can do," Tina V.
Weintraub and James D. Patterson concluded after a study
of Pennsylvania authorities, "which could not be done by a
regular unit of government, except where the need exists
to unify functions and services across municipal or state
boundaries."(2) Regular governments have unrealized
powers here, too, through mergers, annexation, and the
like, but the fact remains that the authority-device is
adaptable to pioneering in this regard.

There are dramatic illustrations of their capabilities
in forming new units across present boundaries on a state-
wide, regional, interstate, and international level, and
some locally. Their full potential, especially in united
projects for municipalities and counties, however, has not
yet been tapped.

Illogical Natural Boundaries

A mere glance at the boundary lines of governmental
units anywhere in the United States, with the possible exception of the State lines of California, will reveal the
fact that form has not followed function. Form came first
in the case of our boundary lines, and in a very casual
fashion. As early as 1787 at the Constitutional Convention,
the need to redraw the boundary lines of the states-to-be
was expressed. In the debate on the issue of suffrage in
the national legislature, Judge David Brearly, of New
Jersey, stated: "What remedy then? One only, that a map
of the U.S. be spread out, that all the existing boundaries
be erased, and that a new partition of the whole be made
into 13 equal parts." James Wilson, of Pennsylvania,
replied: "If N.J. will not part with her Sovereignty it is in
vain to talk of Government. A new partition of the States
is desirable, but evidently and totally impracticable."(3)

New Jersey's boundaries were challenged as creating
a "Cask tapped at both ends," inasmuch as New Jersey
was "placed between Philadelphia and New York" in a way
to create that effect.(4) The early deed for the State had
described the territory in terms of features visible on the
incomplete maps of the day:

all the tract of land adjacent to New England and lying and being to the westward of Long Island and Manhitas Island, and bounded on the east part by the main sea, and part by Hudson River and hath upon the west Delaware bay or river, extendeth southward to the main ocean as far as Cape May at the mouth of Delaware bay, and to the north-ward as far as the northernmost branch of the said bay or river of Delaware, which is in 41 degrees and 40 minutes of latitude, and crosseth over thence in a straight line to Hudson's river in forty-one degrees of latitude; which said tract of land is hereafter to be called Nova Caesaria, or New Jersey.(5)

Bodies of water dominated in the description as they could be identified readily on the maps: "the main sea, . . . Hudson River . . . Delaware bay or river, . . . the mouth of Delaware bay, . . . river of Delaware, . . . Hudson's river . . . ." Straight lines of latitude served to provide the lateral boundaries: "41 degrees and 40 minutes of latitude, and crosseth over thence in a straight line to Hudson's river in forty-one degrees of latitude . . . ."

Neither rivers nor straight lines are calculated to enclose homogeneous areas for purposes of government and politics. Rivers, although easy to designate on crude maps, are not dividing lines for a society, but natural forces for unity. Literature is replete with accounts of people in a valley, held together by the common bond of the river. Roscoe Martin and his colleagues at Syracuse University think that this sense of unity is less apparent in the case of Eastern rivers than for those elsewhere in the country, because in the East people in the valley do not appreciate their dependence on water to the same extent as in Western states. Few "persons living in the Delaware Valley are conscious of the fact," they explain. The very fact, however, that from early days the River has been the political dividing line may, in itself, have conditioned the person to not thinking of the valley as a cohesive whole. "There are too many other associations of greater immediate importance to him by which he locates himself— his municipal government, his community, his county, his state, his bus route, his neighborhood, perhaps his parish, and a dozen others."(6)

At any rate, the fact that the cities tended quite naturally to develop along the rivers meant that as they spread
out they not uncommonly stretched across the river and
thereby extended into two states. New York and Philadelphia are, of course, prime illustrations in which arti-
ficial boundary lines prevent a unified city which has
spilled over on both sides of the river. Serving further to
complicate this picture is the fact that most of the rivers
run generally north to south. The population on the other
hand has usually moved from east to west.

The crest of a mountain would have served far better
as a state boundary line than the river. In 1782 Samuel
Livermore, member of Congress from New Hampshire
under the Articles of Confederation, wrote to Meshech
Weare, President of New Hampshire: "Now for a word about
Vermont. If we should extend west of the river to the ridge
of mountains, it must be done with the good will of the
people living between the river and those mountains otherwise the acquisition would cost N.H. more than it is
worth . . . . Nature sets the mountains for the boundary:
And if Vermont shd. be annihilated or rather disallowed
as a state N.Y. will have a share of it, that is, the part
west of the mountains."(7)

James Bryce pointed out that he "who looks at a map
of the Union will be struck by the fact that so many of the
boundary lines of the States are straight lines."(8) They
are "bounded by surveyors' lines," adds a constitutional
historian, ". . . and . . . the particular state, as a rule,
has no personality based on its physiography, its peculiar
character, or its traditions."(9) The straight lines, of
course, were simply appropriations of lines of latitude
and longitude. They cut, as might be expected, arbitrarily
through groups of people and sections of the country.
They were purely artifical lines not based even on tradition or historical events. The Mason and Dixon line, drawn
by Charles Mason and Jeremiah Dixon between 1763 and
1767 to settle a long-standing controversy between Maryland and Pennsylvania, consists of the "parallel latitude
of 39° 43' 26.3" between the southwestern corner of
Pennsylvania and the arc of a circle of 12 miles' radius
drawn from Newcastle (Delaware) as a center, and along
that arc to the Delaware River."(10)

Still other boundary lines developed by sheer caprice. Tradition has it that Staten Island became a part of New York rather than New Jersey through the offer of the Duke of York to make a part of New York any island in the New York Bay that could be circumnavigated within twenty-four hours. A Captain Christopher Billopp is said to have accomplished the sailing around Staten Island in twenty-three hours, thereby affixing it to New York.(11)

The resultant pattern is that of political jurisdictions confined to unrealistic areas and covering only part of communities which spill across their borders. Two large metropolitan cities are just outside the two poles of New Jersey, one to the northeast, the other on the southwest. New York City serves as the core of a standard metropolitan area which consists of Bronx, Kings, Queens, Richmond, Nassau, Rockland, and Westchester Counties in New York State. Philadelphia is the central city of a metropolitan area of Bucks, Chester, Delaware, Montgomery, and Philadelphia, Counties in Pennsylvania, and Burlington, Camden, and Gloucester Counties in New Jersey. Population has pushed out of New York City into Northeastern New Jersey, out onto Long Island, and up into Connecticut. From Philadelphia it has spilled into Camden and surrounding territory in Southwest New Jersey. Industry has stretched between these two poles along the so-called "industrial elbow" of the State which has become a corridor for travel from New England to the South.

Moreover, there are other than natural features which tend to unite people in ways other than those of early boundary lines.

Metropolitan Areas

The area of jurisdiction most discussed today is the metropolitan. This of course is far more difficult to delineate than are those regions centering on natural objects. Planners foresee New York City extending out fifty miles within twenty years, or, some prophesy, one hundred and fifty.

We do have, however, the so-called standard metropolitan area whose definition has been worked out in detail by the Bureau of the Census. Note the precise description so as to include the central city, the central county, and the outlying counties:

(1) The central city:

    (a) One city with 50,000 or more inhabitants, or

    (b) Two cities having contiguous boundaries and constituting, for general economic and social purposes, a single community with a combined population of at least 50,000, the smaller of which must have a population of at least 15,000.

(2) The central county:

The criteria of metropolitan character relate to the attributes of the county as a place of work or as a home for a concentration of nonagricultural workers. Specifically, these criteria are:

...At least 75% of the labor force of the county must be in the non-agricultural labor force.

...In addition...the county must meet at least one of the following conditions:

    (a) It must have 50% or more of its population living in contiguous minor civil divisions with a density of at least 150 persons per square mile, in an unbroken chain of minor civil divisions with such density radiating from a central city in the area.

    (b) The number of nonagricultural workers employed in the county must equal at least 10% of the number of nonagricultural workers employed in the county containing the largest city in the area, or be the place of employment of 10,000 nonagricultural workers.

    (c) The nonagricultural labor force living in the county must equal at least 10% of the number of the nonagricultural labor force living in the county containing the largest city in the area, or be the place of residence of a nonagricultural labor force of 10,000.

(3) The outlying counties:

The criteria of integration relate primarily to the extent of economic and social communication between the outlying counties and central county.

... A county is regarded as integrated with the county or counties containing the central cities of the area if either of the following criteria is met:

(a) If 15% of the workers living in the county work in the county or counties containing central cities of the area, or

(b) If 25% of those working in the county live in the county or counties containing central cities of the area. (12)

In the five States of New Jersey, New York, Pennsylvania, Connecticut, and Delaware, which served as the laboratory for the study of public authorities for purposes of this book, there are 34 of these Standard Metropolitan Statistical Areas, or 15% of all those in the United States. From New Haven, Connecticut, through Wilmington, Delaware, there are fourteen standard metropolitan statistical areas which are contiguous and which comprise a bloc of what Jean Gottmann calls, "Megalopolis," or the spread city from southern New Hampshire to northern Virginia east of the Appalachian mountains. They include New Haven itself, Bridgeport, Norwalk, Stamford, New York City, Paterson-Passaic-Clifton, Jersey City, Newark, Allentown-Bethlehem-Easton, Reading, Philadelphia, Trenton, Atlantic City, and Wilmington.

Whereas the average population density for the United States as a whole in the 1960 census was 50.5, this section of Megalopolis has densities of 517.5 in Connecticut, 350.1 in New York, 806.6 in New Jersey (the highest in the nation), 251.5 in Pennsylvania, and 225.6 in Delaware. The population in the fourteen areas had increased sharply over the reported figures of the 1950 census:

	1960	1950
New Haven	311,681	269,714
Bridgeport	334,576	273,723

	1960	1950
Norwalk	96,756	65,685
Stamford	178,409	134,896
New York	10,694,633	9,555,943
Paterson	1,186,873	876,232
Jersey City	610,734	647,437
Newark	1,689,420	1,468,458
Allentown	492,168	437,824
Reading	275,414	255,740
Philadelphia	4,342,897	3,671,048
Trenton	266,392	229,781
Atlantic City	160,880	132,399
Wilmington	366,157	268,387
Totals	21,006,990	18,287,267

The population increased in the ten-year span by 2,719,723.

The fourteen areas, curiously, are crossed North and South by four main rivers: the Housatonic in Connecticut; Hudson in New York; the Passaic in New Jersey; and the Delaware, which is part of the boundary between New Jersey and Pennsylvania and between New Jersey and Delaware.

If one could ignore traditions established by long-standing boundary lines in these five States, and in their counties and municipalities, therefore, he would find available other possibilities, both natural and man-made, which could conceivably serve as jurisdictional units for governmental purposes. James W. Fesler insists that "we can define the cotton area, the river valley, the urban settlement area, and the cut-over forest area," and that "an integrated governmental attack on the problem of each such area is most successful if the attack is under the generalship of a government whose territorial jurisdiction embraces the whole of the natural area."(13)

Superimposition of Authorities

It is precisely at this point that public authorities have the advantage. They do not disturb in any way existing boundary lines. Rather, they are superimposed over existing units of government, taking from them perhaps certain functions but leaving them otherwise intact. Traditions are not disturbed, and political and governmental entities are not interfered with. It is not necessary to erase any of the lines of the two States, seventeen counties, and 219 municipalities, which are included within its jurisdiction, in order to establish the Port of New York Authority. Instead, one starts with New York harbor as a natural phenomenon upon which the interests and livelihood of some 13,000,000 people depend. Then, regardless of the boundary lines of the States, counties, and municipalities, the charter specifies that the Port Authority shall have jurisdiction over functions related to the port within a radius of some twenty-five miles of the Statue of Liberty. Each of the two States whose boundary lines have been bridged are then allowed to be represented on the Board of Commissioners of the Authority with six Commissioners.

Within the twenty-five mile radius the Port Authority begins to acquire or construct facilities for accomplishing the purposes for which it has been created. In this way the Port Authority comes not to embrace geographically the entire area, but functionally its many facilities. Its projects are not even contiguous, but scattered here and there. The Port Authority is the Brooklyn, Jersey City, Elizabeth, and Newark piers; truck terminals at Newark and New York; a bus terminal at West 40th and 41st Streets between 8th and 9th Avenues and one at the New York side of the George Washington Bridge; a freight terminal between West 15th and 16th Streets; the Bayonne Bridge, Goethals Bridge, Outerbridge Crossing, and George Washington Bridge; the Holland and Lincoln Tunnels; LaGuardia, Newark, Kennedy International, and Teterboro Airports; the West 30th Street Heliport; and other such facilities. Indeed, it has come to include also offices for trade development purposes in Washington, D.C.; Chicago; Cleveland; and Pittsburgh; and overseas in London; Zurich; Rio de Janeiro; and San Juan, Puerto Rico.

In broader perspective, the Port of New York Authority may be visualized as centering on the port as a natural object. Then, ignoring the State boundary line which

bisects it between New York and New Jersey along the
center of the Hudson River, the Authority proceeds to
develop the port as a unit. It constructs seaports around
the harbor, at Brooklyn, Hoboken, Jersey City, Elizabeth,
and Newark. It constructs airports around the harbor at
Idlewild, Teterboro, LaGuardia, and Newark. It proceeds
from this basic structure to make possible transportation
to and from the port by bridges and tunnels connecting
New York and New Jersey. Finally it erects terminals for
handling the traffic in buses and freight which it has
moved into the port district.

Through the Port Authority's overlooking of the boundary lines, the New York harbor, "one of the greatest
natural harbors in the world," has become the hub for a
vast functional unit of government. As a bi-state unit it
concerns itself with functions related to the development
of the port of interest to people within its twenty-five mile
radius, regardless of their State citizenship.

The same basic concept — that of a functional unit of
government radiating out from a central harbor -- serves
as the basis for the more recently established Port
Authority at Philadelphia, the Delaware River Port Authority. There, the sweep of the Authority's jurisdiction over
all of South Jersey and two counties in Pennsylvania is
more comprehensive than even that of the Port of New
York Authority. In addition to the two bridges, Walt Whit-
man and Ben Franklin, under its control, the Delaware
River Port Authority envisaged a high-speed transit line
from 16th Street in Philadelphia out to Camden, Collings-
wood, Westmont, Haddonfield, Ashland, and Kirkwood, in
New Jersey.

The two Port Authorities have recognized the essential
unity of an area dependent on a natural harbor, but, at
the same time, the polarity of interests of the two separate
ports. Each separately takes advantage of its own particular natural focal point.

A wider-view lens, focused on the whole segment,
or bloc, of Megalopolis chosen for this study, would discern
other authorities which center on factors of nature or

interests. The New Jersey industrial corridor, cutting diagonally through the State, connecting New England and the South, serves as the route of the New Jersey Turnpike under the jurisdiction of the New Jersey Turnpike Authority. This makes possible a transfer of part of the costs of the Turnpike to the users who are merely passing through the State, and relieves those residents of New Jersey of much of its financial responsibility.

Furthermore, the New Jersey Turnpike becomes another link in the chain of public authorities which enable a motorist to drive on turnpikes from Boston to Chicago. Starting at Boston, with the new extension of the Massachusetts Turnpike Authority, thence across the Massachusetts Turnpike Authority to the New York Thruway Authority (as Connecticut does not have turnpike authorities), the motorist becomes further dependent on Authorities as he moves westward: the New Jersey Turnpike Authority, Pennsylvania Turnpike Authority, and Turnpike Commissions of Ohio, Indiana, and Illinois, lead him into Chicago.

Two ports, and the industrial elbow, have been used by public authorities to supersede the more conventional but less rational boundary lines of existing governments. In addition, a River valley comprises the natural area for the Passaic Valley Sewer Authority. Three municipalities, Lavallette, Seaside Heights, and Seaside Park, are joined in one Incinerator Authority. In Pennsylvania, two counties, Lehigh and Northampton, are cooperating in an Airport Authority. The northwest Bergen County Sewer Authority consists of part of a County.

Various public authorities have taken the Delaware River as the focal point of their activities, although the Hudson River has not been so used. In addition to the Delaware River Port Authority, there is a separate Authority, the South Jersey Port District formed in 1926 to enter into contracts with municipalities and counties within the Port District to finance port projects. Included in the District are the New Jersey Counties of Burlington, Camden, Cape May, Cumberland, Gloucester, Mercer, and Salem. The Delaware River Joint Toll Bridge Commission is still another Authority based on the River, this one formed by

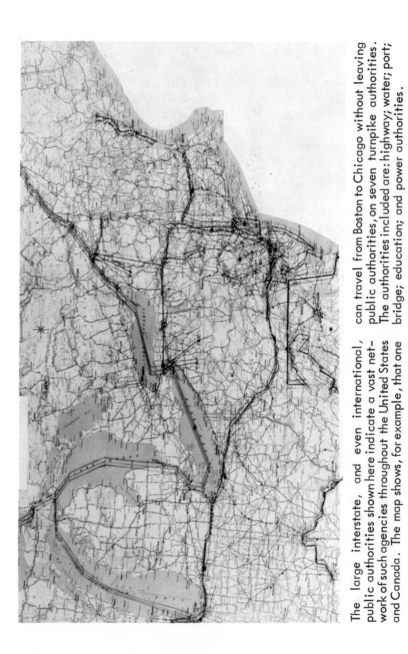

The large interstate, and even international, public authorities shown here indicate a vast network of such agencies throughout the United States and Canada. The map shows, for example, that one can travel from Boston to Chicago without leaving public authorities, on seven turnpike authorities. The authorities included are: highway; water; port; bridge; education; and power authorities.

compact between New Jersey and Pennsylvania in 1934 and amended in 1953. It has the task of operating and maintaining all the State-owned Free Bridges over the Delaware River North of Stone Arch Railroad Bridge between Trenton and Morrisville, and creating, maintaining, and operating, new and additional facilities necessary to the public interest. Its part of the Delaware River runs from the line dividing Philadelphia County from Bucks County on the South, to the boundary line between New Jersey and New York, to the North. Its jurisdictional lines include Bucks, Monroe, Northampton, and Pike Counties, in Pennsylvania, and, in New Jersey, Burlington, Mercer, Hunterdon, Warren, and Sussex Counties.

The Delaware River Basin Commission is the most ambitious cooperative agency based on the Delaware River. Its jurisdiction encompasses the entire basin of the River in a comprehensive program of water distribution, flood control, recreation, generation of hydro-electricity, and the like. Here, again, the difficulties of defining such varied agencies so as to classify them, makes the inclusion of this Commission under the term, authority, a moot point. It has certainly many of the characteristics in its ability to work across existing boundary lines, use methods of its own choosing, float revenue bonds, charge for its services, and operate under a board of commissioners. On the other hand, it may use capital funds provided by the signatory parties for specific projects on a cost-sharing plan. Its board in its method of composition is unique in the history of such agencies in that it makes the United States Government almost a co-equal partner with each of the individual States of Delaware, New Jersey, New York, and Pennsylvania, respectively. Each has one commissioner and one vote. The commissioner representing the United States is appointed by the President of the United States and serves during the latter's term of office.

Conrad L. Wirth, Director of the National Park Service, predicted that this Commission would become a "blueprint for the nation and the world to follow."

This board representation, about which certain officials of the United States Government expressed concern in that

the United States had no more power than any one of the
States, resulted in the addition to the Compact of certain
provisions to protect federal prerogatives, such as: the
stipulation that nothing is to be construed as a derogation
of Congress' power over interstate commerce; Congress
retains the right to withdraw the United States from participation in the Commission or to amend the provisions;
"the Delaware River Basin Commission shall not undertake any project (as defined in such compact), other than a
project for which State supplied funds only will be used,
beyond the planning stage" until it has submitted it to Congress; nothing shall be deemed to restrict the emergency
powers of the President; nothing shall impair the powers
of the President in regard to budgetary and appropriation
matters; nothing "contained in the Compact shall be construed to obligate the United States legally or morally to
pay the principal or interest on any bonds issued by the ...
Commission"; all "laborers and mechanics employed by
contractors or subcontractors ... shall be paid wages at
rates not less than those prevailing on similar construction
in the locality so determined by the Secretary of Labor...";
nothing "shall impair or affect the constitutional authority
of the United States ... in and over the area or waters
which are the subject of the Compact."(14)

The use of the revenue-bond method of finance, and the
degree of independence which the Commission enjoys as
it gets further along in its projects will determine better
whether it meets the terms of the standard definition of
authorities. Its prospects in these regards lead the author
to conclude that it does not at this point of time resemble
a public authority, as defined for purposes of this book, and
therefore should not be included under the term, authority.
Its relationships to public authorities in the area of its
jurisdiction, the river valley, however, make it a pertinent
agency for consideration in this chapter.

Coterminous Boundaries

On the local level such new jurisdictional units are not
unknown, but the development on this level has been less
than spectacular. Indicative of the infrequent resort to
combinations are typical statistics of the trend in the

counties in Pennsylvania, where authorities abound. A characteristic County, Montgomery County, outside Philadelphia, shows the following:(15)

Municipal Authorities	Total Number	Joint Authorities
School	46	17
Water.	5	0
Sewer.	22	2
Multi-purpose	2	0
Parking	3	0
Airport.	0	0
Miscellaneous	2	0
Unknown purpose . . .	2	0
Totals	82	19

Only 23% are authorities in the County in which more than one municipality have joined with another, and all but two of them were for the purpose of building schools on a lease-back basis.

Enabling legislation of most states encourages public authorities to unite municipalities or counties in joint projects. The State Law of New Jersey for County and Municipal Sewerage Authorities is similar to many such attempts. It provides for sewerage authorities for "counties, or municipalities either separately or in combination with other municipalities." It allows, too, for a county sewerage authority to enter into a contract with "one or more municipalities situate within any other county" and to add to the sewerage authority one additional member for each such other county who "shall be a resident of one of said municipalities situate within such other county."

Arrangements for a joint-municipal sewerage authority are made easy, requiring merely for "parallel ordinances duly adopted by each of such governing bodies within any single year . . . ." The ordinances would specify the number of members to be on the authority for each such municipality, but it "shall be not less than one nor more than three."

If a municipality of the county in which a sewerage authority is being established already belongs to such an authority in another county, the "area within the territorial limits of such municipality shall not be part of the district of the sewerage authority of said county." After the formation of the country authority no municipality of that county is allowed to join the sewerage authority of another county except upon the written consent of the sewerage authority of its home county.

Upon the establishment of a county sewerage authority a copy of the resolution creating the authority shall be filed with the clerk of each municipality in the county. A municipality then has sixty days after the filing of the certification of the county authority in the office of the Secretary of State to file a resolution of its own stating that it does not want to be included in the county authority. The municipality may later change its mind and join by filing a resolution to this effect with the Secretary of State, but then "the area within the territorial limits of such municipality shall forever be part of such district."(16)

Despite this encouragement, however, joint sewerage authorities in New Jersey are the exception. Only four are listed for the State in the Annual Report of the Division of Local Government for 1960, but the Division is unable to provide a complete listing of authorities: "The Division has no authority over the budgets of these agencies (public authorities) but does receive copies of annual audits. Thus, the information is only as complete as the reporting thereof."(17)

Connecticut has provided for planning authorities which require memberships by more than one town, city, or borough. As the name, Regional Planning Agencies, implies, two or more municipalities are necessary to achieve its purpose. Even then, "the total number of representatives of such towns, cities or boroughs shall equal 60 per cent or more of the total number of representatives possible of all the towns, cities or boroughs within such region...."(18)

Each municipality on it has two representatives with one additional for each 50,000 persons above 25,000 population. A member municipality may withdraw from the Authority but must give six-months' notice and meet all outstanding obligations. The Regional Planning Agency ceases to exist if the total number of representatives of the member towns, cities, or boroughs is less than 40 per cent of the possible number of such municipalities within the planning region.

Federal legislation, which since the days of the New Deal, has been a great boon to the creation of local public authorities, has from the beginning encouraged their use on a broader scale than existing local governments.(19)

By 1942, William Anderson could report that the great increase in special districts (under which he includes public authorities) was attributable largely to the influence of the Federal Government. "The United States Housing Authority and the Soil Conservation Service ... backed by substantial appropriations made by Congress for aid to local units in their respective ventures, have been mainly responsible for propagating these new species of local units." Without these two types, he explained, the number of special districts actually would have declined by 800, or 10%, from 1930-33 to 1941. He did not approve of the Federal Government's success in this regard, for its "first important venture into the local government arena has resulted in increasing the numbers of local units and in further complicating the structure of local government."(20)

The Federal Housing Act of 1949 directed the administrator to "encourage the operations of such local public agencies as are established on a State, or regional (within a State), or unified metropolitan basis or as are established on such other basis as permits such agencies to contribute effectively toward the solution of community development or redevelopment problems."(21)

More recent federal legislation has enhanced the possibilities for larger units and merger of units for specific purposes through, for one thing, the public-authority concept.

Duplication

Here, however, the authorities run into problems not of their own making. Paradoxically, their greatest advantage, that of being created without disturbing the traditional boundary lines of other units of government, may well be considered also their greatest weakness. What real advantage is there in getting one established if it is to become just another unit of government in an already bewildering maze of units of government? None of the standard maps show public authorities, not even the Federal Government's maps of minor civil divisions. A special map of authorities, used as the frontispiece for this book, reveals clearly the hundreds of new lines of jurisdiction caused by the addition of public authorities to a region.

Do the four public authorities responsible for transportation in New York City, each with fairly consistent jurisdictions, not lose something of their effect when it is considered that there are also eight other city agencies responsible for transportation there, as well as one regulatory agency, three State agencies, six private bus companies, and seven commuter railroads? Is there not a point of diminishing returns beyond which the addition of more units will become increasingly less effective? The prospects for the new Delaware River Basin Commission in unifying the entire valley certainly dim somewhat when one is reminded that already operating in the Basin are 895 governments, and that these will continue to function completely. Is it actually an accomplishment for the Port of New York Authority to extend its functions without disturbing the existing 1400 governments of metropolitan New York?

Rare is it, indeed, when officials, in creating a public authority, abolish any other governmental unit. Not only are none of the 895 governments in the Delaware Valley abrogated by the formation of the broad comprehensive Basin Commission, but neither are several hundred other public authorities which are now incorporated within its borders. Prior to the drawing of the Compact for this multi-purpose River agency, the Syracuse University Research Institute analyzed the Basin in considerable detail, and reported in 1959 the "tendency toward fractionalization of administrative programs" in the Basin with some "252 water supply enterprises in the valley, ... the great majority (of which) are governmental in nature." Many of these are public authorities or special districts, although the Institute admitted

that "an enumeration...of the programs pursued through
(these) special districts" was "difficult."(22)

The Compact does not abolish any of the existing authorities or special districts, but it does recognize their
existence and complications. It attempts to effect a better
coordination of these projects in the Valley among "the
signatory states, their political subdivisions and public
corporations affecting water resources of the basin." They
may continue to exist: "Each state and local agency...
shall continue to have, exercise and discharge such authority, except as specifically provided" therein. The exception,
is worthy of note:

> No project having a substantial effect on the water re-
> sources of the basin shall hereafter be undertaken by any
> person, corporation or governmental authority unless it
> shall have been first submitted to and approved by the
> commission.... The commission shall approve a project
> whenever it finds and determines that such project would
> not substantially impair or conflict with the comprehen-
> sive plan and may modify and approve as modified, or
> may disapprove any such project whenever it finds and
> determines that the project would substantially impair
> or conflict with such plan. The commission shall provide
> by regulation for the procedure of submission, review
> and consideration of projects, and for its determinations
> pursuant to this section. Any determination of the com-
> mission hereunder shall be subject to judicial review in
> any court of competent jurisdiction.(23)

The very success of the proponents of the Delaware
River Basin Commission in getting such an agency approved
and underway may well give rise to other such projects
in the area. As soon as it became apparent that the multi-
purpose Delaware undertaking was to become a reality, a
meeting of persons interested in the possibility of creating
such a Commission on the Susquehanna River was held in
August, 1961, in Wilkes-Barre, Pennsylvania. It was addressed, significantly, by the Executive Director of the
Water Resources Association of the Delaware River Basin,
who spoke on how to organize a Water Resources Association to influence the formation of a Basin authority. The
Philadelphia Evening Bulletin applauded this move

editorially: "The inexcusable pollution of a large stretch of the Susquehanna River points up the need for regional attention to the control and development of the entire Susquehanna River Basin such as now will be given to the Delaware River Basin under the recently-approved federal-interstate compact."(24)

Speaking of the Delaware River Basin Compact, the Poughkeepsie Journal prophesied: "If it works out well -- as it could -- it may point the way out of the jungle of conflict and confusion which frustrates regional attack on regional problems like water resources development, urban sprawl, mass transportation."(25)

In September, 1961, it was announced that the Lower Bucks County Development Corporation, the Lower Bucks County Chamber of Commerce, and the Bucks County Board of Commissioners had joined forces in a campaign to establish a county port authority on the Delaware River between Morrisville and Levittown. They later decided to consider also the alternative of joining with the Delaware River Port Authority instead of creating their own County Authority. "Bucks Countians," said the Evening Bulletin, "these days are looking more intently at the Delaware River than ever before."(26)

These agencies thus compound the elaborate network of governments by several of them using the same factor of nature or interest as their nucleus. The Delaware River seems appropriately suited to the purposes of the Delaware River Basin Commission. But it seems equally well suited to the purposes of the Delaware River Port Authority, or the South Jersey Port District, or the Delaware River Joint Toll Bridge Commission. The New Jersey Turnpike Authority seems ideally well qualified to deal with the problem of the corridor nature of the State with persons crossing through it from New England to the South, but the Turnpike Authority in turn cuts right through the boundaries of a number of other public authorities, such as the Port of New York Authority, the Middlesex County Sewer Authority, South Jersey Port Commission, Delaware River Port Authority, and the Camden County Improvement Authority when it had existed. The Port of New York Authority has had within its boundaries even another Port Authority, at Keansburg, New Jersey.

Connecticut resisted building turnpikes until the New York turnpikes and the New Jersey Turnpike dumped thousands of cars literally into the streets of the small towns of that State. The New Jersey Turnpike Authority, as do many turnpikes, barges right through metropolitan areas, making metropolitan planning even more difficult. The Turnpike slices through the Paterson and Newark Metropolitan Areas in the North and the Philadelphia and Wilmington Metropolitan Areas to the South. The New York Thruway and Westchester turnpikes segment the Northern section of the New York Metropolitan Area.

The Port of New York Authority "has become strongly identified with a single metropolitan area though it sprawls across state lines," but even its boundary lines have not kept pace with the metropolitan "explosion," and they now need redrawing. They twice divide the New York Metropolitan Area, bisect the Paterson Metropolitan Area and the Newark one, and add a corner out of Middlesex and Monmouth Counties of New Jersey which are not in metropolitan areas.

A bill to enlarge the boundaries of the Port Authority to include Morris County had been introduced into the State Assembly by the two Morris County Assemblymen in 1959. The bill would have extended the boundaries widely, to include, in New Jersey, "the remaining portions of the counties of Bergen, Passaic, Morris, Union, Middlesex and Monmouth" and "the counties of Somerset and Mercer," and, in New York State, "the remaining portion of the county of Rockland" and "the county of Orange."(27) This would have filled out the Authority's lines to include all of the metropolitan areas of Jersey City and Paterson-Passaic-Clifton and Newark, and the northern part of the New York Metropolitan Area. It would have included, as well, however, the Counties of Middlesex and Monmouth, in New Jersey, and Orange County, in New York State, which are not within any metropolitan areas.

The Delaware River Port Authority lines are far more realistically drawn, having been devised much later than those of the Port of New York Authority (1952 as against

1921), but even they leave out of the Port area Montgomery and Bucks Counties, which are a part of the Philadelphia Metropolitan Area.

Fractionization

What matter is it, if, each performing its own function, their lines of jurisdiction do criss-cross, as has been indicated? Why should one of them, dedicated to its own specific function, consider the other, if each in itself is capable of accomplishing its purpose? If the New Jersey Turnpike Authority meets the needs occasioned by the corridor-nature of New Jersey, what does it matter that it cuts through several other public authorities? If each of the various authorities centering on the Delaware River performs its particular function of bridges, ports, or water resources, why be concerned that they all use the same natural factor?

The concern is that these many authorities by their sheer numbers may be fractionating an area, rather than using their advantage of overriding existing boundaries to form more logical governmental units. "Freezing a single function or activity into an authority may prevent the unification of all government," commented the late Carl H. Chatters. "(A) careful look ahead is needed in any metropolitan area before the 'fractionating' is frozen even more thoroughly into the governmental structure."(28)

In a news analysis of the jetport controversy in Morris County, the New York *Times* noted the handicaps under which the Port of New York Authority was operating: The "Port Authority operates in effect with blinders on. It is an ad hoc agency, charged with limited, specific duties. No matter how well it discharges them, the authority is not necessarily taking the 'big look' at regional requirements." The 'big look' would require, it explained, answers to the following questions:

> Are there other regional needs, such as recreation or open space, home areas or industry, for which the 10,000 acres would be better suited?

> How is the proposed site served by the region's transportation network, present and proposed?

Does it create new regional problems even as it meets an obvious present need?

Are there better sites further removed from the Port Authority's jurisdiction that would serve the region — and perhaps even a substantially larger area — to better purpose?(29)

In the segment of Megalopolis under concern in this book, only a very few of the public authorities have this area-wide possibility. Closest to it, of course, are the two large multi-purpose port authorities and the Delaware River Basin Commission. If it were to gear its boundaries to standard metropolitan areas, the Port of New York Authority would need to expand its present boundaries, and, as a matter of fact, the inclusion of Morris County which would have been necessary had the decision been made to locate the jetport there, would have been consistent with the inclusion of counties in metropolitan areas within its boundaries. The Delaware River Port Authority would need to add only Montgomery and Bucks Counties in Pennsylvania, and drop Ocean City in New Jersey. The Delaware River Basin Commission encompasses the entire River basin, and has projected a plan for a service area, based on the needs of water from the Delaware River, over fifty-three counties in five States (or, more properly, fifty-two counties and the town area of Fairfield, Connecticut having abolished its counties).

If the Lehigh-Northampton Airport Authority were to extend over into New Jersey and include Warren County, it would encompass the actual standard metropolitan area of Allentown-Bethlehem-Easton.

With these few exceptions, authorities in this segment appear to be unaware of the regional or area problem.

Mergers of authorities are exceptional, but not unknown. The Triborough Bridge and Tunnel Authority developed in such a way. "In 1933 the Triborough Bridge Authority was created. In 1934 the Henry Hudson Parkway Authority and the Marine Parkway Authority were created. In 1938 these two parkways were consolidated into the New York City Parkway Authority which, in turn, was merged with the

Triborough Bridge Authority in 1940. In 1935 the Queens-
Midtown Tunnel Authority was created, but in 1936 it was
superseded by the New York City Tunnel Authority which
was consolidated with the Triborough Bridge Authority in
1946 to form the Triborough Bridge and Tunnel Authority."(30)

The Delaware River Port Authority was the successor
of the Delaware River Joint Commission which had been
preceded by the Delaware River Joint Bridge Commission.

In February, 1962, the New York State Joint Legislative
Committee on Docks in the City of New York, recommended
the creation of a State Port Council to coordinate the activities of the State's six major ports, at New York City,
Buffalo, Rochester, Oswego, Ogdensburg, and Albany.

Rather than cooperative mergers, however, the tendency
has been for competitive relationships. Where mergers
have occurred local jealousies often have mitigated their
efforts. The Parkways of Westchester County, just North
of New York City, are a case in point. The County is tra-
versed by numerous parkways, such as the Cross County,
Hutchinson, Saw Mill River, Taconic Park, and Sprain
Brook. They have proved to be a major concern to Westchester County officials, so much so that in 1957 the Westchester County Parkways were merged into one Authority,
known as the Westchester Parkway Authority. This agency,
however, lacked the borrowing capacity necessary for extensive repairs to the roads, and it engaged in occasional
conflict with the elected County officials. In 1960, therefore, plans were completed for merging the Westchester
Parkway Authority with the Taconic State and Sprain Brook
Parkways, over a period of years, into the State East Hudson
Parkway Authority. The Hutchinson River, Cross County,
and Saw Mill River, Parkways became parts of the new
Authority from its beginning on February 1, 1961; the
Taconic State joined it on April 1, 1961; and the Sprain
Brook Parkway later that summer.

The results, however, did not please residents of Dutchess County, two Counties to the North of Westchester,
through which the Taconic State runs and into which traffic

flows from the former Westchester Parkways through Putnam County. The parochialism, which makes mergers difficult, is evidenced in the opposition of the Poughkeepsie Journal in December of 1961, shortly after the completion of the merger:

> Accompanied by much fanfare the 1960 Legislature set up the East Hudson Parkway authority, on the recommendation of Governor Rockefeller....
>
> We in Dutchess were dubious about the East Hudson authority from the start as it took jurisdiction of the Taconic parkway from under the control of Paul T. Winslow and the Taconic Parkway commission. Both Mr. Winslow and Howland Davis, commission chairman, have deep roots in Dutchess and we knew both would uphold county interests at all times....
>
> Events which have transpired since the enactment of the East Hudson legislation have proved that our original fears were well grounded....
>
> ... (W)ork on the Taconic parkway extension to the Berkshire Thruway spur has been practically at a standstill since the East Hudson authority was superimposed on the Taconic commission, lending strength to the suspicion that the new body is far more concerned about Westchester than it is in completing the long-overdue Taconic links....

Authority Cooperation

With the exception of the municipal authorities in Pennsylvania there has been little indication of an "authorities awareness" even by authority members themselves. By their common core of functions in an area, they constantly come into contact with each other. When, for instance, Mayor Robert Wagner of New York City imposed a ban on the use of private cars and commercial vehicles in the City because of a heavy snowfall on February 1, 1961, a total of 5,552,442 persons rode the subways, an increase of approximately 1,000,000 people, thereby swelling the coffers of the New York City Transit Authority. By the same action, however, the Port of New York Authority and the Triborough

Bridge and Tunnel Authority lost heavily as cars did not use their facilities into the City. The Port Authority's annual report for the year showed that for the first time in years traffic using its bridges and tunnels fell off, from 96,207,000 in 1960, down to 95,654,283 for 1961. The ban on auto traffic for the week of the snowstorm was blamed.

With the opening of the second deck on the George Washington Bridge by the Port of New York Authority it is estimated that 20,000,000 passengers a year will use the bus station on the New York side of the Bridge. Many of these persons will use also the Eighth Avenue IND subway to and from Manhattan. The Port Authority has constructed an underground passageway between the bus station and the West 177th Street Station of the Eighth Avenue line, but the New York Transit Authority will have the responsibility of transporting this greatly increased crowd of subway riders daily.

One rather compelling argument for a bi-state, multi-purpose authority is that, in viewing the port district, for example, as a whole, it can so arrange facilities of common functions that they will not be competing but will be co-ordinated. Before the Port of New York Authority leased the Newark Airport from the City of Newark, for instance, and worked it into the coordinated airport plan involving LaGuardia, Kennedy International, and Teterboro Airports, the competition between the Newark Airport and LaGuardia Airport had almost crippled the former. Now, after its arrangement by the Port Authority in its coordinated pattern, it is a thriving enterprise. Competition within the Port district has been replaced by cooperation.

On the other hand, when the Delaware River Port Authority was created in 1952 for the coordination of certain activities in the Philadelphia-Camden region, it came into sharp competition with the Port of New York Authority. The two large Port Authorities, both created to effect coordination within their respective districts, now have become engaged in vigorous competition between themselves. Furthermore, both of these two Port Authorities are opponents of the St. Lawrence Seaway Authority as it seeks to divert traffic away from New York City and Philadelphia ports to the Seaway. As units based essentially on large economic enterprises, public authorities have competition built into their very functions.

Conflicts among authorities occur at all levels. In Jersey City in 1961 the Jersey City Housing Authority refused to pay a bill of $169,731 to the Jersey City Sewer Authority for sewage disposal services. The latter Authority would not agree with the Housing Authority that, as an authority, it was exempt from taxes and special assessments and that these were included in the bill. The State Superior Court ruled that the disposal charges are a "fee" and that therefore the Housing Authority would have to pay and at the regular schedule of rates.

It was not until 1962, ten years after the New Jersey Highway Authority had been created to run the Garden State Parkway, that it and the New Jersey Turnpike Authority began to work together at all cooperatively, despite the fact that the roads of these two separate Authorities intersect. New Jersey places its authorities within Departments, even though they are autonomous, and therefore both the Turnpike and the Parkway are within the Department of Highways. However, despite these points of contact, only recently have the two Authorities begun to work out mutual programs.

Even this newfound cooperation does not answer the more fundamental question, however, as to why these two Authorities could not consolidate. They are in charge of two highways, both entirely within the one State; and they are within the same State Department. Why, for example, should the New Jersey Highway authority have opened its own $1,000,000 administration building in 1961, just ten miles from the administration building of the New Jersey Tunrpike Authority? Why should there not be cooperative maintenance and snow removal; why should there be salaries for two Executive Directors, at $29,500 for the Director of the Turnpike Authority, and $19,000 for the Director of the New Jersey Highway Authority; why not joint administrative, legal and accounting departments; why may the surplus of the Turnpike not be used to help offset the deficit of the Parkway? Governor Meyner of New Jersey once said

Newark Evening News, February 1, 1960.

that he favored the shift of surplus from the Turnpike to the Parkway, but that there were legal and financial obstacles to its achievement. He thought that "it might be necessary to retire outstanding bonds of both authorities. To do so... might require possibly 800 million dollars and... the premium for premature retirement of turnpike bonds alone might run to 39 million."(31) The bondholder has his commitments. Turnpike bonds are not backed by the State, but Garden State Parkway bonds have the State's full faith and credit.

The New Jersey turnpike problem was further complicated by the creation in 1962 of the New Jersey Expressway Authority to construct the Atlantic City Expressway from Camden to Atlantic City. Even though this new Expressway will cut through both the New Jersey Turnpike and the Garden State Parkway, the New Jersey Expressway Authority is again a separate and distinct unit comprising the third highway authority in the one State.

Conflicts with Governments

Not only do authorities run into conflicts among themselves, but their relationships with existing governments, as might be expected in view of the fact they are superimposed over the latter, are often awkward. This can be seen on all levels.

In 1961 the Borough Council of Somerville, New Jersey, rejected an application by the Township of Bridgewater for permission for a right of way through some two miles of Somerville for the construction of a gravity sewer line. The line would connect with the trunk line of the Somerset-Raritan Valley Sewerage Authority to which both Somerville and Bridgewater belonged.

In the stalemate which ensued, the Bridgewater Township Committee hit upon the idea of constituting a Sewerage Authority of its own, which it did in November of 1962, with the Mayor and members of the Committee as the board for the new Authority. The advantage of the Authority for Bridgewater's struggle with Somerville was that as an Authority, the Bridgewater Board now gained powers of eminent domain over the wider area which it did not have beyond its borders as a Township. The State enabling legislation stipulates that every sewerage authority is empowered to "take for public use real property, within or without the district, which may be deemed by the sewerage authority necessary for its purposes ...."

This power placed Somerville in the position of bearing the burden of proof in the quarrel. After a protracted fight the Bridgewater Sewerage Authority was granted the right to run the line under the land of Somerville in return for a fee of $25,000 for the privilege, and an additional deposit in escrow to insure repairs of damages of another $25,000.

Instead of complementary planning and action, public authorities tend to become obsessed with their single function, or limited purposes, to the exclusion of broader considerations. They pursue these purposes relentlessly. Such preoccupation is made almost mandatory by the promises made to the bondholders that for the period of their bonds nothing will be permitted to interfere with the project for which the bonds were issued.

Transitions to Larger Units

In the retrospect of future years, however, it may just be that public authorities will be credited with a principal role in leading the country toward more logical jurisdictional units of government. Although disappointing to date in fulfilling this potential, certain of them at least have dared to experiment with regional jurisdictions which have much to be said for them. It may even be seen, from the perspective of years hence, that the authorities first pointed us toward more realistic concepts of the metropolitan area. While not accepting the full leap to the metro, they may at least have suggested intermediate levels, such as the county or federation, as necessary compromises.

Noteworthy in this regard is the fact that public authorities are intimately involved in any of the proposed metropolitan solutions: metropolitan multi-purpose district, federation, urban county, contracts, city-county consolidation, and the others.

Public authorities have called attention to the county as a level for functional integration. They have taken functions normally performed individually by municipalities and have transferred them to county-wide authorities. The numbers of county authorities are significant, as are the range of functions that they incorporate, such as water, airports, recreation, improvements, ports, sewerage, and other vital activities. A rather common procedure is for the State enabling legislation to blanket into a county authority all municipalities in the County unless the municipality files within a specified time a resolution objecting to membership therein.

To be sure, this concentration on the county level is fragmentary and may well serve only further to fractionate the county. On the other hand, it may so accustom the residents in turning to the county for their needs that that level could take on increased significance. When, in 1958, the Metropolitan Study Commission of Allegheny County (Pittsburgh) recommended the establishment there of an urban, metropolitan county, it suggested a list of things that should be done as prerequisite thereto. One of the "most important," it said, "is unification of thirty-nine individual transit systems into a county transit authority."(32)

The duration of the experiment has been too short for us to determine whether public authorities will lead toward more realism in regard to jurisdictional boundaries, or rather to a further fractionization of the whole metropolitan scene. William B. Shore sees some encouragement for conceiving of them as transitional means to a desired end; in them, he thinks, is the possibility for approaching a metropolitan government through consolidation of special-purpose governments.

It may be worthy of note that, in the few instances in which metropolitan governments have been organized in the United States, certain public authorities have survived and have been incorporated into the new comprehensive plan.

Although Dade County, Florida, chose to utilize the existing county government for its new Metro, or "Metropolitan Dade County," rather than "create an additional

layer of government such as an authority or special purpose district to provide area-wide services,"(33) it did
continue in effect the Dade County Port Authority for airport development but with the same Board of Commissioners
as the new Metropolitan County. The Charter of Metropolitan Dade County empowers the Board of County Commissioners to:

> establish, merge, and abolish special purpose districts
> within which may be provided police and fire protection,
> beach erosion control, recreation facilities, water,
> streets, sidewalks, street lighting, waste and sewage
> collection and disposal, drainage, and other essential
> facilities and services.... The Board of County Com-
> missioners shall be the governing body of all such dis-
> tricts and when acting as such governing body shall have
> the same jurisdiction and powers as when acting as the
> Board.(34)

The Charter for the Metropolitan Government of Nashville and Davidson County, Tennessee, adopted in 1962, provides specifically for the continuation of the Nashville
Transit Authority and the Nashville Housing Authority. The
"Nashville Transit Authority," according to the Charter,
"shall continue to exist and to function as an agency of the
Metropolitan Government." Although vacancies on the
three-member Board of the Transit Authority are to be
filled by the Metropolitan Mayor, the "entire and complete
supervision, regulation, jurisdiction and control over street
railway companies operating within the Metropolitan Government area, shall be vested solely in and exercised solely
by the Transit Authority." "Neither the Metropolitan Mayor,
the Metropolitan Council, nor any other officer or agency
of the Metropolitan Government shall have or exercise any
authority whatsoever over such street railway companies
or over the Transit Authority," except for appointments
and the like. "The Nashville Housing Authority ... is hereby recognized as existing and functioning within the area
of the Metropolitan Government and as having the same
relationship to the Metropolitan Government as said Nashville Housing Authority previously had to the City of Nashville."(35)

"A Policies Plan for the Year 2000" for Washington,
D.C., envisages the possible need "to establish a new

division of local government (perhaps on Urban Development Agency) in each outlying jurisdiction" to perform functions of assembling land, setting the overall pattern of development, and arranging for the necessary utilities and public works. "Such an agency would also serve as a means of reaping for the public the increased land values resulting from the decision to concentrate development at given locations, thereby providing some funds for the public works and services needed by the new cities."(36)

The "Plan for Improvement" of Louisville, Kentucky, in 1956, called for the annexation of forty-six square miles of territory to the City of Louisville. "There was to be extension of public services to the annexed area in the shortest time possible, as well as extension of the Metropolitan Sewer District sewer trunks throughout the area merged with Louisville."(37)

For the "Greater St. Louis City-County District" of 1959, which was to have absorbed the "existing Metropolitan St. Louis Sewer District" into a new multipurpose district, the very core of the plan had been the expansion of this already existing special district.(38)

In plans for federation within metropolitan areas public authorities play a prominent role. Luther Gulick's proposal for federated municipal councils, in 1957, envisaged representative metropolitan councils to administer or supervise specific functions which have metropolitan aspects. Such a council would make use of service authorities already operating in the area or to be set up. In his elaboration of his plan for federation in 1962, he pointed to the need to transfer certain functions from present jurisdictions "to a more extended jurisdiction." "Such duties," he explains, "can be transferred from cities, villages, and towns to the county, to a new special district, to the state, or even to the federal government, or can be contracted to a nearby government on a service basis. The advantages and disadvantages of these arrangements must be reviewed in each situation."(39)

The Advisory Commission on Intergovernmental Relations, established by Public Law in 1959 "to give continuing

study to the relationships among local, State and National
levels of government," recommended in 1961 the "establishment of metropolitan service corporations or authorities for performance of particular governmental services
necessitating area-wide handling." "The Commission believes that the States should place at the disposal of the
people in the metropolitan areas a variety of possible
measures from which they can make a selection based upon
their own desires and the peculiar needs of their area.
The Commission further believes that functional authorities
constitute one of several methods by which residents of
metropolitan areas should, if they so choose, be able to
proceed."

The Commission acknowledged the "increasing concern
by public administrators, scholars, and political leaders
in the metropolitan areas" about such authorities, and said
that even one member of the Commission had referred to
them as "The Untouchables." Its proposed draft bill to
serve as a guide to state legislatures in making these
metropolitan service corporations possible, contained certain safeguards:

(1) The authorities would be created by a majority vote
of people in the area to be served, with the resolution for
the election coming from the city council of the central
city, or board of commissioners of the largest county, in
the metropolitan area.

(2) The authority would be authorized to carry out "one
or more of several metropolitan functions, such as sewage
disposal, water supply, transportation, planning, etc." The
functions, or function, of the authority would be determined
by a vote of the people in the service area. The authority
could be single-purpose, but preferably not; if it were
single-function in nature other authorities for other functions, would be precluded from that area.

(3) The authority would be governed by a metropolitan
council consisting of the following:

    (a) one member from each component county board

    (b) the mayor of the central city

(c) "one member would come from the mayors and councilmen of each of the three largest component cities"

(d) one member to be selected by the smaller component cities.

(4) "The corporation would have power to impose service charges and special-benefit assessments; to issue revenue bonds; and -- subject to referendum -- to issue general obligation bonds repayable from property taxes imposed for this purpose."

Two members of the Commission dissented from the proposal. Edwin Michaelian, County Executive of Westchester County, New York, opposed its provision for a blanket approval by the State legislature of power to establish these authorities, and argued instead that the "application rather should be made to the State legislature on each individual proposal to establish such a corporation dealing with such specific service or services." "Then, at that time," he said, "a proper appraisal of the situation can be made initially on each such proposed project." John E. Burton, a citizen member of the Commission from Ithaca, New York, dissented, and gave as his reason: "The metropolitan service corporation is a concept of significant merit, but to permit the creation of one by a majority vote of an enlarged area as a whole does not protect adequately the rights of residents of smaller local units of government who might be subjected against their desires and needs, to the power and costs of such an agency imposed upon them by an areawide majority."(40)

The public authorities' greatest claim to recognition must rest primarily on their ability to form more logical jurisdictions for governments. In view of their potential in this regard it is a pity that so few have taken advantage of the opportunities. Most have all too willingly accepted boundaries coterminous with the level of government establishing them. In the New-Haven-Wilmington area under consideration in this book, one can single out the rare bold attempts toward regional areas by authorities: the Port of New York Authority, the Delaware River Port Authority, the Passaic Valley Sewerage Authority, the Delaware River

Joint Toll Bridge Commission, South Jersey Port Commission, the turnpike authorities, and the few mergers of functions of municipalities.

Public authorities appear to be a permanent part of the American governmental machinery. Only in exceptional circumstances have they been abolished, despite proposals to do so. James W. Fesler agreed with William Anderson that their functions should be incorporated into the regular governments. "In fact," said Fesler, "a minimum program of areal reform should consist of the absorption of virtually all special governmental units and their districts into the general governments and their areas." He acknowledged, however, that this would at once raise the question of the adequacy of these regular governments and their areas to handle such problems.(41)

The continued trend, however, still is toward the proliferation of the authorities into more and more functions. Their great advantage here is their adaptability and flexibility. In this respect they reverse the normal governmental procedure in that the more conventional governments are relatively free as to the functions they will perform but bound by regulations as to how to do so, the public authorities are restricted to specific functions for which they are created but are given wide latitude in methods for achieving their purposes.

In the fast moving governmental complex, however, adaptability and flexibility can lead to fragmentation and chaos as well as to greater comprehension and coordination. If the latter are to be the result rather than the former, steps must be taken now to reassess the functional and political roles of the public authorities in the light of the total interrelationships with governments on all levels.

REFERENCES

1. "A Plague of Special Districts," National Municipal Review, XX, No. 11, November, 1933, p. 546.

2. The 'Authority' in Pennsylvania, Pro and Con (Philadelphia, Bureau of Municipal Research, 1949), p. ix.

3. Max Farrand, <u>The Records of the Federal Convention of 1787</u> (New Haven, Yale University Press, 1937), I, p. 180.

4. James Madison, as quoted in Andrew C. McLaughlin, <u>A Constitutional History of the United States</u> (student's ed.) (New York, Appleton-Century Company, 1935), p. 138.

5. <u>Bouvier's Law Dictionary</u>, Baldwin's Students Edition (Cleveland, Banks, Baldwin Law Publishing Company, 1946), p. 846.

6. <u>River Basin Administration and the Delaware</u> (Syracuse, Syracuse University Press, 1960), p. 19.

7. Edmund C. Burnett, <u>Letters of Members of the Continental Congress</u> (Washington, D.C., Carnegie Institution, 1921-1936), VI, pp. 317-318.

8. <u>The American Commonwealth</u> (New York, The Macmillan Company, 1908), I, p. 416.

9. Andrew C. McLaughlin, <u>op. cit.</u>, p. 789.

10. S. E. Morison and H. S. Commager, <u>The Growth of the American Republic</u> (New York, Oxford University Press, 1940), I, p. 313 and 313n.

11. <u>Saturday Evening Post</u>, November 3, 1951.

12. Bureau of the Budget, <u>Standard Metropolitan Statistical Areas</u> (Washington, 1961), pp. 3-4.

13. <u>Area and Administration</u> (University, Alabama, University of Alabama Press, 1949), p. 24.

14. <u>Delaware River Basin Compact</u>, Art. I, 1.6(a), and Part II, Effectuation, United States (from Public Law 87-328, 75 Stat. 688), 15.1, Reservations.

15. Statistics taken from <u>1960 Pennsylvania Municipal Authorities Directory, op. cit.</u>

16. <u>N.J.R.S. Cum. Supp.</u> 40:14A.

17. <u>Twenty-third Annual Report of the Division of Local Government.</u> (Department of the Treasury, State of New Jersey, 1960), pp. XII, XXII.

18. Chapt. 127-8-31a.

19. This federal encouragement came, interestingly, at a time
    when the public corporation device on the federal level was
    declining. In 1941 C. Herman Pritchett said that the char-
    acteristics of the public corporation "have been disappearing
    before our eyes...." "Soon," he prophesied, "there may
    be nothing left...to mark the sport where the government
    corporation once stood." Quoted in Leonard D. White, Intro-
    duction to the Study of Public Administration (New York,
    The Macmillan Company, 1955), fourth edition, p. 136.

20. The Units of Government in the United States (Chicago, Public
    Administration Service, 1942), p. 6.

21. Title I, "Slum Clearance and Community Development,"
    Housing Act of 1949, Public Laws, Ch. 338, July 15, 1949,
    63 Stat. at 414.

22. River Basin Administration, op. cit., p. 51.

23. Delaware River Basin Compact, Art. 3, Sec. 3.8.

24. October 18, 1961.

25. December 6, 1961.

26. Editorial, "Bucks Eyes the River," December 4, 1961.
    During the New Deal the following poem expressed the fear
    of the expansiveness of the authority device in river valleys:
        My fellow countrymen! Hear ye
        Th' eternal President's decree:
        Not one but seven there shall be —
        Seven valleys of the Tennessee.
        New hosts of T.V. Burocrats
        In striped pants and shiny hats
        And dainty gloves and spotless spats
        (They're all deserving Democrats).
        I vowed (before Election Day)
        That I would furnish jobs and pay
        For sixty million; hence I say
        We need a super TVA.
        At first we'll take the one we've got
        And multiply by seven,
        Which may suffice. If it does not —
        Well, seven come eleven!
    John Trebbel, An American Dynasty (New York, Doubleday
    & Company, 1947), pp. 152-153.

27. "An Act to enlarge and change the boundaries of the district known as the Port of New York District and agreeing with the State of New York with respect thereto," Assembly No. 392, State of New Jersey, introduced February 9, 1959.

28. "Another Point of View — A Comment on the Foregoing Paper," The American City, LXX, No. 2, February, 1955, p. 116

29. Clayton Knowles, "News Analysis — Whose Jet Airport?" January 11, 1960.

30. Staff Report on Public Authorities under New York State, op. cit., pp. 106-107.

31. Newark Evening News, February 1, 1960; January 29, 1960.

32. John C. Bollens, The States and the Metropolitan Problem, A Report to the Governors' Conference (Chicago, 1956), pp. 108-109.

33. Government Research Council, Miami-Dade County Chamber of Commerce, "Metropolitan Dade County," August, 1961, p. 1.

34. "The Charter of Metropolitan Dade County, Florida," adopted May 21, 1957, Art. I, Sec. 1.01, par. 2, 11.

35. Metropolitan Government Charter Commission, "Proposed Metropolitan Government Charter for Nashville and David-son County," April, 1962, Art. II, Chapt. 4, Sec. 11.401, p. 50; Art. 64, 2(c), p. d-4; Art. 18, Sec. 18.04.

36. National Capital Planning Commission, National Capital Regional Planning Council, Washington, D. C., 1961, p. 111.

37. Advisory Commission on Intergovernmental Relations, Factors Affecting Voter Reactions to Governmental Reorganization in Metropolitan Areas, Washington, D. C., May, 1962, p. 49.

38. Ibid., p. 65.

39. Luther H. Gulick, The Metropolitan Problem and American Ideas (New York, Alfred A. Knopf, 1962), p. 141.

40. Advisory Commission on Intergovernmental Relations, <u>Governmental Structure, Organization, and Planning in Metropolitan Areas</u> (Washington, D. C., July, 1961), pp. 26-29.

41. <u>Area and Administration</u> (University, Alabama, University of Alabama Press, 1949), pp. 36-37; <u>cf.</u>, William Anderson, <u>The Units of Government in the United States</u> (Chicago, Public Administration Service, 1942), pp. 45-46.

Chapter Seven

Summary Observations

SHOULD A COUNTY or municipal government create a public authority, or special district? The extreme flexibility of the authority-device prevents a categorical answer, but the results of the analysis of their relationships with local governments in the five States of Connecticut, Delaware, New Jersey, New York, and Pennsylvania, suggest unusual caution.

Faced with this question, the local government official should attempt to appraise, for one thing, the meaning the authority might have for his government in the light of the five most commonly advanced claims for the authority method. He must weigh, also, the total impact of numerous such authorities on local governments in the area in which his county or municipality is located. In so doing, he may want to avail himself of the suggestions in this regard concerning each of the five points offered by experts over a wide area and tested within a given area by actual case studies and observation. The results of one such study, presented in this book, tend to point to the following observations:

(1) The first point frequently proffered in their favor is that authorities make possible the financing of desperately

needed capital construction which otherwise would be impossible under the present restrictive ceilings on debt, and/or taxation, set by the states. This is done by floating bonds in the name of the authority, usually without obligation to existing governments, which will be self-liquidating through the collection of charges for the use of the authority's facilities. Once the debt is so paid off, the authority will be dissolved and the function revert to the parent government.

More public authorities are created to circumvent debt ceilings of the states than for any other one reason. They do provide a very simple expediency for so doing. They may be organized usually by a resolution by the county governing body, or an ordinance by the municipal council, under a general enabling act or special legislation of the state legislature. In their own name they may then issue revenue bonds for the function for which they have been created. The indebtedness does not become an obligation against the parent government or any other. It is to be paid for by user charges for services rendered in connection with the function. This is a simple direct way for a county or municipality to get action on a necessary function.

The local government official, however, must always weigh expediencies of the moment against the long-range effects. He must determine how much of the cost of capital construction should be borne by the present generation who need it now, and what proportion should be carried over to succeeding generations who also may benefit from it.

Looking ahead, then, inasmuch as authority functions generally involve long-term construction, the future prospects are much less favorable than the immediate results. Revenue-bond financing is more expensive than general obligations. Although it is true that the bonds do not show against the obligations of any government there is serious reason to doubt that a government could stand by and permit an authority to fail without stepping in to rescue it, because, for one thing, the matter of its own bond-rating might be affected, at least indirectly. This casts some doubt on the validity in actual practice of the assurance to the government that its "full faith and credit" is not being used for such borrowing. Indeed, if the parent government should fail to come to the help of an ailing authority it would, in a very real sense, be inviting intercession in the public functions of the authority by a group of 25% of the bondholders who could ask that a receiver be appointed to run the authority in any way necessary to recapture their investment and interest.

The single-purpose revenue-bond, again contrary to general obligations, minimizes the flexibility of function by the authority, as it has pledged to the bondholder that that function will be pursued until the bond and interest thereon has been redeemed. This dedication produces "vertical functional autocracy," or an obsession for the continuance of that one function at the possible expense of needs which subsequently become apparent during the time of maturity of the bonds. If, on the other hand, the function becomes increasingly important during the period of bond maturity and builds up a surplus of revenue, that revenue has to remain under the control of the authority, and the parent government finds itself thus locked out of money which could be shared for other needs.

There is the possibility, not yet subject to proof, that the authority-device may have a built-in resistance to self-liquidation through the continued need to issue new revenue bonds for periods of perhaps forty years which cannot be sold unless the terminal date for the authority is pushed further ahead.

The resort to revenue-bond financing through the public authority calls into an influential role in the public functions of a community two groups: the bondholders, on the one hand, and the users of the facilities, on the other. The bondholders are, of course, an absentee group scattered throughout the country or world. The users may be local residents or outsiders depending upon the nature of the function.

As some 50% of local-government indebtedness has come to rely on its own revenues for repayment, one wonders about the impact in time of recession or depression.

(2) Advocates of public authorities, as a second point, explain that, as agencies each engaged in one particular

function of importance to the community, they have a greater attraction to professional and business persons who think in terms of specialization in their everyday occupations, thereby drawing into participation in civic governmental affairs the better citizens representing middle-class and upper-class interests.

Surveys of board memberships of authorities and the interest of middle and upperclass residents in the kind of activities the authorities sponsor both support the contention that these agencies do attract superior citizens. The authority provides a bridge between the citizen's exclusive specialization to which his profession or business leads and the single technical achievements of the authority. The frame of reference for his participation on the authority board therefore is much more closely associated with the normal pattern of his thinking than is that of a county board or municipal council where he is faced with varied questions requiring the approach of the generalist.

The decisions board members are called upon to make in regard to the authority functions are among the most important in the life of the community. These are not mere administrative agencies, but units of government empowered to plan vast projects, finance and operate them even to the extent of fixing charges and rates. The problem of the representativeness of the boards is, therefore, of great importance. The facts show that priceless little attention has been paid to this matter. A variety of methods of appointment range the scale from direct election to appointment by the executive from lists submitted by interest groups. The result, accordingly, is that boards appear not to have a basis of representation. A very few in this country reflect functional representation, and a few others have resorted to the naming of the members of the parent governing body to the authority board. Either method, to be sure, is better than no basis, and yet neither seems calculated to mold into a coalition the four "constituencies" of the public authority: the bondholders whose investment must be protected, the users who make the maintenance and operation of the function possible and enduring, the residents of the area in which the authority functions who are greatly affected by its decisions and actions, and the governing body that gave it birth and endowed it with certain of its powers.

Even if the board could be made representative, if not on the traditional American bases of population and geography but on some more meaningful grounds for the current interests of a community, the boards still would be siphoning from potential interest in the regular governments of county and municipality the best citizens who might become more interested in the latter if they were to plan, construct, and operate themselves the functions which are more meaningful and dynamic. Participation by professional and technical people is desirable, but it is unfortunate that they are now lured to semi-independent agencies which serve to fractionate planning and coordinated efforts at the very time that there is such a pressing need for the complementary role of standard governments.

(3) Two other arguments for authorities may be analyzed as part of the same characteristic: namely, that, relying as they must, on financing themselves through the sale of their bonds, rather than on taxation, they must conduct the affairs of the authorities in a more "business-like" manner than must a department of the government and must, for the same reason take their functions "out of politics."

The public authority is a "quasi" agency, in that it is partly public. The meaning of this unique role may be interpreted either as a boon for efficiency and nonpartisanship, or as a method of escape from both public and private controls or checks, and therefore a method of irresponsibility. The positive interpretation would have it that the public authority is endowed with the responsibilities of the public interest but the initiative and motivation of private enterprise. The negative would infer that the authority lacks the restraints of both the public and private sectors in that it does not have to be aware of an electorate organized to unseat its officials, nor of stockholders controlling enough shares to check its policies and operation. The authority-concept is not that there is a third area distinct in itself between the public sector and the private sector, but that there is need for an institution that can move between the two areas and synthesize some of their common interests.

Attempts to determine whether such a peculiar unit of government as the authority is more "business-like" than a department of government, even in the management of the same kind of function, falls of its own weight because of the innumerable variables involved. There is no basis for comparison.

One can, however, single out advantages enjoyed by the authority and not available to the government department: the authority is able to invade the private sector to a far greater extent than the government department in that it may apply to enterprises so private in nature that the government in the past has done little more than attempt to regulate them, powers of eminent domain, tax exemption, the extension of public credit, and the granting of monopolies, all of which are denied in whole or part by state constitutions to private business. The authority can work with business of concern to the public in ways that a government department would not dare undertake. Through this device, local governments have been able to attract industry, or keep it from leaving the community.

The authority created to accomplish this result for the local government, may become in the process and in the continuation of the business involved, an actual competitor of the government which established it. This arises through the tax-exemption principle of the authority. The local government is unable to tax the new business, but may receive at the best only a payment in lieu of taxes, based on the value of the land before the industry was built up on it. The tax immunity, the privilege of the authority, is extended to the private business attracted by the authority thereby insulating the latter from taxation by the government.

(4) The issue, above all others, raised by the creation of the authority is its accountability. Is it accountable to the private sector, or to the public sector? What are its public responsibilities in its role of performing a function of government? Through its non-political emphasis on efficiency, the public authority has succeeded in insulating itself, whether consciously or not, from the public.

This detachment is encouraged by the type of function being performed by the authority. Many of the inconveniences of city and suburban living today find expression in the needs for transit, garbage disposal, toll-highways, and noisy jetports, which are the functions of authorities.

Recent attempts to give identity to these units which operate under the generic term, "authority," have met with little success. They have not created a public image, and, accordingly, have become further isolated from public relationships.

It is this high degree of freedom from concern for a "constituency" or electorate which must be balanced against the authority's claim to efficiency. Efficiency is but one desiderata of a governing unit; another is the sensitivity to public will.

Any thought that policy-making agencies responsible for decisions of the scope made by public authorities could be "taken out-of-politics," even were that desirable, is dispelled readily by an examination of the functioning of these agencies on the local level. They are involved in politics in a way perhaps unique in American government, in that they seem to have become a meeting place for the forces of traditional party politics and the newer elements of the middle-class ideal suburban politics. In three ways, they enter the political realm: (1) Often from the very struggle over the appointment of board members, they are engaged, to a surprising degree, in regular party-line politics; (2) Superimposed as they are over existing governments, their relationships with such older units are, by their very nature, awkward, and the authorities become caught up in the cross-currents of political struggles of these governments; (3) They attract to their boards technical, professional, and business persons who will not participate in party politics, but who may well be in the process of becoming part of a newer policy-making process of banker, lawyer, engineer, and public relations specialist.

(5) The fifth claim for the public authority is that it makes possible, through its flexibility, the formation of more logical lines of jurisdiction, no longer tied to boundaries drawn a century or more ago, but able to center now instead on combinations of municipalities or counties, or

on natural factors, such as port or river valley thereby accommodating area and administration for the effecting of functional needs.

Potentially its greatest strength, this use of its acknowledged flexibility, has been demonstrated rather dramatically on the international, interstate, and regional, levels, but has been a tool of authorities on the local level in distressingly few instances. State enabling and special legislation, as well as federal laws which have greatly spurred the proliferation of authorities on the local level, have encouraged the use of these agencies over wider areas in combining municipalities and counties in joint functions, but relatively few such joint authority projects have emerged.

Above the local echelons, authorities have made greater use of natural features, such as ports, river valleys, corridors, and bays, than on man-made metropolitan statistical areas or inter-community regions. Even those based originally on natural forces, have not been enlarged as the potential of the producing factor has enlarged, or as more persons have become increasingly dependent on the natural phenomenon.

Experiences with such new jurisdictional units for the operation of functional needs which seem more unrelated, or unconfined, to traditional levels of government, as exciting as they have been, already begin to cause conflicts of duplication with existing governments and, indeed, with each other. Authorities are superimposed as overlays over an area, with no other units being dropped. They add, therefore, to the already existing maze of jurisdictional lines.

Such authorities, with enlarged scope, may, in retrospect, appear to have been transitional units leading toward needed expansion of scope of governmental jurisdiction. It may not be insignificant that, where they have been used locally, they have tended to assign more functions to the county than the municipal level. And, where they have been used in urban areas, they have tended to encompass an urban county. In the very few examples of metropolitan-wide governments in the country, a county-wide authority or special district has preceded their formation.

Greater direction of efforts of authorities in creating units which relate more meaningfully today to area administration, is a need which can not much longer be postponed unless the result is to be the widespread fractionating of regions, especially in metropolitan areas.

These long-term observations as to the effects of public authorities on existing governments, serve to challenge the advantages these agencies have for meeting expediencies of great concern. Their appreciation by the local government official should encourage him to place the burden of proof on those advocating the creation of an authority.

These disadvantages also should cause him to reexamine his own government to determine whether it could not handle the function, and, if not, why not. He should explore, as well, other possibilities, such as transfer of functions to another standard government, service contracts, annexation, merger, city-county consolidation, the urban county, federation, and the like.

As early as 1914 The American Political Science Review had pointed to the "inadequacy" of the regular governments to meet the "obligations . . . imposed by an increasingly complex community life" as the principal reason for the "creation of special municipal corporations of greater flexibility and with more homogeneous interests."(1) Very much the same opinion has been advanced as recently as 1961 by Jean Gottmann in his study, Megalopolis: "Authorities have been especially important and helpful in Megaloplis, and they express precisely the inadequacy of other governmental units to take care of the new problems arising from regional integration."(2)

The greatest single spur to the proliferation of public authorities was a letter which President Franklin Roosevelt sent to the Governors of all the States in December of 1934 recommending the creation of "municipal improvement authorities without power to tax, but with power to issue bonds payable solely from the income of revenue-producing improvements, such as water, sewer, and electric light and power systems."

It should not be overlooked, however, that in that same letter, the President's first recommendation called for the "(s)implification of the procedure for the authorization and financing by municipalities of public-works projects, and conferring of additional powers upon municipalities to undertake such projects and issue bonds to finance the same."(3)

Local governments will not improve their positions by divesting themselves of essential functions and assigning them to semi-autonomous units operating within the co-terminous confines of the government itself.

A major attack on the continued proliferation of these agencies was made by the California legislature in its 1963 regular session. Faced with 1,962 special districts at that time and prospects of their increase throughout the State, California enacted legislation establishing Local Agencies Formation and Annexation Commissions for each county in the State.

The Interim Committee on Municipal and County Government of the Assembly of the State of California had made a study of special districts from 1959-1961, and had concluded: "In the past the need for single purpose special districts to provide a municipal type service to the rapidly growing unincorporated fringe areas of California was great but as cities and counties have expanded their services to take care of such problems, the need for such a district decreases."(4)

The legislation of 1963 provides for a commission in each county which has to consider and approve any proposal for the formation of a new city or special district or the annexation of any territory to an existing city or special district before such action may be taken.

The commission is to be comprised of two county officials, who may be county supervisors, appointed by the Board of Supervisors, and two city officials who must be from the city councils, appointed by the mayors of all the cities meeting as a committee for selection. The four members then appoint a fifth member to represent the general public.

The criteria to be considered by the commission in deciding whether or not to approve a new city or special district, or the annexation of territory to them, include the following factors:

(1) Population; population density, land area and uses; assessed valuation, topography; the likelihood of significant growth of the area and adjacent incorporated and unincorporated areas during the next ten years.

(2) The need for organized community services; the present cost and adequacy of governmental services and controls of the area; proportional future needs of such services and controls; proportional effect of the proposed formation and of alternative courses of action of the cost and adequacy of services and controls in the area and adjacent area.

(3) The effect of the proposed formation or annexation and of alternative action on adjacent areas, on mutual social and economic intersts and on the local government structure of the county.

The County Officer, journal of the National Association of Counties, commented: "A state suffering the most rapid growth has thus taken a major step at the state level, to coordinate such growth, and give full awareness and fuller responsibilities to unit of government already in existence. It may be a major triumph for counties."(5)

In this direction, rather than in the continued uncoordinated proliferation of public authorities and special districts with boundaries coterminous with those of existing governments, lies the hope for the strengthening of local government.

REFERENCES

1. Vol. VIII, November, 1914, p. 614.

2. (New York, The Twentieth Century Fund, 1961), p. 759.

3. Letter from Franklin D. Roosevelt to Governor Guy B. Park, Missouri, undated. Letter from Governor Guy B. Park to President Franklin Roosevelt, December 27, 1934. On file, Franklin D. Roosevelt Library, Hyde Park, N. Y.

4. Assembly of the State of California, Special District Problems in the State of California. Final Report of the Assembly Interim Committee on Municipal and County Government, Assembly Interim Committee Reports, 1959–1961, vol. 6, no. 15, p. 47.

5. Vol. XXIX, no. 10, October, 1963, p. 395.

Bibliography

PRIMARY SOURCES

The researcher on public authorities must resign himself, at the outset, to the fact that his role will be that of
"digging out" data. Systematic records of authorities are
rare. Pennsylvania's organization of such information is
unusual.

The point of departure for this "digging" should be the
the Census of Governments, of the Bureau of Census. The
1962 edition goes beyond that of 1957 in giving recognition
to the authority-device. The trend is toward the more
liberalized acceptance of authorities as independent, rather
than dependent, agencies. "This adjustment," the Bureau
explains, "mainly concerns municipal authorities in Pennsylvania, school building corporations in Indiana, and some
municipal authorities in New Jersey...."

Statistics are given for special districts, without dif-
ferentiating them from public authorities, but for each
state lists of the more prominent actual public authorities
are given.

The Urban Survey Corporation of Boston has made
further use of information compiled by the Census of

Governments in its Directory of Special Districts, published in 1964. The volume includes 18,323 special districts,
with information about them in six categories. Of interest
to readers of this book is the fact that one such distinguishing characteristic used in the Directory is that of whether
or not the agency has the power to tax.

Specific lists of public authorities within the states
have to be compiled from a number of sources, depending
upon the state. Pennsylvania is no problem, as the 1960
Pennsylvania Municipal Authorities Directory, published
by the Division of Documents in Harrisburg, lists all municipal and joint-municipal authorities in the State by categories of functions and by counties. In New York State lists
were prepared for the Staff Report on Public Authorities
under New York State by the Temporary State Commission
on Coordination of State Activities in 1956. The Staff of the
Law and Legislative Reference Bureau of the New Jersey
State Library assembled "A List of Authorities in New
Jersey: State, Regional and Local" in 1953, and each year
now the Annual Report of the Division of Local Government
for New Jersey shows those authorities that have reported
bond revenue issues or audit reports, but this is by no
means a complete listing of authorities. In almost all the
states records have to be put together from information
in various departments, such as State or Treasury, or
kept by taxpayers' associations. Regional housing authorities keep lists of the federal housing authorities.

Clues to the departments of state government which may
have records on authorities are found in the laws of the
state relating to authorities. They are created by general
or special enabling acts passed by the state legislature.
The researcher will have to examine different titles of
state legislation, as most states do not codify their laws
on authorities. Titles bearing on Highways, Sewerage, Local
Government, and others, may contain the enabling acts.
New York State has grouped its provisions for public authorities under a section so labeled, "Public Authorities,"
and there is available for that State McKinney's Public
Authority Laws. The Pennsylvania Municipal Authorities
Association has published The Pennsylvania Municipality
Authorities Act and Related Laws, as of 1962.

Local ordinances on the municipal or county level will supply details of the creation of individual authorities under the state enabling acts.

Almost all public authorities prepare annual reports in some detail, and, of course, have a prospectus for each bond issue. Minutes generally are not available. The Port of New York Authority has an excellent library collection of works on authorities.

Primary sources for facts relating to the social, economic, and political aspects of areas in which public authorities function, may be obtained from two standard works by the United States Government, Statistical Abstract of the United States, and County and City Data Book. For the study of authorities in metropolitan areas, the Bureau of the Budget of the Executive Office of the President has a list of Standard Metropolitan Statistical Areas. Economic facts concerning these areas are contained in Donald J. Bogue, Population Growth in Standard Metropolitan Areas, 1900-1950, and in his more comprehensive reference book in which he and Calvin Beale break the country into economic regions, including metropolitan areas, under the title, The Economic Areas of the United States. The political complexion may be gleaned in part from voting statistics down through the county and Congressional District level in the four volumes of America Votes by Richard J. Scammon.

BIBLIOGRAPHIES...

Books and articles on public authorities are indexed in the Metropolitan Communities -- A Bibliography, through 1955 in Volume I, and 1955-1957 in Volume II, although the references to authorities is not exhaustive. Materials on government corporations are indexed for the Federal level in Catheryn Seckler-Hudson, Bibliography on Public Administration, 4th edition, 1953.

Two of the largest public authorities have published bibliographies on their own which are useful. The Tennessee Valley Authority published its references in 1945, as Government Corporations, a Selected List of References, and The Port of New York Authority has available A Selected Bibliography 1921-1956, listing over 1,000 references, revised in 1960.

GENERAL STUDIES OF PUBLIC AUTHORITIES...

The starting point here should be Research in the Use of the Government Corporation, 1940, by the Committee on Public Administration of the Social Science Research Council. Its "Outline of Suggested Topics" still has relevance, as very few of the suggestions have been met. This Report lists, among pioneer works, Harold VanDorn's Government Owned Corporations, 1926; John McDiarmid, Government Corporations and Federal Funds, 1938; Ruth G. Weintraub, Government Corporations and State Law, 1939; and others. W. Brooke Graves' American Intergovernmental Relations, published in 1964, provides excellent background. Standing out in more recent studies are: Council of State Governments, Public Authorities in the States, published in 1953; Dr. William Ronan and his staff of the State Commission on Coordination of State Activities, Staff Report on Public Authorities under New York State, 1956; John C. Bollens, Special District Governments in the United States, in which in 1957 he established the importance of special districts, and discussed in a separate chapter public authorities. Nathaniel S. Preston's unpublished doctoral dissertation at Princeton University, "The Use and Control of Public Authorities in American State and Local Government," is a scholarly contribution which suggests a classification of public authorities. Marvin L. Fair refers to public authorities in Port Administration in the United States, 1954. The symposium on Public Authorities published by the School of Law of Duke University in the Autumn of 1961 is as good an introduction and analysis of the overall problem, in this and other countries, as one could find.

The Advisory Commission on Intergovernmental Relations was preparing in 1964 a comprehensive study of special districts.

General legal studies of public corporations include, in addition to Ruth Weintraub's and Nathaniel Preston's studies, a number of representative works: Burton Andrews, The Law of Public Corporations -- The Leading Cases in New York and Annotations, 1951; Millard Caldwell, "Legal Aspects of the Regional Plan for Higher Education," Higher Education, January 1, 1950; Mortimer S. Edelstein, "The Authority Plan -- Tool of Modern Government," Cornell Law Review, January, 1943; James A. Hankerson, "Special Government Districts," Texas Law Review, October, 1957; David E. Lilienthal and Robert H. Marquis, "The Conduct of Business Enterprise by the Federal Government," Harvard Law Review, February, 1941; R. R. Nehemkis, Jr., "The Public Authority: Some Legal and Practical Aspects," Yale Law Review, November, 1937; C. Herman Pritchett, "The Government Corporation Control Act of 1945," The American Political Science Review, June, 1946; Jerome J. Shestack, "The Public Authority," University of Pennsylvania Law Review, February, 1957.

Recommendations for model charters for more effective control of public corporations are found, for the Federal level, in Sidney D. Goldberg, The Government Corporation; Elements of a Model Charter, by the Public Administration Service, 1953 and, for the state level, "Governmental Structure, Organization, and Planning in Metropolitan Areas," by the Advisory Commission on Intergovernmental Relations, 1961.
STUDIES OF PUBLIC AUTHORITIES IN INDIVIDUAL STATES...

The Staff Report on Public Authorities under New York State, previously referred to, is an outstanding statewide analysis. A few other States have studied those within their borders. Dr. Frederick L. Bird, who has one of the two standard works on the Port of New York Authority, has published for the Bureau of Government Research of the University of Rhode Island a thirty-eight page pamphlet on Local Districts and Authorities in Rhode Island. Emmett Asseff prepared a study in Louisiana, Special Districts in Louisiana, published by the Louisiana University Press in 1951; Stanley Scott and John C. Bollens collaborated on Special Districts in California Local Governments, for the Bureau of Public Administration of the University of California in Berkeley, in 1949; The New Mexico Legislative Council Service published in June, 1962, its Special District

Governments and New Mexico; the University of Texas published in 1959 Woodworth G. Thrombley's Special Districts and Authorities in Texas. Bennett M. Rich has a short section on public authorities in New Jersey in The Government and Administration of New Jersey, 1957, and four years earlier Herman Mertins had written an unpublished undergraduate honors thesis on "Authorities in New Jersey," for Drew University. Tina Weintraub and James D. Patterson summarize the effect of municipal authorities in Pennsylvania in The 'Authority' in Pennsylvania, Pro and Con, for the Bureau of Municipal Research of Philadelphia. The North Carolina State Ports Authority, by Charles E. Landon, was published by Duke University in 1963, involving statistical and other analysis of the economic problems involved.

STUDIES OF INDIVIDUAL AUTHORITIES . . .

The Tennessee Valley Authority has inspired more good literature than any other public authority, far more than the Port of New York Authority. The drama of the remaking of the valley has lent itself to such writings. David Lilienthal's Democracy on the March has been printed and reprinted. More practical studies of its phases of operations include: Harry L. Case, Personnel Policy in a Public Agency: The TVA; Gordon R. Clapp, The TVA, An Approach to the Development of a Region; James Dahir, Region Building: Community Development Lessons from the Tennessee Valley; Roscoe C. Martin, TVA, The Firt Twenty Years; C. Herman Pritchett, The Tennessee Valley Authority; and Philip M. Sleznick, TVA and the Grass Roots.

There are no comparable studies of the Port of New York Authority, despite the fact that it traces back to 1921. The two standard works, Erwin W. Bard, The Port of New York Authority, and Frederick L. Bird, A Study of the Port of New York Authority, concentrate largely on the economic aspects and the structure. Barbara Jahreis, in an unpublished undergraduate honors thesis at Drew University, made a compilation of criticisms of The Port of New York Authority, and carried on her studies in a graduate thesis at Columbia University. Martin B. Dworkis conducted a project study in the Graduate School of Public

Administration and Social Service, New York University, of a more behavioral nature in which opinions of various interest groups were ascertained concerning the Port of New York, including the Port Authority, under the title, "The Port of New York and the Management of its Waterfront." The comprehensive objective study of The Port of New York Authority has yet to be written, indicating again the dearth of studies in the field of public authorities. The Hearings of the so-called "Celler Committee," Subcommittee No. 5 of the Committee on the Judiciary of the House of Representatives of the United States Government in 1960, published as Serial No. 24, Parts 1 and 2, "Port of New York Authority," contain information of an ancillary nature to the attempt of Congressman Celler to get intra-Authority papers from the Port Authority which in the long range may have more value than the point of the hearing itself.

The St. Lawrence Seaway Authority and Power Project, as international projects, are attracting attention. Although still sufficiently new to attract mostly euphemistic accounts, the story of its construction is dramatic from both an engineering and political viewpoint. The original documents are found in Documents on the St. Lawrence, edited by R. R. Baxter. The Canadian side of the story is told by Lionel Chevrier, The St. Lawrence Seaway, and the American side for the power project, in an unpublished doctoral dissertation at New York University by Edward Kresky, "The New York State Role in the Development of Power from the St. Lawrence River."

Syracuse University has specialized in studies of water basin authorities under the direction of Roscoe C. Martin. Not only do we have his recapitulation of the first twenty years of the Tennessee Valley Authority, referred to above, but the preliminary study of the Delaware River Basin in the detailed River Basin Administration and the Delaware, which was instrumental in the creation of the unique Delaware River Basin Compact.

A case study, and a discussion of the "jurisprudential" implications of the case of the Wisconsin Development Authority, Jurisprudence and Statecraft, by Samuel Mermin, published by the University of Wisconsin Press in 1963, points to the need for additional case studies of this type authority, as well as all others.

Mention has been made of doctoral dissertations in the field. It is encouraging to note that more are beginning to be written on public authorities. Another valley authority, "The Lower Colorado River Authority -- A Study in Politics and Public Administration," was analyzed by Comer Clay at The University of Texas. At the University of Chicago Roderick K. DeCamp wrote his doctoral dissertation on "The Chicago Transit Authority: A Study in Responsibility."

Redding S. Sugg and George Jones have collaborated on a book, The Southern Regional Education Board: Ten Years of Regional Cooperation in Higher Education. Sugg, with Richard Leach, had published The Administration of Interstate Compacts, which supplemented Interstate Compacts, 1783-1956, which had been published by the Council of State Governments.

CASE STUDIES OF PUBLIC AUTHORITIES . . .

The raw materials for further analysis of public authorities is building up slowly in case studies of individual authorities. Although relatively few, they have considerable promise for the future. In the Inter-University Case Program, the following cases concern public authorities or related agencies: John DeGrove, "The Florida Flood Control District," ICP Series No. 58; William J. Gore and Evelyn Shipman, "Commuters vs. the Black Ball Line -- Washington Purchases the Puget Sound Ferries," No. 42; Herbert Kaufman, "Gotham in the Air Age," CPAC Studies, 1950, revised 1952; Arthur A. Maass, "The Kings River Project," CPAC Studies, 1949; Roscoe C. Martin, "From Forest to Front Page," No. 34; Donald E. Pearson, "The Whittier Narrows Dam," No. 17; Edwin A. Read, "The Coterminous Boundaries Dispute," No. 33; Ellen St. Sure, "The TVA Ammonia Plant," CPAC Studies, 1950; Owen Stratton and Phillip Sirotkin, "The Echo Park Controversy," No. 46; and Paul Tillett and Myron Weiner, "The Closing of the Newark Airport," No. 27. In his Cases in State and Local Government, Richard T. Frost includes cases on two authorities: Don Becker's case study, "The Fight for the

Seattle Metro," and David D. Gladfelter's "Jets for the Great Swamp." Acknowledgement is made in the preface of this book of unpublished case studies prepared by students of Drew University in New Jersey, New York, and Pennsylvania.

POLITICAL STUDIES OF PUBLIC AUTHORITIES . . .

Political analyses of public authorities remain virgin ground, but books on metropolitan politics almost without exception refer to authorities. The year, 1961, witnessed the publication of an unusual number of such works, including: Edward C. Banfield, Political Influence, which contains two studies of public authorities: "The Chicago Transit Authority," and "The Exhibition Hall" of the Metropolitan Fair and Exhibition Authority in Chicago; Robert A. Dahl, Who Governs? Democracy and Power in an American City; Robert C. Wood, 1400 Governments; Aaron Wildavsky, Dixon-Yates -- A Study in Power Politics; Stanley Scott and Willis Culver, Metropolitan Agencies and Concurrent Office-Holding: A Survey of Selected Districts and Authorities; Roscoe C. Martin and others, Decisions in Syracuse; Peter H. Rossi and Robert A. Dentler, The Politics of Urban Renewal; and two books of excerpts: Edward C. Banfield, Urban Government, and Oliver P. Williams and Charles Press, Democracy in Urban America. The fact that all these books came out in 1961 is significant, for it indicates a new consideration of metropolitan politics and stresses the need for the inclusion of public authorities in such an emphasis. Other books had hinted at this need: Edward C. Banfield, and Morton Grodzins, Government and Housing in Metropolitan Areas, in 1958; Robert C. Wood, in his earlier book, Suburbia, Its People and Their Politics, in 1959; and Wallace Sayre and Herbert Kaufman, Governing New York City, in 1960. As early as 1949, James W. Fesler had called attention to how public authorities complicate government and politics, in his Area and Administration. Luther Gulick discusses the problem of authorities in relation to his plan for metropolitan federation, in The Metropolitan Problem and American Ideas, published in 1962.

PERIODICALS . . .

The fact that there is such a dearth of books on public authorities casts increased emphasis on periodical literature in the field. A considerable number of writings here suggest arguments for and against authorities, but usually without supporting evidence or systematic treatment. Periodicals to be consulted are: The National Civic Review (formerly the National Municipal Review), The American City, The Pennsylvanian (formerly The Authority), The American Political Science Review, Public Administration Review, Daedalus, The County Officer, and The New Leader.

Persons beginning research on public authorities would do well to read first the following selected articles: Two articles in The American City, February, 1955: "Is 'Authority' Financing the Answer?" by Harold F. Alderfer, and "Another Point of View, A Comment on the Foregoing Paper," by Carl H. Chatters; Juan Cameron, "Whose Authority?" in The Atlantic Monthly, August, 1959; Edward C. Banfield, "The Political Implications of Metropolitan Growth," Daedalus, Winter, 1961; Arthur W. Bromage, "Political Representation in Metropolitan Areas," The American Political Science Review, June, 1958; Kirk Porter, "A Plague of Special Districts," National Municipal Review, November, 1933; Paul Studenski, "Fiscal Headaches for Metropolitan Areas," GRA Reporter, 1st Quarter, 1955; Horace A. Davis, "Borrowing Machines," National Municipal Review, June, 1935; Joseph E. McLean, "Use and Abuse of Authorities," National Municipal Review, October, 1953; Victor Jones, "The Withering Away of the City," Public Management, December, 1950; Luther Gulick, "Public Authorities and How to Use Them," The Tax Review, November, 1947; William H. Markus, "Removal of Municipal Authority Board Members," The Authority, September, 1961; Austin J. Tobin, "The Administration of a Port Authority," The Bond Buyer, October 11, 1952; and William B. Shore, "Developments in Public Administration," Public Administration Review, Winter, 1961.

Index